Literary Criticism and Cultural Theory

Edited by
William E. Cain
Professor of English
Wellesley College

A Routledge Series

Literary Criticism and Cultural Theory

William E. Cain, *General Editor*

Novels, Maps, Modernity
The Spatial Imagination, 1850–2000
Eric Bulson

Novel Notions
Medical Discourse and the Mapping of the Imagination in Eighteenth-Century English Fiction
Katherine E. Kickel

Masculinity and the English Working Class
Studies in Victorian Autobiography and Fiction
Ying S. Lee

Aesthetic Hysteria
The Great Neurosis in Victorian Melodrama and Contemporary Fiction
Ankhi Mukherjee

The Rise of Corporate Publishing and Its Effects on Authorship in Early Twentieth-Century America
Kim Becnel

Conspiracy, Revolution, and Terrorism from Victorian Fiction to the Modern Novel
Adrian S. Wisnicki

City/Stage/Globe
Performance and Space in Shakespeare's London
D.J. Hopkins

Transatlantic Engagements with the British Eighteenth Century
Pamela J. Albert

Race, Immigration, and American Identity in the Fiction of Salman Rushdie, Ralph Ellison, and William Faulkner
Randy Boyagoda

Cosmopolitan Culture and Consumerism in Chick Lit
Caroline J. Smith

Asian Diaspora Poetry in North America
Benzi Zhang

William Morris and the Society for the Protection of Ancient Buildings
Andrea Elizabeth Donovan

Zionism and Revolution in European-Jewish Literature
Laurel Plapp

Shakespeare and the Cultural Colonization of Ireland
Robin E. Bates

Spaces of the Sacred and Profane
Dickens, Trollope, and the Victorian Cathedral Town
Elizabeth A. Bridgham

The Contemporary Anglophone Travel Novel
The Aesthetics of Self-Fashioning in the Era of Globalization
Stephen M. Levin

Literature and Development in North Africa
The Modernizing Mission
Perri Giovannucci

The Tower of London in English Renaissance Drama
Icon of Opposition
Kristen Deiter

Victorian Narrative Technologies in the Middle East
Cara Murray

Victorian Narrative Technologies in the Middle East

Cara Murray

LONDON AND NEW YORK

First published 2008
by Routledge
2 Park Square, Milton Park, Abingdon, Oxon OX14 4RN
52 Vanderbilt Avenue, New York, NY 10017

Routledge is an imprint of the Taylor & Francis Group, an informa business

First issued in paperback 2012
Typeset in Adobe Garamond by IBT Global.

Library of Congress Cataloging-in-Publication Data

Murray, Cara.
Victorian narrative technologies in the Middle East / by Cara Murray.
p. cm. — (Literary criticism and cultural theory)
Includes bibliographical references and index.
ISBN 978-0-415-95791-5
1. English literature—19th century—History and criticism. 2. Technology in literature. 3. Middle East—In literature. 4. Literature and society—Great Britain—History—19th century. 5. Literature and society—Middle East—History—19th century. 6. East and West in literature. 7. Narration (Rhetoric)—History—19th century. 8. Islamic countries—In literature. I. Title.
PR871.M87 2008
820.9'3552—dc22 2007052707

ISBN13: 978-0-415-54079-7 (pbk)
ISBN13: 978-0-415-95791-5 (hbk)

To the Murrays
and
Quique Lanz Oca

Contents

Acknowledgments

I am grateful to the many friends and colleagues who have talked with me about roads, canals, romances, novels, and other technologies over the past five years. I would like to extend my heartfelt thanks to those who supervised the doctoral dissertation on which this book is based: Anne Humpherys, Rachel Brownstein, Timothy Alborn, and Gerhard Joseph. Less-official support was offered in the same period by Glenn Burger, Gordon Whatley, Marshall Berman, Maria Fahey, Lopamudra Basu, Crystal Benedicks, Sean O'Toole, and Rachel Oberman. I am pleased that William E. Cain, General Editor of the Routledge Literary Criticism and Cultural Theory Series, solicited my manuscript, and I am thankful for Erica Wetter's assistance at Routledge. I am deeply appreciative for the two years that I spent at the Center for Place, Culture, and Politics. I credit the spirited debates there for sharpening my thinking about empire and other catastrophes. I am particularly indebted to: Omar Dahbour, Peter Hitchcock, Ira Dworkin, Christopher P. Iannini, Jennifer Ridgley, Saadia Toor, Brenda Biddle, Megan Schauer, and Julia Benedict. I especially want to thank Neil Smith, the director of the Center, for his commitment to turning all spaces into places of impassioned critique. Colleagues at Queens College, CUNY, where I worked as a visiting professor as I revised this manuscript, provided support of all kinds: Nancy R. Comley, Jason Tougaw, Carrie Hintz, Talia Schaffer, and Duncan Faherty. And I thank my new colleagues at the University of Houston-Downtown who have made me feel at home in Houston as I completed this book: William Gilbert, Nell Sullivan, Chuck Jackson, Nicole LaRose, Kat McLellan, Bailey McDaniel, Antonio Garcia, and Dan Shea. I am especially grateful to my parents, Jim and Jean Murray, for all of their support and encouragement. Final thanks are due to Enrique Lanz Oca, without whose love and geographical expertise I would be lost.

Introduction

The Suez Canal and the Technologies of the Novel

In a pivotal scene in David Lean's 1962 movie *Lawrence of Arabia,* T.E. Lawrence, played by Peter O'Toole, emerges like a ghost from the Sinai desert at an abandoned British outpost. He has just crossed the desert on foot with two young Bedouin servants in order to report the news to the Cairo headquarters that he had successfully led a group of Arab nationalists to take Akaba from the Turks. In the crossing he lost his servant in quicksand and his compass in a storm. The camera fixes on his gaunt corpse-like face, covered in dust, still and emotionless as he pauses before the empty outpost. A metal fence squeaks in the wind; a door bangs open and shut. His desert travail seems to have ended here in this apocalyptic landscape. But as he walks through the wreck of the station, he hears the sonorous blast of a ship horn; and as he emerges on the other side, he stands transfixed as a large ship steams by in the desert. The music starts, and the movie cuts to a busy street in Cairo.

With this scene the Suez Canal makes its first appearance in a Hollywood epic. Its role here, however, is nothing new. Since the Canal was completed in 1869, it had been portrayed, paradoxically, as a technological miracle. That what was hailed as the nineteenth-century's greatest technological feat took place on Eastern soil was no matter because the Canal was seen as Western—despite the fact that it was made with Eastern monies, labor, and know-how. As Emily Haddad has recently argued, the Canal could not be depicted as Egyptian because of its "affiliation with order and progress," and the British failed to see Egyptians as modern, even in the face of their participation in the building of such modern projects as the Suez Canal (382).

Throughout its long representational history—appearing in travel narratives, guidebooks, and newspaper accounts—the Canal had always been depicted as severed from its environment. In nineteenth-century drawings, severe straight lines and high banks wall it off from the more fluidly rendered desert through which it cuts. Sketches of the modern cities and ports erected to service the Canal further emphasize its separation from Egyptian village life. The Canal's geographical and cultural detachment fostered the idea that technology itself was Western, even before technology became a full-fledged concept. According to Leo Marx, the concept of technology emerged in the early twentieth century in order to describe a complex system, such as a railroad, rather than just a part, such as a steam engine (466). The new term conveniently disguised the social and political choices involved in making that complex system at the same time that it redefined progress in technological rather than political or social terms (467). Marx shows how the concept of technology arose in order to obscure agency, and he illustrates its antidemocratic roots, deeming technology a "hazardous concept" (469).

If Marx is correct, then we have reason to uncover the historical circumstances that contributed to the making of this hazardous concept. Marx argues that technology emerges out of the complex organizational tasks involved in building railways, offering the transcontinental railway in the United States, completed in 1869, as a prime example.[1] I suggest, however, that we must also consider how colonial projects shaped the concept. During the period in which technology was emerging as a concept, the Suez Canal and the Bombay-Calcutta railway were under construction, projects that must have also contributed to our modern notion of technology. Narratives of the Canal not only propagated the idea that it was Western but that technology itself was a Western concept. Convictions that technology was Western made it possible for Western nations to stake claims on the global highway that was born upon the completion in 1869–1870 of the world's newest technologies: the Suez Canal, the Union-Pacific Railway, and the Indian Peninsular Railway.

In addition to being a symbol of Western technology's global right-of-way, the Canal also helped to promote the benefits of spatial and temporal transformation. If, as David Harvey has argued, "time-space compression"[2] was vital for the expansion of capitalism, then the Canal's ability to cut travel time in half and bring the colonies to Britain's doorstep promised great gains for capitalist development (240). Furthermore, the Canal embodied these transformational processes by becoming a monument on the Western tourist trail. Henri Lefebvre has demonstrated that as development transforms spaces it also transfers ownership.[3] As the West changed the desert into a waterway, the Suez Canal became a sign of the promises of a new world order to all who journeyed to behold it.

Lean's iconic movie scene of a modern ship cutting through an ancient desert dramatizes a related concept of the Canal as transition. By carrying Lawrence out of the timeless desert into a modern city, Lean's ship canal literally facilitates a transition from East to West.[4] The technical work of this transition from desert to modern city is to make that move seem effortless. The ideological work of the Canal's transitional role in the film and throughout its representational history is to smooth over modernism's rough waters—to make it seem as though any Western project in the Middle East, whether the building of banks, cities, or railroads would benefit all involved, even as many of those projects led instead to famine, bankruptcy, and foreign invasion.[5] In this way the Canal has always promoted modernization's glib promises.[6]

For *Lawrence of Arabia's* contemporary audience, the Canal dramatically symbolized a transition of another sort. In 1956, just five years before the film's release, Gamal 'Abd al-Nasir, then President of Egypt, nationalized the Canal that had long been controlled by Great Britain. Although al-Nasir's nationalization of the Canal became one of the most powerful symbols of the postcolonial era, I want to suggest that at least part of the panic that al-Nasir's actions caused in the West had to do with a rupture in a nearly century-long representational tradition. When al-Nasir claimed Egyptian ownership of the Canal, he challenged the idea that Western representations of the Canal had always worked to propagate, namely that technology was a Western concept and that modernization was the property of the West alone.

The Western response to al-Nasir's actions indicated a major shift in the modern geopolitical landscape. England and France joined together in opposition and induced Israel to provoke a conflict with Egypt on their behalf that would serve as a pretext for an Anglo-French invasion of Egypt, a military action that ultimately did not occur. With the threat of a world war on the horizon, the newly deemed "Suez Canal Crisis" was born. In subsequent years a number of books appeared examining the immediate causes of the crisis. However, these studies largely ignored England's 1882 bombardment and invasion of Alexandria to seize the Suez Canal. Only recently have historians begun to analyze the crisis of 1956 within the context of its much longer history.[7]

In this book I revisit Britain's early incursions into the Middle East, for this first canal crisis has often been referred to as the initiation of a more robust form of imperialism in the century. Edward Said is just one of the many scholars to point out the significance of Britain's seizure of the Suez Canal to the development of Western imperialism. Although historians had long recognized that this aggressive act paved the way for the scramble for Africa that took place at the end of the decade, Said set up a startling new teleology. According to him, Britain's 1882 invasion of Egypt was not the event that began a new imperial fervor in the region; rather, it punctuated a long history of cultural practices (*Orientalism* 31–36). In his well-known argument, Said asserts in *Orientalism* that through writing about the Middle East, Europeans practiced a textual mastery over colonial subjects that led to physical possession. Whereas Said posits 1882 as the teleological endpoint of cultural imperialism in the Middle East, I suggest that we consider an earlier date, the 1875 purchase of the Canal, anticipating that a somewhat differently configured teleology may reveal imperialism's more quotidian aims.[8]

Prior to 1875, the British wanted nothing to do with the Suez Canal, a baffling stance considering not only the geopolitical relevance of the Canal, but its ideological importance. By looking at texts written during the decades leading up to Britain's purchase of the Canal, a period which was characterized by a thorough rejection of the project, I shall show that cultural works did much more than just create a sense of mastery, as Said has argued. They helped to produce a way of doing business that in turn made imperialism business as usual. I examine the ways in which literary genres are technologies of development. I focus primarily on novels, but I also consider biographies and travel narratives produced during the four decades leading up to Britain's purchase of the Suez Canal: the 1840s when the British speculated wildly in railways domestically; the 1850s when the nation first began to export capital abroad but refused to invest in the most talked-about business opportunity of the age, the Suez Canal; the 1860s when the Canal was built (1859–1869) without British monies; and the 1870s when the British Prime Minister, Benjamin Disraeli, purchased a majority of the shares of the Canal for England with widespread support of her people.

The popularization of imperialism that begins in England during the 1870s, evidenced by the popular support of the purchase of the Suez Canal, would have been impossible without major shifts in cultural attitudes toward character, investment, and technology. The study of England's initial resistance to the Canal project and its final embrace reveals the attitudes that needed to be in place for such an imperial project to be realized. Although this book uses the purchase of the Canal as a focal point, it is not a book about the Suez Canal, per se. Rather, it is a book that seeks to identify the cultural components of an important shift in the way that British imperialism came to be practiced during the nineteenth century. The Canal is important because it is a material object around which discourse about imperialism circulated. I argue that we cannot understand the popularization of imperialism without looking at the way that narratives worked as one of the technologies that made imperial projects possible. I therefore focus on the interrelated formal techniques of the novel, travel narrative, and biography.

CONCEIVING THE IMPERIAL WAY: 1850–1869

Why didn't the British build the Suez Canal? After all, they had every reason to do so, and they had the technology and the expertise: they had a well-prepared set of vessels to navigate the Canal and an industry poised to build the new steamships that the Canal necessitated; they had an educated and skilled body of workers; they had the capital; they had the right political connections with Turkey and Egypt; they also stood to gain from the newly opened markets of East Africa and the more accessible markets of the Near and Far East. Most important of all, they had the motivation: they needed a direct route to their largest colony, India, and after the 1857 Sepoy Rebellion, they felt this need urgently, for a canal would provide a quick and direct route for the deployment of British troops.

Still, the British did not invest in the Canal, a fact that is more perplexing when one realizes that the projector Ferdinand de Lesseps counted on them to purchase 20 percent of its shares and made propaganda tours of England throughout the 1850s. During his 1857 visit he spent three months in England and held twenty-two meetings in eighteen cities (Farnie 43). He talked to the press, business groups, and politicians and distributed elaborate pamphlets and a book written by his English secretary. As in France and elsewhere, he appealed to the people, bypassing big banks and powerful financial institutions, attempting instead to gain the support of small investors. He was received cordially, even enthusiastically, yet no individuals subscribed.

Granted, the British were otherwise engaged. They were busy building railways in India, and they were constructing their own railway to Suez.[9] Yet neither of these facts sufficiently explains their reticence to invest in the Suez Canal. Even with the British building railways in India in the 1850s, there is little evidence to suggest that capital was not also available for investment in Egypt. In fact, British investment in Egypt had increased dramatically during the decade. Said Pasha did not grant the British a concession for their railway until a year after he granted one for the Canal, so the British reluctance cannot be attributed to an effort to avoid competition for their railway. Even before a British railway was a possibility, the press strongly disapproved of the Canal. As early as 1851 Lord Palmerston famously proclaimed, "It shall not be made, it cannot be made, it will not be made; but if it were made, there would be a war between France and England for the possession of Egypt" (Farnie 29). Lord Palmerston was not alone. In fact, the body of literature about the Canal, including newspaper and journal articles and Parliamentary reports, is characterized by its naysaying.

The journalistic accounts of the Suez Canal during the twenty years of its planning and development supply insights into a staunch and nearly universal British resistance. Yet only six years after its completion, Disraeli purchased the Canal to universal fanfare.[10] This sea change in public opinion may have resulted from the fact that the Canal was now not only functioning, but British. Yet, there is more to it than that. The decade of the purchase also coincides with an entirely new public acceptance of British imperialism called by many the "New Imperialism."[11] The Canal is unique because it was an international project, not just in its positioning between two seas, but in its conception, investments, labor, management, technology, and in its proposed use. Britain's long rejection and final acceptance of the Canal then indicates the nation's readiness to accept its place in the new world order, an order which would depend upon international alliances, joint ventures, and shared technologies.

Contemporary discussions in British newspapers and journals about the possibility of building a canal across the Isthmus of Suez focused a nation's newly surfacing questions about global commerce. Fears about everything from cosmopolitan characters to international cooperation and transnational finance were aired through writings about the hypothetical canal. Journalists who approached the question from an economic standpoint failed to predict the importance of the new global transportation networks for the encouragement of capital flow and the control of the empire. Nor did they understand how the shortening of travel times and the demolition of spatial barriers, what David Harvey refers to as "time-space compression," could serve the ends of capital. It was often in the guise of a more literary sort of journalism that ideas about global commerce became the subject of free-ranging discussions. In the pages that follow, I argue that although the meticulous calculations of economic journalism failed to project a new commercial route around the world, the technologies of the novel came to the aid of global capitalism.

I. Economic Projections: The Limits of the Capitalist Imagination

The near unanimity of the press during the 1850s and the 1860s is striking, especially given the diversity of opinions that were usually expressed in Victorian journals and newspapers. Across political lines writers agreed:

the Suez Canal could not be built. Even though two out of a team of three engineers from France, England, and Austria who went to Egypt in 1847 to study the prospects asserted the project's feasibility, the British press cast doubts. The sole engineer against the Canal was the British Robert Stephenson, son of George Stephenson, the "father of the railways" and inventor of the "rocket" locomotive. Stephenson deemed the project "impracticable" and his assessment was repeated in nearly every article on the subject throughout the next two decades. Nine years later in 1856, another international committee of engineers, from a wider array of European nations, traveled to Egypt to study the prospects again. This time there was a consensus: the Canal could be built. Even the British engineer agreed. The British press, however, dug in their heels.

Articles about the canal project follow a similar pattern throughout the 1850s and 1860s. They first recite the history of attempts to build a canal, arguing that although canals connecting the Mediterranean and the Red Sea (by a different route) had been cut in ancient times, few remained open for long.[12] They then jump to modern history, citing Napoleon Bonaparte's French expedition of 1798. Under Napoleon's direction, J.M. Lepère made the first survey of the Isthmus of Suez in 1799 and concluded that the Mediterranean was thirty feet below the Red Sea, precluding the possibility of a workable canal because the currents would be too strong. Then comes Lesseps, attempting to do what Napoleon could not.[13] In the British journalists' narratives, Lesseps's plan punctuates a long line of failures. If that fatal positioning is not enough, they drive their point home by reciting a litany of obstacles that Lesseps is sure to face. The most common include the lack of labor, the difficulty of Red Sea navigation, impossibilities of building in shifting sand, and the complications related to constructing a port on the Mediterranean end. Three years after work on the Canal began, *The Times* aptly captures the unanimity of the English public on the matter: "Opinion in England is that it is not at present possible to open a shipping canal across the isthmus for the use of traffic, nor can it be maintained in working order" (29 November 1862). Although it may appear that these negative articles about the Suez Canal are not useful as sources because they only betray a prejudiced obstructionism, I suggest that the most earnest journalism in this vein reveals just how much is at stake in conceiving the Canal.

Shortly after Lesseps gained a second concession in 1856 from Said Pasha, improving upon the terms of the 1854 concession after a new survey of the Isthmus was performed by an international group of engineers, H. Reeve in the *Edinburgh Review* responded with an article which became the most influential of the era. It was regularly cited throughout the following decade as evidence that Lesseps's project was not viable. H. Reeve's piece, in contrast to the vast majority of the ones that came before, intimates that building a canal may very well be a possibility: "Although these gigantic schemes seem so utterly impracticable, it is by no means intended to assert that the canalization of the Isthmus is not a possible or even a feasible idea" (126). Reeve concedes that a canal can be built—technically speaking. As the international committee of engineers from England, France, Holland, Prussia, and Austria had just returned from Egypt and declared the project feasible, Reeve does not contradict them—at least not their expertise. Instead, he asserts that engineers know nothing about commerce. Thus, he redefines the canal question by suggesting that it is not a matter of technical expertise, but a matter of money.

Reeve's article proceeds by showing how dredging, building the pier at Port Said, and keeping the locks in repair all may be performed, but only at exorbitant costs. Reeve points out that such large amounts of money could never come from France alone. Lesseps's pamphlets, however, are clear on the matter of finance: this was not a French project; it was to be financed, built, and maintained by an international company appropriately named the "Universal Company of the Suez Maritime Canal." Lesseps sought money from investors in France, Spain, Portugal, Italy, Holland, Russia, Austria, the Netherlands, Tunisia, Egypt, and the U.S.A. and printed up shares in Italian, English, German, and Turkish. However, he focused most of his energies on raising money in England because he knew that her people had the most capital to invest. That Reeve so blatantly refuses to admit the international makeup of the company into his comprehension of the project suggests a wider discomfort with international finance and global alliances.

Reeve's article also emphasizes that the Canal, if built, would never "pay." That is, even if the monies were raised, the Canal could not make a profit for its shareholders. Most interesting is why. Lesseps's plan, outlined in his 1855 pamphlet that Reeve quotes extensively, projects a tenfold increase in world commerce. But Reeve strongly disagrees. Reeve forcefully maintains that commerce would barely budge and presents detailed arguments to show why. Opening a new road to the Near and Far East, Reeve claims, would only facilitate the import of luxury items, products that represent a number "so infinitesimally small as to defy commercial calculation" (134). In hindsight it is easy to see how Reeve was wrong; his comment, however, shows that the Canal spurred public discourse about the nature of commerce.

Reeve further argues that the Canal would have no use at all and presents many reasons why. Ships, he asserts, would prefer to sail around the

Cape to avoid the turbulent Red Sea waters. And what is true of sailing vessels is also true of steam, he asserts. Although passengers and mail had been transported by steam for nearly twenty years, goods, he projects, would never be carried by steamboats, for all past experiments had failed. His arguments about sail or steam, the Cape or Red Sea, are really about whether or not the Canal would spark commerce. They lead him into questions about the relation of distance to time and to cost and cause him to argue against Lesseps, who proclaims that the Isthmus route, half the length of the Cape way, would amount to a savings in travel time which would translate into a savings in price: "Finding by their [Lesseps and Co.] maps that the distance in miles through the Canal would be only half, they jump at once to the conclusion that prices will be reduced in an equal ratio, and commerce in consequence doubled or quadrupled" (134).

Reeve embarks upon even more complicated questions about commerce, including how insurance relates to shipping and product costs, ultimately claiming that it would cost as much to send products around the Cape from Aden to England, a distance of 12,000 miles, as it would to send them from Aden to Suez, a distance of 1,400 miles. By studying contemporary trade patterns, he further predicts how much the Canal is likely to affect commerce. The largest increase in shipping in the recent past, he shows, was to Australia: from 1844 to 1854 it had grown by more than seven times. Reasoning that since it would take longer to go to Australia by the Canal than by the Cape, he predicts that the Canal was destined not to increase commerce by much—a dubious assertion not only because he was wrong in his estimates of comparative travel time, but also because he based his argument on the assumption that Australia would continue to be England's fastest-growing trading partner and that no other nation would emerge to rival Australia.

Reeve concludes that due to delays in navigation, turbulence on the Red Sea, the unimportance of luxuries, the cost of insurance, and persistent trade patterns, the Canal would not increase commerce by more than 2 percent, if at all. Consequently, he predicts that English shareholders will discover that "the route round the Cape is infinitely preferable for commercial purposes, we may rest assured that the Canal will never be executed; or, if it were opened, it would as in ancient times, soon be closed again, as it could never pay its working expenses" (131).

Reeve argues that engineers know nothing about commerce, but the popularity of his argument suggests that such ignorance was more widespread. His seventeen-page article presents a variety of proofs for why an increase in commerce does not depend upon the establishment of international finance, global cooperation, new inroads in communication, or the development of new products and markets. His models are inflexible. He does not imagine that steam technology could be adapted to carry goods, although it was, shortly after the opening of the Canal. Nor does he predict that better routes and cheaper prices might stimulate the consumption of luxuries. And it fails to occur to him that Australia may not be the only growth market.

Despite Reeve's failure to predict correctly, the influence of his article warrants attention. It became so influential, I suggest, because it set out to answer the unanswered questions of the age: How does commerce work? Who pays for it? What makes it grow? If commerce were the key to the strength and vitality of the world's largest free-market economy, it would need to become less of an abstraction. Reeve's article attempts clarification. Asking his readers to do the math along with him, Reeve shows how the Canal will only save 2 percent on goods and then calculates again to demonstrate how 2 percent was not enough to stimulate trade on a global scale. Even if the Canal were to save as much as 5 percent, he facetiously asks, what effect would that have on world commerce? "Would it enable Indian cottons to compete with Americans, or Bengal sugars with those of Havanna? Would it induce the Indians to use more goods from Manchester, or the French to drink tea instead of coffee, or to change their fiscal laws as regards sugar or silk?" (134). The implied answer is "no"; it would not affect "world" trade (here configured as British) in the least. With the benefit of hindsight, however, these questions do not seem as absurd as he meant them to be.

II. Imaginary Projections: Trafficking the World

One of the rare pieces written in support of the Canal appeared six years prior to Reeve's in Charles Dickens's *Household Words.* Two companion pieces published in April and May of 1850, both titled "Short Cuts across the Globe," urged on the building of a Panama Canal and a Suez Canal respectively. The articles, jointly authored by William Weir and W.H. Wills, briefly discuss the technical obstacles to a canal and their remedies, optimistically concluding: "These difficulties, though great, are not insuperable. The advanced state of marine architecture and engineering ought surely to be able to cope with them" (May 168). Next, Weir and Wills summarily dismiss the financial obstacles, suggesting that the idea that the projects would not "pay" is preposterous. Unlike Reeve, however, they do not discover their proof in tedious accounting. Instead, they find it in traffic.

The articles emphasize that the world now has sufficient traffic to support a Suez and a Panama Canal. Weir and Wills never define traffic; however, they appear to combine older notions of the word, having to do with trade or commerce, with more modern ones developed in the nineteenth century. According to the *OED,* which finds its first modern usage in 1825, traffic is "the passing to and fro of persons, or of vehicles or vessels, along a road, railway, canal, or other route of transport."[14] Thus, the modern sense newly incorporates the movement of people as well as goods implicit in the older usage and is dependent upon the new travel technologies. Another significant difference between modern "traffic" and its earlier meaning is the new emphasis on the repetitive movement of going to and fro. In order to illustrate the importance of traffic to the establishment of technologies such as railways, Weir and Wills use the example of the London and Liverpool railway, built in 1836. They claim that it was not built "until the intermediate traffic between these termini had swelled to a sufficient amount in quality and value to bear reimbursement for establishing such a mode of conveyance" (April 66). Without traffic, they contend, "its execution would have been impossible, even though men had known how to set about it" (April 66). They then project this model to South America, where they would like to see a canal built at Panama, claiming that areas hitherto not in communication with each other are likewise now joined by traffic. What they have to say about South America is applicable to Egypt since the two articles work in tandem to make an argument about technology and global shortcuts.

Traffic in their South American example connotes a general movement of people. Weir and Wills present a picture of a vibrant place newly crisscrossed with human activity. Peoples are no longer isolated, and villages are no longer remote, they say. Instead, peoples are in conversation with one another across mountains and valleys and plains. Their way of seeing South America contrasts with one observed by Mary Louise Pratt, who describes the attitudes of European travelers to South America and Africa in the eighteenth century as the "emperor of all I survey." In this model, explorers scurry up mountains to have a bird's-eye view of the surrounding territory and lay claims to all that they see. By contrast, Weir and Wills represent South America as a busy landscape with a network of villages laced together by well-traveled paths.

Weir and Wills's vision resembles Benedict Anderson's theorization of Central and South American landscapes during the nationalist movements in the early nineteenth century. Although Anderson's theory has been of interest to literary critics because of the way that it implicates the novel in nation building, I shall argue that Anderson also provides a useful way to understand the novel as a technology that functions like a railway or a canal. In Anderson's depiction, Creole functionaries crisscrossed that landscape on their pilgrimages to the capital cities of Mexico, Chile, or Peru. Unlike their counterparts in Spain, they were barred from access to the seats of power in Madrid. As a result, Creole functionaries neither move laterally to make the trans-Atlantic journeys to Madrid, nor, consequently, vertically to advance their career. Cut off from career advancement, they were fated to repeat their to and fro movements between the centers of administration located in the cities of South and Central America. During these local pilgrimages Creole functionaries began to perceive themselves as interconnected with other Creoles on like journeys. Yet these pilgrimages "had no decisive consequences until their territorial stretch could be imagined as nations, in other words until the arrival of print-capitalism" (Anderson 61).

Print gave Creoles the ability to imagine their territorial stretch as a national landscape and to envision themselves as part of that nation. Anderson argues that the novel and newspaper provided the "technical means for 're-presenting' the *kind* of imagined community that is the nation" (25). The "technical means" of the novel and newspaper is found in their employment of "homogeneous, empty time," a term Anderson borrows from Walter Benjamin to mean time based upon temporal coincidence and measured by the clock or calendar. Characters may never meet, yet they are joined together in readers' minds through their temporal coincidence in the text. Anderson shows how print culture facilitated the breaking down of the great landscape divides and ultimately sparked peoples to imagine communities of the like-minded across vast distances.

Weir and Wills show that this connective way of thinking was not just found in the domain of novels and newspapers. It is possible that Weir and Wills projected a novelized vision onto South America. But I would rather suggest that the novel, the newspaper, railways, and telegraphs share similar technologies, capable of turning vast territorial stretches into well-trafficked imagined communities. Indeed, one of the publicity stunts that George Hudson, the Railway King, pulled to celebrate the opening of a new line was to have a newspaper delivered from the town at the start of the line to the town at its end. He awed crowds who could not fathom reading a paper from another town on the same day that it was published. Hudson's stunt demonstrates the similarities between the technologies of the railway and the newspaper. And through Anderson's understanding of the Creole pilgrimage, we can see how words like "traffic" point to a new technology at work, performed by good roads, trains, telegraphs, and novels, which give shape and form to landscapes. Throughout this book I will consider the ways in which the novel, travel narrative, and biography take part in a technological remapping of the globe.

Weir and Wills envision a much larger landscape than do Anderson's Creoles. They do not stop at the borders and imagine only nations, but widen their compass to contemplate "the realization of the unity of mankind" (May 68), for "every short cut across the globe brings man in closer communion with his distant brotherhood, and results in concord, prosperity, and peace" (May 68). Their bold confidence in technology bores through borders and imagines distance dissolved entirely:

> The distances which separated the different nations and parts of the globe are gradually vanishing before the achievements of modern invention, and we can traverse them with incredible speed; the languages of all nations are known, and their acquirements placed within the reach of everybody; thought is communicated with the rapidity, and even the power of lightening. (May 68)

In their writing we hear echoes of the railway and telegraph. And indeed this way of thinking was quite common to the railway era, when it was often feared that speed would abolish space, as Wolfgang Schivelbusch points out (34).

Technology's ability to sweep away borders comes into conflict with the nationalist projects of the age which sought to shore them up. The Suez Canal brought this contradiction to the forefront. Lesseps's internationalist language is what most irritates Reeve about the project, who charges that Lesseps and Company:

> stand forward in the garb of philanthropy as the champions of civilization, anxious to bring into communication nations that have now no means of intercourse with one another; to use their own motto, "*Aperire gentibus terram;*" and, by breaking down what they conceive to be the barrier between the East and the West, to spread wealth and good will to the remotest corners of the globe. (134)

French visionary style, inspired by the Saint-Simonians, clearly irked the British. When talking about their own technological projects, British writers often opted for a less ambitious style. Samuel Smiles, the most prolific propagator of the great engineering projects of the century, emphasizes the humble speech of his British engineers. Such antipathy towards visionary style had as much to do with a cultivated hatred of the French as with the fears of technology's internationalizing potential. Accordingly, Smiles consistently belittles the extranational projects of his engineers. He wants to keep a national handle on technology and to portray only the canals, tunnels, and break walls found within Britain. Smiles uses his biographies of British engineers and his descriptions of their new projects to bridge the nation and fortify its borders.

Reeve attempts to freeze that fortified nation in time, and by doing so maintain the global *status quo.* His world picture is static. It traces one path—the Cape route—with two points at either end—Australia and England. And it uses one question, "Will it pay?" to determine all movement. Weir and Wills dismiss that question outright. They don't get bogged down by the economic details. Instead, they imagine a dynamic world interconnected by a multiplicity of paths. But their more cosmopolitan way was not chosen by England. It was Reeve's view that was quoted, advocated, and developed by journalists throughout the following decade. This was not, however, the whole story. While newspapers shut off the possibility of a dialog about this international undertaking, novels did not.[15] Nineteenth-century novels, with their interest in the habitual movements of people through space, provided a forum for considering the kind of questions that the Suez Canal raised. I am not suggesting that novels offer literal representations of the Canal. Instead, I argue that the novel's generic form is one of the technologies that allows globalization.

III. Literary Projections: The Novel's Globalizing Strategies

At the center of the British failure to imagine the Suez Canal during the 1850s and the 1860s is England's ambiguous relation to the rest of the world. J. A. Hobson, the first theorist of imperialism, argues that it was the inability of nation states to live within their "natural banks" and to foster expressions of "humane cosmopolitanism" across those banks with other nations that ushered in the New Imperialism in the 1870s (6). Hobson's analysis of imperialism is useful because it describes England's situation—its inability to accept those kinds of visionary bridges across worlds that Weir and Wills projected.

Franco Moretti puts forth a view similar to Hobson's in *Atlas of the European Novel,* only he places the blame squarely on the novel. He argues that the nineteenth-century British novel's refusal to cross boundaries and insistence upon fortifying the national borders turns England into an island of provincialism. At the opposite pole from Moretti is M. M. Bakhtin, who sees the production of encounters at the border as the essence of the novel form. It is at the borders that voices meet and bubble up into a fountain of heteroglossic discourse. For Bakhtin, the novel accepts, accumulates, and absorbs frontiers, drawing in all genres and all social voices placing them in dialog with each other; indeed, it thrives upon borders. Although these two approaches to the border may seem difficult to bridge, it should be noted that they both situate the novel in a wider world, as do many theories of the novel.[16] Whether one sees the novel's function as patrolling borders or crossing them, the novel, long associated with nation building, actually arises out of international situations. Indeed, Anderson's theory depends upon the articulation of pan-nationalism before nationalism sets in. The Creoles travel around the undifferentiated territories of South America before they can perceive their own national landscapes of Chile, Peru, and Mexico. Thus what print captured and formulated into a national form began as a much more expansive process.

Another way of thinking about the novel's propensity to encourage reflection beyond the border has been proposed by Amanda Anderson. She argues that during the nineteenth century, novelistic discourse, as well as ethnography and sociology, served to cultivate the sort of critical distance and detachment that would enable a critique of more provincial viewpoints. Cosmopolitanism within the Victorian context, Anderson writes, gives voice to a "reflective interrogation of cultural norms" (21). She does not see this interrogation as the exclusive domain of the novel, as does Bakhtin. Rather, she finds it evidenced in a wide array of Victorian writings, although the majority of her examples do come from novels. Anderson's point, however, is not that all Victorians cultivated a cosmopolitan viewpoint, but rather that Victorians were ambivalent about detachment, and that such ambivalence reflects their feelings towards modernity. Anderson's observations are useful here, for they enable us to locate the project of the Victorian novel somewhere between the creation of Moretti's isolated island and Bakhtin's babbling border.

The nineteenth-century British novel shores up borders, and it breaks them down, although it may not do so with equal energy. But its ability to do both, to shape space and organize peoples in the ways that Moretti, Bakhtin, Anderson, and Anderson describe is what I am calling its particular technology. Throughout this book I examine the ways that the novel both expands and delimits the nation, borrowing from abroad—coopting, corrupting, or using what it borrows and exporting its generic techniques only to import them again in a varied form. I focus upon the novel's importing and exporting of characters, investments, and technology and argue that these concepts undergo radical changes from the 1840s to the 1870s that encourage a new approach towards imperialism.

The Victorian concept of character develops its primacy because of the instability that the newly globalized market exposed it to. Thus, the Victorians not only expanded their repertoire of characters but altered their notions of what constitutes character based upon market needs. As character is reevaluated, sentiments about investing alter. From the largest and most devastating of the domestic speculative booms in the 1840s to the exportation of capital in the 1850s and 1860s, Victorians gained a new confidence in investing. Technology was the beneficiary. It, in turn, altered Victorians' relation to time and space, bringing the colonies closer to home and the idea of colonization nearer to the heart. Most importantly, the invention of technology as Western at the very moment that technology was emerging as a concept served to justify a new logic of global ownership, for it was through Western claims upon the world's newest technologies that the globe was girdled.

The novel's generic ability to incorporate a plentitude of voices and speech types, in fact its compulsion to do so, makes it the form in which to find the most unsavory of characters. One such character is the projector, or the person who organizes and raises money for large projects. In the early nineteenth century he was often depicted as a schemer, a cheat, or a gambler. Yet projectors were vital for the building of the railways, canals, and tunnels that sutured the nation together. Moreover, if such projects were to continue to be built into the 1850s, 1860s, and 1870s in the colonies and beyond, the British would need to revalue this much-maligned figure. This revaluation happens in the space of the novel.

Chapter 1 examines the way that Charles Dickens takes up the real-life figure of George Hudson, the notorious railway projector in *Little Dorrit.* I argue that Dickens struggles with the presentation of this deplorable character, but ultimately takes advantage of the novel's flexible form to make this deplorable type presentable. Reading Dickens's new capitalist hero alongside of Ferdinand de Lesseps, the projector of the Suez Canal, I assert that between Hudson, who was most productive in the 1830s and 1840s, and Lesseps, who was most productive during the 1850s and 1860s, a change took place in the valuing of the men in charge of the productive factors that is reflected in the import of the French word "entrepreneur." As international capital became necessary for building large projects, the man who was able to cross national borders, and collect capital—the entrepreneur—became a prized national character.

Chapter 2 explores the relation between capital investments in the Middle East and literary ones. I seek to understand the connection between the export of technologies of the novel and the export of railways, telegraphs, and steamships of the same period. I consider Benjamin Disraeli's 1847 novel *Tancred* because of its unique generic structure that combines romance and the *Bildungsroman* in the space of the Middle East. I argue that through the combination of these forms and then their imaginary export to the Middle East, *Tancred* does its political work—turning the Middle East into a zone of imaginative investment for the British public.

Throughout this chapter I use genre theory as a tool to understand the positive revaluation of market practices that occurred in Britain between the 1840s and the 1870s. This shift coincides with and is intimately connected to the concurrent revaluation of imperial practices that turned "imperialism" from the dirty word of the 1840s into the national ideal of the 1880s. Considering generic practices as technologies reveals how aesthetic practices that are often theorized as domestic, the *Bildungsroman* for example, actually have imperial import.

Further explaining the Western development of Egypt, Chapter 3 considers travel narratives written by female visitors to Egypt in the 1860s while the Suez Canal was being built. During this period, the West also invested in the intensification of cotton growing, the building of irrigation works, canals, roads, and ports, and the remodeling of Cairo to look like Paris. In *Colonising Egypt* Timothy Mitchell shows how along with these developments, Westerners imported their own technologies of seeing, ways of bifurcating the world into an object and its representation, a vision that manifested itself in the rise of world fairs and exhibitions which often sought to represent the world in miniature. I look at the way this reorganization of vision is further internalized through technologies developed in the novel form and imported into the travel narrative. I am particularly interested in the widely theorized concept of the "everyday" that is often associated with the novel form. I argue that in the 1860s Western women venture inward, leading to an exploration of Egyptian interior spaces. I consider the travel narratives of two women, Emmeline Lott and Lucy Duff Gordon, who lived in Egypt and recorded what they saw in journals and letters home, and argue that they adapted novelistic methods of everyday accounting in order to describe, delimit, and change their world.

I conclude by examining the international cooperation involved in imperial projects. Chapter 4 considers Jules Verne's 1872 *Around the World in 80 Days* within the context of newly emerging international globe-trotting aesthetics. Whereas in my first chapter I allude to the international cooperation found in the borrowing of words and ideas like "imperialism," and "entrepreneur," and show the way that the British borrowed from the visionary imperialist and entrepreneur Ferdinand de Lesseps, in my final chapter

I look at a genre born of international cooperation—the round-the-world travel narratives of the 1870s. The dramatic emergence of this international genre in the 1870s followed on the heels of the completion of three of the most innovative technological enterprises of the century: the Suez Canal, the Great Indian Peninsula Railway, and the Pacific Railway. By 1870 travelers could more easily circle the globe, traveling with agility and speed.

This genre of narratives records the bourgeois global re-visioning on the cusp of the arrival of a more aggressive style of imperialism. When the bourgeoisie circle the globe, they meet face to face with their newest imperial technologies. In writing about their global shortcuts, they write about technologies that exist because of a new relation to the colonies, and they develop writing strategies and narrative techniques that represent that relationship. The technology that they survey, and intimately get to know, is what enables their class to take hold of the globe more firmly. I reveal how the genre that they write encodes that knowledge and vision in its narrative and thematic structures. Reading from various examples of this form, such as William Simpson's 1874 *Meeting the Sun: A Journey All Round the World,* I argue that this genre, which first appeared in 1869 and was most famously improved upon by Jules Verne's *Around the World in Eighty Days,* is characterized by its push towards improvement, for it always develops methods to narrate faster and shorter ways around the world. In the process, the round-the-world travel narratives disseminated the new ideology of speed in a way that ameliorated Victorian fears about the loss of space, time, and story.

* * *

The round-the-world accounts assuage the fears of a shrinking globe that had been in ascendance since the coming of the railways. In them the fears that the Suez Canal raised about international alliances are also finally put to rest. The purpose of these narratives is to catapult goods and peoples around the globe in the fastest way possible—demolishing all temporal and spatial borders along the way. Within their pages time and space are conquered, new inroads in communication are celebrated, international partnerships are championed, global cooperation is exulted, and a cosmopolitan hero is born. Phileas Fogg travels the world with a Frenchman and an Indian woman, and becomes one of the first British men in literary history to take an Indian bride. But what an odd sort of cosmopolitanism this is, for on his long journey, Fogg famously never even looks out the window.

A particular sort of cosmopolitanism is produced at the end of the century, born of Britain's complete confidence in its global dominance. When, as Hannah Arendt argues, the bourgeoisie are safely ensconced in political power, they begin to export that power abroad, an act which she believes initiates the New Imperialism (126). I posit that it also marks the arrival of a frictionless cosmopolitanism, in which the British are at last so secure in their global dominance that they feel free to venture out and get to know the other. This sort of cosmopolitanism, born of being "at home in the world," as Timothy Brennan observes within the context of U.S. imperialism, obscures the "national and ethnic dissonances" of the peoples that the British encounter (8). Achieving this sort of cosmopolitanism comes at the expense of the other.

Yet the round-the-world narratives also suggest that there is not just one type of cosmopolitan, nor is there just one technological trajectory, as Martin Heidegger makes clear. Heidegger argues that technology is a way of thinking that converts all objects into reserve energy, so that a hill is never just a hill, but always a mound of coal ready to be exploited. Although Heidegger warns of technology's vampiric nature, he also insists that this way of thinking is not inevitable. Alternatively, technology can be a creative force, an art. I conclude this book with the circumnavigation narratives precisely because within them a counternarrative begins to unfold. If these narratives represent the birth of technology as Leo Marx understands it, namely a concept that obscures agency, then they also open up a space for new historical agents to seize control of the technologies that have been foisted upon them. A different sort of technological vision parallels the technological conquest of the globe that these narratives promote with their tireless quest for improvements.

The round-the-world accounts give voice to those who want to take back technology—whether it be a railway, canal, or a novel—and do with it what they will. In this genre we see the inklings of a resistance to imperialism. The round-the-world genre intimates a world in which the world's inhabitants can do what Jules Verne's Londoners most fear they will, "tear up the rails" and tell their own tales. Or they can lay claim to what has been built with their own blood. The threat of taking back technology is more pervasive than just the reclamation of property, for it involves the reclamation of an ability, a means by which to remake and rewrite the world.

Chapter One

French Imports

The Entrepreneur in England, Deciphering de Lesseps

When the Suez Canal was completed to world fanfare in 1869, the British were shocked that they did not make it themselves. As we have seen, there was no reason that they could not have built it. They had the most prepared set of vessels to navigate the Canal and an industry poised to build new steamships. They had a skilled body of workers and engineers. And they had the right political connections with Turkey and Egypt. Most importantly, they had the need, a direct route to India. So why didn't the British build the Suez Canal? Perhaps they did not have the right character. In this chapter I posit a relation between market forces and novelistic enterprise in the shaping of the nation's imperial character/s. And I argue that the demands of empire helped to renew the character of the British novel.

Despite the surfeit of attention that has been paid to character throughout the last century, Fredric Jameson asserts that character has not been considered nearly enough as a product of unique historical situations (*Marxism and Form* 195). Following his lead, I show how the idea of the entrepreneur was negotiated in popular culture and literature from the speculative mania of the 1830s to the arrival of the world-famous entrepreneur, Ferdinand de Lesseps, in England in the 1850s to his international triumph in 1869. From the beginning the projector was a troubling character, precisely as a result of the historical situation in which he first emerged. In a period of rapid and unregulated development that characterized the building of the railways, someone who could get things done without the aid of the government was what was needed. Yet such a figure threatened to sully the "national character" at the very moment that this concept was being produced.[1] It was the entrepreneur's inextricability from the market, or what J.B. Say, the French political philosopher who first theorized his role, called his "unerring market sense," that made him such a dangerous figure.

Novelists had a particularly difficult time with the entrepreneur. From Charles Dickens's Mr. Merdle to Anthony Trollope's Augustus Malmotte, portrayals of finance capitalists are unforgiving. Characters who engage in speculations and investments are represented as exceedingly selfish. Their origins are obscured (although they are often portrayed in an anti-Semitic or Franco-phobic manner). They are frequently denied the most basic novelistic techniques used to create interiority such as free indirect discourse, interior monologue, and extensive dialogue. And they are an exceedingly unproductive lot, for they fail in their projects, have no children, and are prone to suicide.

Novelists struggle with the entrepreneur's representation because it threatens to reveal one of the major ideologies of the era, character, to be just that. If character was constructed in the period as emanating from the individual, then the entrepreneur, who was articulated by the market system, challenged that very notion. But as the extension of capital beyond the limits of the nation becomes necessary at midcentury, the entrepreneur's capabilities become newly valued, and novelists find a solution for representing him. In the face of empire building, novelists discover ways to rehabilitate the nation's most productive figures.

HUDSON'S STATUE: TOWARDS REPRESENTING NATIONAL CHARACTER

In 1845 George Hudson was one of the most celebrated men in England. Journalists wrote that his wealth and his influence were unparalleled. He was a new man representing a new age: a large-scale projector of the railways that were quickly spreading across the nation. By the boom year of 1845, Hudson had distinguished himself from the many other promoters who were speculating upon and investing in the new industry by successfully completing all of his projects. Whereas many projectors active in the 1830s lost credibility by promoting bubble schemes or becoming involved in ill-advised speculations, Hudson rode the waves of the speculation booms and avoided the fallout of the busts, so that during the peak years of the railway expansion period of the midforties, known as the "railway mania," Hudson too was at his peak. His enterprises encompassed industry, finance, land acquisition, and politics. By 1845 he had controlled four railway lines; promoted docks, colliers, and glassworks and dealt in iron. He had promoted and managed two banks. He acquired two Yorkshire estates, and by some reports the largest privately owned house in London. He had recently gained a seat in Parliament, and there wielded an influence that was unprecedented. Stories about his latest projections, land purchases, and arrival to

Parliament appeared in newspapers across the nation, while faith in his projections was at an all-time high. Just evoking the name of Hudson could fill a subscription list.

His wealth, power, and importance to the nation are best represented by the testimonial which was collected by various boards of directors of railways and thrown open to the public in October of 1845. Testimonials were popular public declarations of a person's achievements or service, which usually involved collecting a sum of money and presenting a gift. So prevalent were testimonials in the early Victorian era that Charles Dickens included a satire of the tradition in his 1857 *Household Words.* In "A Testimonial in Praise of Testimonials" Rev. James White mocks the nation's propensity to pay tribute in this manner to just about anyone. But Hudson's testimonial was by no means of the mundane variety: in three short months £25,000 to £30,000 was raised for the Railway King. Silverware, china, and linen, the mainstays of testimonial purchases, were not to be considered: Hudson would receive a much larger, public offering. The form that it would take quickly became the talk of the nation, as Thomas Carlyle sourly noted at the end of the decade: "The £25,000 subscribed, or offered as oblation, by the Hero-worshipers of England to their Ideal of a Man, awoke many questions as to what outward figure it could profitably take" ("Hudson's Statue" 221). Most likely the tribute would take the form of a brass statue, a prospect that made Carlyle cringe, but kept the nation talking. In a flurry of articles that appeared in newspapers across the country people discussed the size, shape, and significance of the impending Hudson Statue.

Yet, in the end, the nineteenth century left behind neither a statue nor a biography of Hudson. Despite one contemporary journal's proclamation that "the biography of Hudson would sell in thousands at the railway station" (Troup 320), his first book-length biography did not appear until 1934, more than half a century after his death in 1871.[2] By 1850 Carlyle knew that no statue of Hudson would ever be built, and that the question of what to do with the monies collected in his name would go unanswered. The testimonial question, he said, was "never finally settled; nor ever now to be settled, now when the universal Hudson ragnarok, or 'twilight of the gods,' has arrived, and it is too clear no statue or cast-metal image of that Incarnation of the English Vishnu will ever be molten now!" ("Hudson's Statue" 221). Carlyle was clearly right.[3] Yet, the reason that Carlyle supplies for Hudson's lack of memorial, "the universal Hudson ragnarok," is not so obvious.

Historians give two reasons for Hudson's downfall. First, Hudson was a victim of the turbulent and unpredictable economic cycles that characterized the railway expansions. Moreover, he was unlucky enough to be actively projecting during the year of the most radical of the economic downswings, 1847. In 1848 the British economy began to contract even further, and railway travel for the very first time began to show a decline. And second, Hudson's fraudulent business practices finally caught up with him. From 1849 on, boards of directors from the lines that he had formerly directed began to bring him to trial on various accounts of fraud. Like many of the speculators, promoters, and investors who were felt to be responsible for destroying the fortunes of a wide segment of the population, he was meant to pay the price. In his trials that began in 1849 and lasted throughout the 1850s Hudson was accused on many counts including forgery, falsification, fixing prices, cooking accounts, mismanaging funds, taking dividends from capital, creating false speculation sheets, misallocating funds, and bribing members of Parliament. Although Hudson was never convicted of any of these charges, the accusations ruined his reputation and career. By 1850, the Railway King was permanently dethroned. Although he maintained his seat in Parliament throughout most of the next decade, he had no real political power; his seat was increasingly vacant, and his incompetence in Parliamentary matters became a public scandal. Stories of Hudson's outrageous blunders appeared in all venues, from regional and national newspapers to journals and national lampoons. One popular story is that during the discussion of the spending of public money on the funeral of the Duke of Wellington in December of 1853, Hudson referred to "the delight the occasion afforded to such a vast number of our countrymen who witnessed the scene" (qtd. in Lambert 285).[4] Most sources claim that his only interest in Parliament now was in keeping himself out of debtor's prison. Although the trials of the early fifties were damaging to Hudson's reputation, Carlyle's vituperative attack in his *Latter Day Pamphlets* of 1850 caused the most harm. In "Hudson's Statue," Carlyle hurled negative epithets at Hudson, and one in particular stuck: "big swollen Gambler." It is hard to find a source after 1850 that does not cite Carlyle's words.[5]

1850 also marked Hudson's last successful projection. To much fanfare and a crowd of 50,000 he opened the Sunderland docks; after that he disappeared from public life. He lived the next twenty years in and out of exile, slowly shedding his various properties, and dabbling occasionally in projection. In Spain he tried to project a trunk line, but he failed to raise the appropriate funds. He moved to Paris, and there shuffled from cheap hotel to cheap hotel. Back in England there was almost no word of him. On returning from a trip to Paris in 1863, Dickens caught sight of him and penned the following:

> Taking leave of Manby was a shabby man of whom I had some remembrance, but whom I could not get into place in my mind. Noticing when we stood out on the harbour that he was on the brink of the pier, waving his hat in a desolate manner, I said to Manby, "Surely I know that man." "I should think you did," said he: "Hudson! He is living—just living—at Paris." (qtd. in Lambert 296)

In 1863 Dickens had all but forgotten one of the most talked-about men of his generation, and by the time of Hudson's death, it is as though the man who changed the landscape of England forever never existed.[6]

Hudson's displacement in history is the concern of most of his biographers. In 1834 Hudson's first biographer, Richard Lambert, accuses Hudson's native town of York of a "deliberate excision of the Hudson page from York and English History" (13), and he blames that excision on the public shame about Hudson that ensued after his speculations began to fail in 1848. Of that shame, he says, "So many had put their faith in him that when that faith was violently and suddenly uprooted, the only refute—after a shortlived outburst of execration—seemed ashamed silence" (Lambert 15). Lambert begins his book by lamenting that instead of constructing a memorial to Hudson, York constructed one to his rival, the solicitor who had a hand in Hudson's downfall, George Leeman. And he finishes his biography by suggesting that Hudson's memory may be lost forever: "In Scrayingham churchyard the tall grass half hides the Hudson family grave, and the grey lichen eating into the stone all but obliterated the names carved about its base" (Lambert 299). In spite of Lambert's efforts to restore the memory of Hudson to the nation, he seems to have failed. The man who Lambert said had "a dazzling popularity and influence unexampled in our commercial history" (14) remained uncelebrated: Lambert's biography stirred little response.

The turn of the twentieth century, however, saw a surge of interest in clearing Hudson's name, and three biographies with that aim were published within a ten-year period. In his 1995 biography, Brian Bailey accuses "politically correct" historians and scholars of refusing to recognize capitalist subjects. Bailey asserts that Hudson falls into the ranks of the early speculators, projectors, and investors who were vital to capitalism and who should therefore be memorialized. He sees the dubious fundraising and accounting methods that precipitated Hudson's fall as part and parcel of the period. Lambert, he hints, had not gone far enough in his rescue of Hudson, and Bailey's biography is an attempt to correct Lambert's slight. Robert Beaumont's 2002 biography is written in the same spirit. Although Beaumont admits that Hudson's financial techniques were "downright crooked," he ultimately justifies them by asserting that he "was simply playing by the political rules of the day" (33). It is Hudson's peers and subsequent historians who, he asserts, are to blame for not recognizing that reality.

Hudson's biographers introduce reception as the major factor in understanding Hudson's fall. I would like to consider Hudson's downfall in terms of the national reception of him during the period in which his reputation was being drastically revised. What did Hudson represent to the British in the mid-to-late forties? And why was that representation rejected? We know that Hudson was a scoundrel of sorts, and yet we also know that many a scoundrel has had his memorial. Hudson is most interesting to study because nobody wanted to claim him for history. I shall argue two related points: first, that it was important for Victorians to understand Hudson not just as a man, but as a character type. Understanding Hudson's character became key for a nation grappling with a new lot of characters: the speculators, projectors, and investors of the 1830s and 1840s associated with domestic railway building. Contemporaries complained that it was not always easy to detect the character of these new arrivals: "All the received tests of respectability seemed to be of no avail, and people literally could not tell whom they might trust" (Evans 3–4).[7] And second, Hudson was a representative man, but of a type that England was not yet ready to own. England was not prepared for what it was to become, nor for the men it needed to revere in order to get there. The study of the rejection of Hudson will show the confusion and ambivalence that England had about the type of man that would be necessary for the promotion of England's future projects. In other words, Hudson had no statue or biography during the Victorian age precisely because he is representative of the type of man that capitalism increasingly needed: the morally ambiguous, yet economically productive character, an enterprising man who could get things done on a large scale—who could, for example, promote the Suez Canal. The nation's inability to represent Hudson troubles Harold Perkin's argument that the entrepreneurial ideal reigned supreme during the first half of the century.[8]

I. Understanding Hudson's Curious Work

One peculiar characteristic of Hudson was the amount of work that his name alone could achieve: "A hint that 'Hudson' was going to 'take up' such-and-such a line, would send the shares up in the market with magical buoyancy" (Francis 215).[9] But the magic of the Hudson name was only symbolic of an entire economic process that was mystified and mystifying. Nobody as of yet understood overall the large-scale, unregulated investing, speculating, and jobbing that was occurring at unprecedented rates in all parts of the nation in the 1830s and 1840s. To understand the power of the Hudson name, one must understand what he did for a living. Indispensable to this knowledge is the biography. Although Hudson had no full-length biography during the period, biographical information was nevertheless in circulation.[10] Certain details of Hudson's life were commonly known and often repeated in newspaper accounts. The following is a redaction of popular biographical sketches of his life that appeared in contemporary sources: Hudson was a farmer's son born in Hawsham, near York, who at an early age was apprenticed to a draper at York because of his father's death. There he worked his way into a partnership and finally became one of the most successful drapers in York. Before he reached thirty, a relative died and left him £30,000; soon after he entered political life in York and became Lord Mayor. He was involved in all sorts of endeavors from the promotion of banks to docks, but he excelled in the field of railway speculation, and by 1845 he had built many lines in England. In 1845 he became M.P. of Sunderland and bought one of the largest homes in London.[11]

This skeletal biography, circulated as common knowledge, served to produce a sense of Hudson's character. Two of his most frequently repeated traits were his "energy" and "activity," terms commonly used to bolster the myth of the self-made man from 1825 on (Perkin 307). Yet in Hudson's case, these characteristics are not drawn from known biography but instead are used to help understand the unfamiliar parts of his life. One leap in Hudson's story was particularly difficult to comprehend: his jump from a man with an inheritance of £30,000 to one whose wealth is so extensive as to be uncountable.[12] This leap, I suggest, was explained through the vague traits of being "energetic" and "active."

Much of the writing about Hudson in the period is marked by the attempt to describe his characteristics. Paradoxically he is described as unpolished, peremptory, brusque, simple, abrupt, pushing, bustling, talkative, polite, able, organized, clear-headed, and monosyllabic. How can one be both monosyllabic and talkative? Or polite and unpolished? Equally puzzling is how his clear-headedness could be determined if he is monosyllabic. Such confusion arises because Hudson's character is merely a redaction of descriptions of his work. And his work was something that few understood. In the following we can see how two of his professions, draper and amalgamator of railways, engendered two contradictory traits, what *Fraser's* calls "brusquerie" and politeness:

> If he gave his orders to an errand-boy with the same rough peremptoriness that in after years conveyed the railway dictator's will to some non-amalgamating line, he would unfold a roll of linen to some fair and favoured customer with the same profusion of courtesy, the same incoherent professions, the same short, heavy duckings and bowings, with which he will now apologize to the Chancellor of the Exchequer . . . ("Outlines in Parliament" 217)

Understanding Hudson's character thus involved knowing his daily work life, which is just what many of his curious countrymen attempted. After his move to London in 1845, people began to make pilgrimages to his Albert Gate home to watch him at work: "You found him immersed in a multitudinous sea of papers—estimates, evidence, correspondence—surrounded by clerks, giving audience to deputations, or members of parliament, or engineers" (qtd. in Francis 219). What he did and how he did it fascinated people: "He would throw his head on the back of his chair, cover his eyes with his hands, arrange expenses, and form the most elaborate combination of figures" (qtd. in Lambert 73). In the context of his home office his character is revealed in terms of his business: "Your business must be cut and dried. He listened, not always patiently or politely, but with sundry fidgettings and gruntings, to your story, gave you your answer in a few brief monosyllables, turned his back, took up the affair that came next, and—you were shewn out" (qtd. in Francis 219). Because he is so good at what he does, he behaves brusquely: "His experience and clear insight make him impatient of details—he cuts off the most anxious applicant or the most convincing statement with a 'Yes!' or a 'No!' or a 'That won't do!' and, having got so much distilled from the royal lips, the sooner you abscond the better" (qtd. in Francis 219).

The Victorians were fascinated by what Hudson did for a living because he represented the rise of a new social breed. *The Times* captures the newness of his plight: "Now Mr. Hudson's position was not only new to himself, but absolutely a new thing in the world altogether" (qtd. in Beaumont 129). Yet what Hudson did for a living represented a challenge to narration, for the morality of his endeavors was ambiguous. Therefore, vague and sometimes contradictory traits were ascribed to him. Hudson's "energy" came to stand in for a whole group of work activities that were not fully understood by the general public, and his "brusquerie" mystified market practices by not giving him a voice, for Hudson when he did "speak" voiced the ideology of monopoly capital and unregulated industry better than any other. "I think the public would rather be in the hands of companies than of government," he confidently asserted to Gladstone (qtd. in Beaumont 71). He is credited with "winning" the middecade arguments with Gladstone, who advocated state-controlled expansion of railways, while Hudson argued that monopoly and unregulated growth were the best way to promote railways.[13] The result was that because England's transportation system was largely left to the market and not to government planning, and few laws were in place to regulate market practices, a breed of sometimes reputable, often disreputable characters arose and flourished—the jobbers, speculators, investors, and projectors who helter-skelter raised the monies for the projects. Hudson was representative of these men. And what he stood for became unbearable for the nation, so much so that it struggled with his representation, ultimately choosing not to represent him at all.

II. Debating Hudson's Public Worth

Through the discourse surrounding the Hudson Testimonial of 1845, we can best see the anxieties about what Hudson represented. The testimonial coincided with two events that raised his status as a national figure: the purchase of his London home, an act that was symbolic of a move from the periphery to the center, and his entrance into Parliament. Both of these events raised Hudson's national presence, but it was the testimonial, which was opened to the general public through various boards of directors, that made Hudson's significance a public concern. When the testimonial opened in October, subscriptions poured in from all parts of the nation until it closed three months later with £25,000 to £30,000 received. The testimonial opened up a site for people to evaluate the type of man whose activities were frequently called "unparalleled" and "unprecedented." Up until this point, critical discussion had not often reached the public realm; there were even suggestions that it was impolitic to criticize the "King" publicly.[14] However, through the testimonial responses in the form of letters to newspapers across the country, Hudson was converted into a representative figure.

The advertisement for the testimonial that appeared in the nation's principal papers in October stressed the public nature of Hudson's work:

> The committee feel that it is wholly unnecessary for them to attempt to urge the powerful claims of Mr. Hudson to the gratitude and respect, not only of all who are shareholders in the several lines of railway with which he is concerned, but of the public generally. His pre-eminent services are universally appreciated and acknowledged: and of the success that has attended his labours the public have experienced the most abundant and satisfactory proof. (*The Times* 6 October 1845)

Within only a couple of weeks, £20,000 had been raised towards the testimonial, and money kept pouring in. But as some paid tribute to the hero, others began to question his worthiness. The critique warrants attention because although it often took the form of *ad hominem* attacks against a "greedy" and "selfish" man, more was being challenged than just Hudson. In the following response to the Hudson Testimonial, for example, what begins as an attack upon Hudson's character ends with a question about Hudson's relation to the nation:

> George Hudson, a man reared behind a counter in York, with scarcely two ideas in his head, was left money by some relative or other, and speculated in railway scrip and railway shares, by which means he accumulated vast wealth, bought estates from Dukes, lords and commoners, and latterly he sought and found admission into the House of Commons as M.P. for Sunderland. He never did any great thing for his country. All he has done has been for himself. (*The Times* 23 March 1846)

Implied here is that testimonials were spaces through which national character was represented, debated, and defined.

Often the responses to Hudson's testimonial take the form of comparison pieces. As above, the "greedy," "selfish" Hudson is compared to an unselfish man such as Sidney Bernard or Thomas Waghorn. Sidney Bernard was an English surgeon who boarded the *Eclair,* a ship that contracted a plague off the port of Madeira and was forbidden to dock, and then guided the ship home, only to perish on the way. *The Times* commented, "A more signal act of cool disinterested heroism is not on record" (28 November 1845). Similarly, Thomas Waghorn was perceived as contributing to the public good. According to *The Times,* he dedicated his life to building a road through Egypt. In 1846, in a piece contrasting Waghorn and Hudson, Waghorn came out on top:

> Thomas Waghorn, a brave officer, has crossed the burning sands of Egypt again and again to find out a short route between England and India. Whereas that journey, a few years ago, could not be accomplished in less than two, three, four, and sometimes six months, Thomas Waghorn has succeeded in throwing it open within the space of 30 days. (23 March 1846)

Further, *The Times* described Waghorn as "opening up a communication between millions of the human race. He is adding to the grandeur and glory of England" (23 March 1846). By comparison, Hudson was perceived as achieving nothing for England and nothing for the human race.

Bernard had no testimonial despite his lofty contributions to humanity: "Alas, for Sidney Bernard and the gallant volunteers of the *Éclair;* alas, for their widows and orphans! No testimonial is proposed to record their daring humanity; no subscription is raised for the families of the dead" (*The Times* 19 November 1845). And Waghorn was only a little better off, complained *The Times.*

> He is enriching its [England's] merchants—stretching out incalculable bounds for their enterprise; and what have they done for him? There was laid down at the bar of the Royal Exchange, the other day, a subscription paper for some 'testimonial' to Thomas Waghorn. It lay there for four days—it lies there still. Some 10 or 12 Glasgow firms have subscribed in all £70 to it. Blush, ye mammon-worshippers of George Hudson! And let our ears tingle ye ungrateful recipients of the matchless services of Thomas Waghorn! (23 March 1846)

Comparing Hudson to Bernard and Waghorn made clear that Hudson was not a humanitarian, but it accomplished far more than that.

Underlying the testimonial critiques is the question: what type of man should represent our nation? This suggests that the real agenda in the comparison is the creation of a "national character." The problem is that the projector, speculator, or investor cannot be ignored in this project at this time. Yet to have a projector represent the nation would be, in *Punch's* words, "monstrous." However, Hudson's testimonial and the critique that followed did in fact turn him into a representative figure of the age, as *Tait's Edinburgh* observes at the end of the decade: "Mr. Hudson will be accepted as the most appropriate illustration of the speculative and railway spirit in the current decennial period" (Troup 320). But the cultural response to Hudson shows not just reservations about him but also about the role of the projector in the nation.

By 1849 it was clear that Hudson's statue would not be built, yet Carlyle still wrote a piece of invective against its erection one year later. Carlyle saw clearly that Hudson was representative of the age, or perhaps more importantly, he saw that the character of the age was reflected in Hudson: "If Odin, who 'invented runes,' or literatures, and rhythmic logical speech, and taught men to despise death, is worshipped in one epoch; and if Hudson, who conquered railway directors, and taught men to become suddenly rich by scrip, is worshipped in another,—the characters of these two epochs must differ a good deal!" (238) Carlyle may have argued that he wanted

Hudson's memory expunged—"If you would have sunk a coalshaft . . . deep coalshaft, there to bury him and his memory, that men might never speak or hear of him more" (226)—yet what he argued more effectively was that he wanted an age expunged. Carlyle desired to rid the epoch of the projectors, investors, and speculators that made it distinctive; he wished to stamp out the laissez-faire morality that defined the times. In short, he wanted to rid the age of its character.

MERDLE'S COMPLAINT: MARKET FAILURE AND THE LIMITS OF CHARACTER

Few Victorians were more vocal in their dislike of Hudson than Charles Dickens, who said, "I find a burning disgust arising in my mind—a sort of morbid canker of the most frightful description—against Mister Hudson. . . . There are some dogs who can't endure one particular note on the piano. In like manner I feel disposed to throw up my head and howl, whenever I hear Mr. Hudson mentioned" (qtd. in Bailey 70). Yet there are few writers who grappled more productively with the Hudson tradition. Dickens recognized on some level that England must celebrate its risk-takers and capital raisers if it were to compete on an international level. In the late fifties, the promoter was beginning to be revalued, and this revaluation process can be seen in Dickens's *Little Dorrit* (1855–57). *Little Dorrit* presents the social death of the character of the projector, a phenomenon that we already saw with Carlyle's "burial" of Hudson. But *Little Dorrit* reconstitutes this character into a socially acceptable form.

Dickens ushered the Hudson type into literature with the figure of Merdle, of whom he said, "If I might make so bold as to defend that extravagant conception, Mr. Merdle, I would hint that it originated after the Railroad share epoch, in times of a certain Irish bank, and of one or two other equally laudable enterprises" (*Little Dorrit* xxi). Merdle was not meant to represent Hudson, but rather John Sadleir, the Irish MP. Sadleir was a railway and bank promoter who had perpetrated extensive fraud and committed suicide in 1856 after the discovery of his involvement in the Tipperary Bank scandal. However, Dickens was critiquing a type, not a man, and Hudson's indecipherability was more representative of that type than Sadleir's transparency. Everybody knew what Sadleir was—he was a scoundrel and a swindler—but Hudson's contribution to society was not fully understood. Despite Carlyle's attempts to limit his cultural significance, the ambiguity surrounding Hudson was still alive. Merdle's character relies on a cultural moment of indecipherability of the Hudson type.

Merdle is a mystery that muddles its way through Dickens's text. The essence of his character is the muddle that his name evokes.[15] Dickens introduces him in a chapter called "Merdle's Complaint," in which Merdle has a complaint, but nobody knows what it is, not even his doctor: "I can find nothing the matter with Mr. Merdle. . . . He may have some deep-seated recondite complaint. I can't say. I only say that at present I have not found it out" (*Little Dorrit* 212). Merdle is inscrutable, and it is precisely this inscrutability that is essential to the Merdle plot, which can function only if nobody understands what he does. "Nobody, as aforesaid, knew what he had done; but everybody knew him to be the greatest that had appeared" (476). Merdle's profession is as incomprehensible as the money system itself: "Nobody knew with the least precision what Mr. Merdle's business was, except that it was coining money" (331). Slyly, the text avoids clear labels: Merdle is vaguely called "a world-famed capitalist."

Merdle's inscrutability is reinforced by novelistic devices. In the exposition of his theory of heteroglossia, Mikhail Bakhtin turns to *Little Dorrit* to demonstrate the hybrid nature of discourse in the British comic novel. Hybrid utterances belong grammatically and compositionally to single speakers, but actually contain mixed within two utterances, manners, or styles (Bakhtin 304). Bakhtin quotes from *Little Dorrit* to demonstrate this:

> It was a dinner to provoke an appetite, though he [Bar] had not had one. The rarest dishes, sumptuously cooked and sumptuously served; the choicest fruits, the most exquisite wines; marvels of workmanship in gold and silver, china and glass; innumerable things delicious to the senses of taste, smell and sight, were insinuated into its composition. *O, what a wonderful man this Merdle, what a great man, what a master man, how blessedly and enviably endowed*—in a word, what a rich man! (304)

Bakhtin explains that the passage starts with a "parodic stylization of high epic style," and then beginning with the italicized portion moves into "concealed speech of another." This concealed speech represents a chorus of enthusiastic Merdle worshipers, and society in general, but is undercut by a return to an authorial utterance, "in a word, what a rich man." With these words, the hypocrisy of the social chorus is unmasked. Bakhtin says that here the merging of authorial speech with common opinion exposes the hypocrisy and greed of the common opinion.

It is telling that Bakhtin chooses *Little Dorrit* and specifically Merdle to explicate his theory of heteroglossia. Of the eight examples of heteroglossic utterances that he takes from *Little Dorrit,* seven of them are focused on

Merdle. Indeed, Bakhtin turns to *Little Dorrit* because Merdle is a heteroglossic composite. Of course, heteroglossia is the essence of the novel form for Bakhtin; nevertheless, Dickens's use of it in the creation of Merdle is extreme. It is as though Dickens does not want to take responsibility for his creation. This is not the case with other characters in the novel, not even the most despised characters: Miss Wade, Blandois, Gowan, and Casby. Merdle is unique in that he does not exist outside of the context of the heteroglossic utterance.

Thus, stylistically, Merdle is a Hudsonian conundrum. On the one hand, the lack of authorial sanctioning makes him the most unstable character in the novel. On the other hand, he has foundations firmly rooted in society. His character, like Hudson's, is a pure social formation; born, as Dickens claimed, of the Railway share epoch, he is a unique historical record of the social voices of speculative mania. With Merdle Dickens found a way to narrate *laissez-faire* morality. Moreover, this endeavor takes the form of a "character." And in the production of this character, Dickens absolves himself of authorial responsibility, allowing Merdle to arise from the depths of the novel itself.[16]

Bakhtin theorizes character as a formalistic device. Characters do not exist; instead, "character zones," or spaces around which heteroglossic discourse centers, populate the novel. Such zones are open, permeable, and dialogic. Merdle, a purely heteroglossic production, then, is the most characteristic character of Dickens's novel. Ironically, he is brutally expelled from its pages. Although Bakhtin's understanding of character is profoundly at odds with the bounded and impermeable construction of character during the nineteenth century, it does reveal much about the problems inherent in representing Merdle. In order to understand why Merdle cannot ultimately be represented, we must briefly return to Hudson.

Merdle's suicide highlights an important facet of the understanding of character in the period: individuals are responsible for their own character. If this is so, then the social making of Hudson/Merdle challenges these beliefs. Throughout the Hudson trials of the 1850s, writers began to raise questions about whether Hudson was solely responsible for his actions. The general tenor of such accounts was that Hudson did only what society wanted him to do. Monkton Milnes's musings are typical: "Hudson has done exactly what the shareholders all the time wanted him to do, and which plan, if it had succeeded in making the branch lines remunerative, would have been regarded as a measure of courageous prudence, but which, having failed, is now called swindling" (qtd. in Beaumont 112). Even Hudson's frequent critics, the editors of *The Times,* argued that the system, not Hudson, was at fault:

> The system is to blame. It was a system without rule, without order, without even a definite morality. Mr. Hudson, having a faculty of amalgamation, and being also so successful, found himself in the enjoyment of a great railway despotism, in which he had to do everything out of his own head, and among lesser problems to discover the ethics of railway speculation and management. (qtd. in Beaumont 128–129)

Here the editors inadvertently expose the fantasy behind character. If character is the responsibility of the individual, then it is easy to fix a broken capitalist system because all that is troublesome about that system can be named, contained, and exiled. But the system, which is responsible for making Hudson and Merdle, will always come up with new creations, new voices, new forms. To represent them is to expose the ideology of character.

Merdle's emergence from the belly of the novel makes it difficult to fix his meaning because we have so few authorial markers to hold onto. One way to know a person is to know what he does for a living; however, the plot of *Little Dorrit* insists on an inexact knowledge of his profession.[17] He, like Hudson, is a projector, investor, speculator, but these words are vague. Further, in the novel, the vagueness about who Merdle is allows others to be ensnared by his schemes. Notice this slippage between the description of Merdle and his schemes: "He's a man of immense resources—enormous capital—government influence. They're the best schemes afloat. They're safe. They're certain" (487). The person who is most affected by Merdle's schemes is Arthur Clennam, who has just returned from operating his family's business in China. After twenty years, he comes home to extricate himself from the business and to "set things right." Clennam, characterized by his carefulness, is the very last person we expect to find investing with Merdle. Yet he invests all of the money of his friend and business partner, Daniel Doyce, into Merdle's projects, a move which lands Clennam in debtor's prison. Instead of putting things in order, he succumbs to the chaos of the market. How does the text explain such an incongruent step? What causes him to take this financial misstep can be traced to a conversation that he has with his friend Pancks about Merdle's enterprises. A fundamental lack of understanding about the workings of the market economy of the thirties and forties allows Clennam to make this grave error. Clennam asks Pancks:

> "Is it not curious, Pancks, that the ventures which run just now in so many people's heads, should run even in little Cavalleto's?" "Ventures?" retorted Pancks, with a snort. "What ventures?" "These Merdle enterprises." "Oh!

> Investments," said Pancks. "Aye, aye! I didn't know you were speaking of investments." (*Little Dorrit* 486)

"Ventures," "enterprises," "investments" are all words suggesting similar activities; however, they have slightly different meanings. Pancks considers Clennam's original question, but does not answer it. Instead, he gets stuck on a word; he continues: "Yes. Investments is the word" (486). In turn Clennam doesn't follow; instead he returns to his original question, but chooses the wrong word, "speculate": "Right in sharing Cavalletto's inclination to speculate with Mr. Merdle?" "Per-fectly, sir," said Pancks. "I've gone into it. I've made the calculations. I've worked it. They're safe and genuine" (487). Still Clennam doesn't stay with the word "speculate," and when the subject comes around again, Clennam chooses another, "And you have really invested," Clennam had already passed to that word, "your thousand pounds, Pancks?" (488) Stranger than Clennam's conversion from the word "speculate" to the word "invest" is the narrator's need to make note of it ("Clennam had already passed to that word.") The conversation finishes with the word "invest" and Clennam decides to "invest" with Merdle.

This self-conscious wordplay shows the importance of the developing terminology of business in the period as well as an underdeveloped understanding of that terminology. Pancks steers the conversation away from certain words like "venture" to which he reacts with a bold snort. He is aware of the connotations of such words, while Clennam is not. "Venture" is a risky word and it is an old word, having too many associations with the merchant-venturers, who beginning in the sixteenth century criss-crossed the seas with their wares, risking in the process life and material loss. "Venture" could be the death knell of a new economy. To raise the massive amounts of money necessary to create railways throughout England, capitalism needed to cast its net wider than the few hero-adventurer types who would risk life and product for material gain. Too few people wanted to take on that adventure; instead they wanted something, as Pancks states, "safe." Pancks knows intuitively that "investments" is a better word, a safer word, yet he does not seem to understand the nature of the word "speculate."[18] The meaning of "speculate" was ambiguous, and was more indicative of the general lack of understanding about capital raising in the period. In some cases, "speculate" was used synonymously with "invest." But in many cases "speculate" had more risk attached, and had associations with get rich quick schemes and fraudulent activities. In this latter usage, "speculator" describes the first one on the scene—buying quickly and quickly unloading what they bought as in this 1849 usage: "Railway speculators who invested merely for the day, to sell again to-morrow, if the market rose" (Troup 321).[19] The "investors" followed, seeking a smaller but more permanent return on capital. Thus when Pancks steers Clennam away from words like "venture" and "speculate," he is demonstrating a developing consciousness of a morality of the market that is associated with safeness and stability.[20] Pancks knows more about the market because he, as a rent collector, has been exposed to money matters. Clennam, on the other hand, a "stranger in England," has no recent knowledge of the economy. He is not aware of England's radical speculative growth cycles, and the new aggressiveness of the free market economy. But most importantly, he has no knowledge of this new market's principal characters, as he learns to his and Daniel Doyce's sorrow. For soon after this scene between Pancks and Clennam, we discover that Merdle's Complaint had been "simply Forgery and Robbery" (*Little Dorrit* 594). Merdle murders himself with a penknife to the jugular in a public bath. With that, the text seemingly absolves itself of its major conundrum. Dramatic as his death may seem, Merdle's death comes from a re-labeling of him—from Banker to Forger, from Projector to Swindler. His character is killed along with its ambiguity.

Even after Merdle's death Dickens continues to be concerned with the problem of Merdle. More precisely, he is concerned with Merdle's progeny and with the nation's productive future. How will the nation continue to raise the capital needed for its large projects without relying on criminals (or the criminalization of men) like Merdle? How will the nation learn to evaluate and understand its risk-takers and capital raisers so as to compete productively—and safely—on an international level? Amanda Anderson has argued that Dickens's nationalism in this novel is ambiguous, for he critiques provincialism and promotes critical distance throughout. But within the context of Dickens's business plots, even his critical stance towards provincialism serves the nation. Through his business plots, Dickens discovers a creative solution to capital reproduction, and one that seems to be a specific response to the Merdle/Hudson phenomenon. He posits a new sort of character, one who can take care of the nation's business without taking on the ugly undertones of such associations.

I. Business Matters

Little Dorrit posits a strange cartography. Among its gloomy streets and its repressed and stifling prisons and governmental institutions exists a variety of Victorian business activity, almost all of which could be described as is the Clennam family business, "out of date and out of purpose" (37). The Clennams, the Dorrits, Monsieur Blandois, Casby, Pancks, the Plornishes, and

Daniel Doyce all dabble in business. A business debt structures the first half of the novel, for Mr. Dorrit sits in prison because he had signed a bond for "the performance of a contract that was not at all performed" (471). Because of the debt he incurred, his business in "spirits, or buttons, or wine, or blacking, or oatmeal, or woolen, or pork, or hooks and eyes, or iron, or treacle, or shoes" (471) went bust, and he went to prison. Further, Arthur Clennam returns home to a family business with which he wants nothing more to do.[21] Housed in a gothic setting of nocturnal perambulating, subterranean meetings, and family secreting, this home business is "on the decline" and marked by a sense of decay and lack of currency. In the end, it mysteriously collapses, taking with it all of its supporters. Monsieur Blandois, who often visits the house on "what he calls business," disappears under the rubble. This French wife-killer and swindler ran a dubious blackmailing business. Another type of business is represented by Casby, the real-estate mogul, the patriarch who has Pancks collect his rents, giving him "all of the dirt of the business" while he takes "all the profits." Pancks exposes him as the rackrenter that he really is, and shears him of his flattering locks. Exhibiting a wide-ranging vocabulary for such cheats, Pancks publicly outs his dirty dealings, calling him a driver, screwer, wringer, squeezer, shaver, deceiver, sneak, and bottle-green smiler. Even the unemployed working-class Plornishes are set up in business in the Bleeding Heart Yard by Mr. Dorrit who helps them establish a local store, but they are plagued with cash-flow problems, for their poor neighbors buy on credit which they never pay off.

Indeed, the outlook of business of all sorts in this novel appears to be grim: business seems to be losing its productive capacities. But actually the novel represents business in all of its stereotyped connotations in order to finally present a viable model. The way that the word "business" is in play can be seen in its application to Mr. Meagles. Mrs. Gowan, an aristocrat with no money of her own, contemptuously describes Mr. Meagles, the banker who supplies her son with money through his marriage to Mr. Meagles's daughter, Pet, "as a man of the world and one of the most business-like of human beings" (435). The narrator then explains that what Mrs. Gowan means by "business-like" is "artful schemer" (435). By the end of the novel, however, Mr. Meagles proudly claims, "I am a man of business" (677), suggesting that that term has been shaken of such negative connotations.[22]

For the type of revitalization that we see here to occur, two of its inhibiting objects must be disposed of. First, business must be cleared of provincial attitudes that hold back its growth. The houses of Dorrit and Clennam represent a stagnant provincialism about business practice. Both of these businesses live within the family name. Dorrit's comfort in his prison cell suggests a provincial mindset. The Clennams, who branched out to China, came home empty-handed. They are literally housebound. Mrs. Clennam is a prisoner of her home, never leaving it until the day of her dramatic death. When the Clennam house crumbles to the ground, the Clennam firm is no more. And second, business must be rid of deep-rooted cultural prejudices that are raised by its mere presence. These attitudes hold that all business activity is synonymous with fraud or gambling, and that dabblers in the market are either swindlers or, as Carlyle called Hudson, "gamblers swollen big." Blandois and Casby, for example, are produced as unambiguously corrupt swindlers and frauds.

Blandois represents the fear of free-trade's potential: the creation of uncontrollable flows across borders; he crosses no less than six borders. He is a self-proclaimed "cosmopolitan," and he is at home in the world as his accentless speech shows. His threat is not only the threat of the Other—the not-French, French swindler, who sucks the lifeblood from the country, while filling his own purse—but also the threat of unfettered trade. Casby, on the other hand, represents the opposite. His home-based business of collecting rents is profoundly English. The profundity and richness of the vocabulary that Pancks hurls at him shows how long his type has been around. He symbolizes economic stagnation resulting from an old way of doing business. Clennam notes that Casby was "as unchanged in twenty years and upwards, as his own solid furniture" (121), and he associates Casby's establishment with his own unchanging family business ("The house . . . is as little changed as my mother's" (120)). In the end, however, Casby's treatment differs from that of Blandois and Clennam's mother. He is not expunged, but rather changed: his appearance is altered when Pancks cuts his hair.

Merdle should be understood in relation to these two men. Like Blandois, he is a man without a country, and he stands for the threat of the free flow of goods and ideas. Although he is of a much newer breed of businessman, he has become affectively tied to these other two through his greediness, lack of human concern, and hypocrisy. The cultural prejudice against Blandois and Casby also bleeds onto him. The fate he suffers, though, is that of the foreigner, suggesting which prejudice is more dangerous.

Of all the businesses in *Little Dorrit,* the Plornish "grocery and general trade" store is most puzzling. It neither gets expunged nor reformed. Instead, it impossibly hobbles on with all of its credit problems, miraculously producing goods from behind the counter, which are faithfully consumed, never paid for, and always replenished. Further, the store represents the influx of a new type of product into the Bleeding Heart Yard to which its working-class inhabitants were "unaccustomed"—the luxury item. Perhaps the Plornishes represent the fantasy of modern Empire: endless consumption without an evaluation of the cost. At the very least, their presence raises the question: where do they get their money? Since Mr. Dorrit set them up in business, we may assume that it is he who continues to fund them, but his untimely death negates that possibility. The mystery that the Plornishes provoke, especially how the consumption habits of the Bleeding Heart Yard will continue to be met, lead us to turn to the only other business in the Yard, located at its "other end." If the Plornishes raise questions about consumption, the Doyce and Clennam Company does so about production. Dickens frames the latter as a problem of management.

Doyce's business goes through more changes than any other in the novel, but they are only registered at the management level. In the beginning of the novel Doyce is the owner of the foundry; he also performs the duties of projector, manager, inventor, engineer, and keeper of books. Soon, however, a deal to split the ownership of the factory with Clennam saves Doyce from going out of business. The novel ends with the promise of the adoption of a third partner, Pancks, projecting the firm's growth into the future and suggesting that this business is the most productive of the novel.

II. Business Models

Though Clennam, the character with the strongest anti-business sentiment in the text comes home from abroad precisely to abandon his family business, he is recouped by this text, and re-established in business in a new way. Clennam's relation to a changing business climate is established when he returns to his family business in which "nothing has changed" in over twenty years and refuses to move into the Clennam House of business. Instead, he lives separately and establishes "daily business hours" (47) at the Clennam House, two acts which represent a more modern way of doing business. But more importantly, Clennam's new role is established when he becomes partners with Daniel Doyce, who is an inventor, engineer, and projector but is not fit for the business side of business, as he explains to Clennam ("No inventor can be a man of business, you know" (161)). He is a projector and an inventor, not a calculator and keeper of books. The split between these two functions is most strongly upheld by Doyce when he explains his need to partner: "So I find that I must have a partner who is a man of business and not guilty of any inventions" (161). Thus the Doyce/Clennam partnership is a solution to an economic problem. It is also a solution to Clennam's personal problem, invigorating him and giving his life modern meaning by providing him with a "promising career" (222).[23]

The Doyce/Clennam partnership is most significant, however, because it makes business a national concern. Doyce, in particular, understands his business to be the improvement of the nation, for he wants to do "something serviceable to the nation" (168). Doyce's patriotic conception of business differs from what is expected of Clennam when he returns to his family business. Mrs. Clennam believed that he "would infuse new youth and strength into it, and make it a great profit and power" (44), that is, profit put to the private use of the revival of the family fortunes. In contrast, Doyce only has the "public interests" at heart. But because the Circumlocution Office does not recognize public interests, Doyce reasons, he must seek work abroad, saying of England and its governmental Circumlocution Office: "Have you ever heard of any projector or inventor . . . whom it did not discourage and ill-treat?" (103). Thus he goes abroad to a place where projectors and inventors are encouraged, while Clennam runs their business at home. Unfortunately Clennam is no more fit for business than Doyce; his calculations are off. He speculates with Merdle and ends up in jail. The partnership, as configured, is shown to be unproductive.

The text dramatizes this unproductive partnership in order to fix it. It uncouples the business/inventor pair in order to reunite them in a much stronger and more productive form. In the final chapters, Clennam sits depressed and in prison, not unlike Mr. Dorrit before him. Outside of the prison walls Little Dorrit is poising herself to marry him. Although everything is in place for the anticipated marriage, something must be done before it can happen, as Mr. Meagles explains: "We must have Dan here . . . we must have Doyce here. I devote myself, at daybreak tomorrow morning, to bringing Doyce here" (678). So Doyce is fetched from abroad and brought back to England. But upon return he makes a proposal of his own, telling Clennam that "a new and prosperous career was opened before you and me as partners" (686). Of course Doyce and Clennam were already partners, but with these words Dickens raises their partnership to a new status. He places it on the level of marriage, having Doyce and Clennam's partnership take place in the same temporal frame as the Clennam/Dorrit wedding. Thus, *Little Dorrit* ends with a second marriage, the partnering of Doyce and Clennam, the successful joining together of the engineer/inventor/projector with the man of business. By closing with these dual marriages, Dickens equates domestic happiness with business prosperity, suggesting that the nation's well-being depends upon a productive business model.

LESSEPS'S VISIT: FOREIGN IMPORTS AND THE REVITALIZATION OF NATIONAL CHARACTER

Little Dorrit is divided into two unlike parts. The first begins in a French prison and swiftly relocates to the prison cells and suffocating rooms of

England, and the second begins in the Swiss Alps and weaves through Europe, following the spatial logic of a grand tour. While the first part is claustrophobic and close, the second is loose and open. Structurally, it is almost two separate novels. Actually, this two-part structure can be understood as a part of the business plot. It enables Dickens to reconsider business in a wider perspective, adding life blood to English business, by encouraging a flow of people and goods across borders. Critics have commented upon the items that the Meagles bring home from abroad with which they decorate their home. Indeed, the Meagles' exotic baubles distract one from the other goods that flow into England from abroad in this novel. The most important inflowing commodity is information. For example, Blandois receives the information that makes his blackmail trade possible in Antwerp. Meagles gathers important information in France when he collects the suitcase that holds the long-concealed codicil to the will that threatens to alter Little Dorrit's life. And most importantly, Daniel Doyce comes home from his sojourn into "barbaric" lands with knowledge that is vital for his business and necessary for his country.

In fact, Doyce comes home much improved: richer, more prosperous, and better able to take care of business. Furthermore, Doyce has done the impossible: he has circumvented the Circumlocution Office. The fact that it took years to put Mr. Dorrit's financial affairs in order but it only took Doyce a few days to clear up Clennam's accounts makes one want to know exactly what Doyce learned abroad. The little we are told of Doyce's experience in an unnamed Arab-speaking land is impressive: "Dan is directing works and executing labors over yonder, that it would make your hair stand on end to look at" (685). In 1891 Richard Theodore Ely wrote in his *An Introduction to Political Economy,* "We have been obliged to resort to the French language for a word to designate the person who organizes and directs the productive factors, and we call such a one an entrepreneur" (170). I suggest that abroad Dan Doyce learned to be an entrepreneur.

I. The Arrival of the Entrepreneur

Throughout the fifties the Frenchman Ferdinand de Lesseps visited England to promote the Suez Canal to the British public. He canvassed the country visiting business groups, newspapers, and politicians in every major city. He carried with him maps and drawings and plenty of calculations. The business community embraced him, but the government and its officials did not.[24] After consulting the prominent railway engineer, Robert Stephenson, Lord Palmerston labeled Lesseps's project "impracticable," and nearly no British people invested in his shares.[25] Although he was not able to persuade them to purchase his wares, they did seem interested in a more intangible offering. His arrival into England was simultaneous with another: in the fifties the British imported the French word "entrepreneur" into common parlance. Before then, it had only been used academically by British political economists who had borrowed the term from the French in the 1830s.[26] Lesseps, arriving in England on the heels of the economic downswing of the late 1840s, came to represent the ideal of the entrepreneur to the British public just at the moment when the nation was in need of such a representation. He embodied the spirit of enterprise and investment, and represented culturally what figures like Hudson and Merdle did not.

According to Bert F. Hozelitz, the most common term in use in nineteenth-century England to describe men like Hudson and Merdle was "capitalist." But this word was overly general, while other words, such as "projector" and "promoter," perhaps more precise, became increasingly opprobrious.[27] Whereas Hozelitz suggests that "capitalist" was used by the British throughout the nineteenth century until "entrepreneur" was adopted at the century's end, I argue that earlier than this Britain's colonial expansion necessitated the importation of a term that was more specific and positive than the ones in existence. "Speculate," "promote," and "project" were three commonly used words in the beginning of the century. Although they always had had a seamier side, these words became less flattering as the century progressed. "Promoter" from the French *promoteur,* which had been in use since the mid-fifteenth century, and had the relatively neutral meaning of "one who or that which promotes, advances, or furthers any movement or project; a furtherer, an encourager" (*OED*), began to take on negative undertones in the nineteenth century. Thus by the 1870s readers of *World* had to be assured that: "A promoter, *quoad* promoter, is not necessarily a bad man" (*OED*). "Projector," borrowed from the French *projecteur,* was popularized in the seventeenth century. Like "promoter," its early usage was relatively free of negative connotations. It simply meant "one who forms a project, who plans or designs some enterprise or undertaking; a founder" (*OED*). However, soon it accumulated negative connotations.[28] By 1729 "projector" is adopted in a truly ironic form to name the profession of the speaker of Swift's "A Modest Proposal." Henceforth the projector is potentially suspect. In the nineteenth century "promoter" and "projector" are imbued with hybridity. On the one hand they signify productivity and generation; on the other the cool calculation of a schemer or cheat.

The word "entrepreneur," however, took on positive connotations early. It gets the business done without the negative undertones of its predecessors. According to the French philosopher J.B. Say, who is often credited with introducing the concept of the entrepreneur into economic literature in his 1803 *Traité* (translated as *A Treatise on Political Economy* in 1834), an entrepreneur is the "master of all that was known in a particular branch of industry, and who had collected the requisite capital and labourers" (Berg 91). As the organizer of production, he is at the center of a web of relations, holding together landlord and capitalist, technician and laborer, producer and consumer (Koolman 273).[29] Say is the first to justify entrepreneurial income, which he does on three counts: as a return for the moral qualities of the entrepreneur, for ensuring that an enterprise had capital, and for undertaking risks of enterprise. Consequently, the entrepreneur draws on three sources of income: a wage payment, interest on capital, and a premium for risk (Berg 91). Say criticized Adam Smith for ignoring the difference between gains of superintendence and the return on capital, arguing that the profits from superintendence were dependent upon skill, activity, and judgment. By thus justifying the entrepreneur's income, Say newly values this actor, giving him a role to play (justified by a wage) at the center of the economy, instead of at its periphery on the high seas. The primary quality of the entrepreneur, according to Say, is judgment and an "unerring market sense" in the face of market uncertainty and flux (Koolman 275).

Lesseps was a visible example of this new type. He was revered for his skill at bringing together diverse elements, for his incessant activity, and his superior judgment. Like the word he came to embody he was a much-needed injection to a nation that had larger projects, imperial projects to undertake. Although Lesseps's project was not the biggest engineering feat of the century, it was widely believed to rely upon the most skill in its execution, for it involved the coordination of various elements including an international body of labor, investors, and politicians. Though the British had nothing to do with the canal project, its promoter was the subject of public discourse throughout the second half of the century.

One can perceive this preoccupation in the first nineteenth-century British biography of Lesseps, published in 1876, by Percy Hetherington Fitzgerald, biographer of James Boswell, Laurence Sterne, and Charles Dickens. Fitzgerald marks Lesseps's difference from the likes of Hudson in the innovative way that Lesseps raised funds for his project: "Lesseps did not lack applications from the horde of pseudo-financiers and rich gamblers that bred and flourished under the Empire; but he had determined from the outset that they should have no part in the enterprise; he would not even allow the legitimate magnates of the stock exchanges of Europe to lend him their rather costly assistance" (119). Fitzgerald distinguishes Lesseps in two ways. First, he applauds him for turning his back on institutional support, singling out Lesseps's skill at seeking out financial sources from middle-class investors. Second, Fitzgerald stresses Lesseps's lack of greed. Cordoned off from the greed that marked his predecessors, Lesseps came to represent a new type, a man not tainted by the same rapaciousness as Carlyle's big swollen gamblers. If England was going to extend the type of projects that Hudson and his compatriots did in the forties into the fifties, sixties, and beyond, and do so without negative consequences, it needed some respectable role models, even a hero.

Fitzgerald makes Lesseps into a romance hero, complete with more difficulties to overcome than Bunyan's Christian on the way to the Celestial City. He writes, "The story of the Suez Canal, together with that of its persevering projector, who has finally succeeded in triumphing over all obstacles and all opposition, has ever seemed to contain something romantic, and to be worthy of being made the subject of regular narrative" (Fitzgerald vii). In Fitzgerald's "regular narrative" Lesseps overcomes all odds, including lack of labor, lack of water, lack of towns and a port, lack of funding, and lack of support from the Ottoman Empire. But most importantly, Lesseps overcomes the lack of support from the British Government. Like Doyce and Clennam, Lesseps succeeds in spite of the English government. He too circumvents the Circumlocution Office.

By 1876 Lesseps could safely be hailed a hero. Since the British had purchased the majority of the Canal shares from Egypt just one year earlier, celebrating Lesseps became a form of national affirmation. However, the story of Lesseps was long in the making. I shall argue that the state forges the entrepreneur into a national hero long before Fitzgerald does. Fitzgerald embellishes state discourse and packages it in a narrative form well suited for the cultural affirmation of the individual, biography.

II. State Production of the Entrepreneurial Hero

Harold Perkin argues that the "entrepreneurial ideal" emerged in the beginning of the nineteenth century and that by midcentury it held sway. Soon, however, a professional middle class, affiliated with the expanding state bureaucracy, rose to challenge the entrepreneurial class, and by 1880 these new professionals gained precedence.[30] Building on Perkin's thesis, Lauren Goodlad argues that middle-class identity at midcentury should be understood as a contest between entrepreneurs and professionals. She states that this contest defines the new "national character" of the age, complicating Mary Poovey's earlier argument that "national character" must be understood in relation to the rise of the professional classes. I shall argue, however, that professionals and entrepreneurs reinforce each other's power. The state and the class of professionals that it engenders make the entrepreneur into a heroic figure. The entrepreneur, in turn, reinforces the state's power with his newly articulated national vision.

Lesseps's story begins to unfold in the British press in 1854 when he surprised the world by obtaining a concession for building the Canal from the Viceroy of Egypt, Said Pasha. For the international press, this was an ingenious political coup, for Lesseps had single-handedly bypassed the formidable power of the Ottoman Empire by obtaining permission straight from the Egyptian ruler. But the British government adopted an obstructionist policy towards him and his project. *The Times* explains how the government used their influence with Turkey to interfere with Lesseps's project:

> When the Pasha and the company had agreed upon the project why should England interfere, or how? The thing was done in this way:—Egypt is not exactly an independent state. Its Viceroy has a Sovereign above him, and that Sovereign has always seen good reason for listening to the counsels of England. So the British ambassador spoke to the Sultan and the Sultan spoke to the successive Pasha of Egypt, and M. de Lesseps occasionally found obstacles in his path. (15 August 1863)

Ironically, by blocking Lesseps at all roads, the British government created a fascinating "romance" narrative, one in which a Doycian hero emerges to counter the government's blockage. In summing up Lesseps's early problems with navigating between the Viceroy of Egypt and the Sultan of Turkey, which were aggravated by Britian's attempt to obstruct the project by manipulating the Sultan, for example, William Hamley notes in *Blackwoods:*

> M. de Lesseps procured a concession from the Viceroy sanctioning the commencement of the works; but this concession was not good without the Sultan's ratification, and great pressure was put upon the Sultan to induce him to withhold his approval. The difficulty was at length overcome through the perseverance and insistence of M. de Lesseps, who forthwith made a demonstration by commencing the works. (741)

In the face of British-induced adversity, Lesseps's heroic traits of "perseverance" and "insistence" emerge. The more the British government and press criticized Lesseps, the larger his implied heroic character grew. In Britain's principal papers, every obstacle that Lesseps faced, whether real, theoretical, or just imagined was published and dwelled upon. Commenting upon this phenomenon, Hamley provides a sense of the things that were said about the Canal in the British press:

> "The Canal will be a stagnant ditch," said some. "It will be filled by the sand of the Desert." "The bitter lakes, through which it is to pass, will be filled up with salt." "The Mediterranean entrance cannot be kept open." These, and many more, were the cheering prophecies that M. de Lesseps was complimented with in English journals. (741)

Beginning in 1854 when the concession was granted, and continuing until 1869 when the Canal was completed, the press carried stories about the insurmountable problems that Lesseps would face. They did not foresee that as they stacked up the problems, they fortified the character when he overcame each declared obstacle. The press insisted that Lesseps's efforts at digging the Canal would be futile, for the land had no rock-base and would continually fill up with sand. But Lesseps employed native building techniques to pat dry the sand and let it dry in the sun, thus creating a solid base that did not cave in as expected. The press predicted that he would not be able to find enough workers in labor-poor Egypt to build his canal, and that even if he could procure the labor he would not be able to provide the workers with enough water in the desert. But he negotiated a contract with the Pasha to provide him with four-fifths of all labor that he would need, which the Pasha fulfilled by *corvee.* And he engineered a channel bringing fresh water into the desert. They predicted he would never be able to replace the Egyptian workers after the Pasha pulled them out to work in the newly robust cotton industry in 1863, and that this blow would be fatal to his relations with the Pasha. But Lesseps brought labor in from Southern Europe, Syria, Greece, and Albania and when he still didn't have enough workers he replaced labor with machinery, massively employing the dredger and the elevator to international critical acclaim. Then he mended the poor relations with the Pasha, and continued to work. Time after time, Lesseps faced real problems with real solutions. Thus British obstructionism produced a truly resistant "character," as Hamley admitted in *Blackwoods* in 1869:

> If there had been only smooth sailing—if there had been no imputation, no misrepresentation, no prophecy of failure, no scoffing—then the perseverance, energy, and confidence of M. de Lesseps could not possibly stand out as they now do. The opponents of the scheme have

given opportunity to M. de Lesseps of proving himself to be one of the great. (740)

III. The Entrepreneur's Articulation of a National Vision

A distinctive vocabulary began to settle around Lesseps. He possessed energy, perseverance, and confidence. He had zeal and faith. And he was visionary. Some of these characteristics are nineteenth-century commonplaces, such as energy. Samuel Smiles, who wrote biographies about engineers, industrialists, and ironworkers throughout the 1860s and 1870s, attests to the importance of energy in the character of his subjects. Perseverance and determination were also important for Smiles. As important as Smiles's writings were in teaching the habits that enabled national projects, he was unable to advocate the ethos necessary for raising large-scale capital for the construction of international projects.

Perseverance, as we have seen, became important to the entrepreneurial ideal. Although Smiles's understanding of perseverance changes over time, he never develops a model of perseverance that breaks out of the national mold. In *Self Help* (1859), Smiles equates perseverance with patience, especially while working. Word pairings such as "long laboured," "incessant industry," "indefatigable industry," and "incessant toil" show that Smiles's "perseverance" is synonymous with habitual work. Obstacles that the persevering must overcome are predominately figured as bad habits: laziness, drunkenness, sleeping late. Smiles's uses the idea of "perseverance" to inculcate good work habits. In Smiles's *Lives of the Engineers* (1862), perseverance takes on a different meaning. In this work Smiles documents the biographies of the prominent canal, road, bridge, and railway builders of the eighteenth and nineteenth centuries, using techniques so similar to Fitzgerald's that it seems probable that Fitzgerald borrowed from it in his depiction of Lesseps. Smiles documents how each engineer overcame nearly insurmountable obstacles to achieve his goals. George Stephenson, the railway engineer famed for his successful introduction of the locomotive, for example, faced severe difficulties:

> It was declared that its formation would prevent cows grazing and hens laying. The poisoned air from the locomotives would kill birds as they flew over them, and render the preservation of pheasants and foxes no longer possible. Householders adjoining the projected line were told that their houses would be burnt up by the fire thrown from the engine-chimneys; while the air around would be polluted

> by clouds of smoke. . . . Boilers would burst and blow passengers to atoms. (*Lives* 195–196)

In the face of such obstacles, George Stephenson took on the motto "Persevere!"

Although Fitzgerald may have borrowed from Smiles, his representation of Lesseps is more than just a throwback to Smiles's old-fashioned engineers. In other words, Fitzgerald is not just coopting Lesseps and forcing him into an accepted British model. Fitzgerald's projector differs from Smiles's engineer for Smiles carefully maintains a separation between the qualities of the engineer and the projector in order to separate the hard-working engineer from the taint of money-making.[31] Smiles's separation of the engineer from the capital raiser is one of his accomplishments in *Lives,* and can further be seen in his depiction of George Stephenson. Smiles clears Stephenson of George Hudson's taint, for Hudson famously projected a line on which Stephenson worked. To this end, Smiles repeatedly claims that Stephenson "would have nothing to do . . . with stock-jobbing speculations" (471). Not only does Smiles maintain the difference between Hudson and Stephenson, he also shows how the Stephensons were unlike the engineers better known for their international speculations, the Brunels. Whereas the Stephensons were "inventive, practical, and sagacious; the Brunels [were] ingenious, imaginative, and daring. The former were as thoroughly English in their characteristics as the latter perhaps were as thoroughly French" (397).

Smiles excludes the "French" Brunels from his *Lives.* He sticks to the "English" variety of engineer whose "humble" and "inarticulate" character he can celebrate. He portrays George Stephenson as an "untaught, inarticulate, genius" (*Lives* 203). Smiles leaves the capital raising and the articulation of a project upon which it relies to the projectors who populate only the background of his account. Smiles's engineers are a humble lot. If he does not make this clear in his repeated usage of the word "humble," the many drawings of their humble cottages that illustrate his writings do. And he does not allow his engineers to stray far from this domestic image that he takes pains to create. For example, he frames the story of Robert Stephenson's youthful mining venture in South America in the mid-1820s as an utter disaster, replete with a shipwreck and a spooky chance encounter with Richard Trevithick, the famed builder of the first railway locomotive, who has become so poor in South America that he must beg money from Stephenson to get home. Stephenson himself does not stay long in Marquita, where he has been hired to work as an engineer in a silver mine, for he gets homesick and goes home.

Robert Stephenson died in the year that work on the Suez Canal began, but he was one of the most influential critics of the Canal. When he pronounced that the project was "impracticable," his expert opinion was then touted by every politician or journalist who took up the subject. Hence, when the Canal was completed in 1869, Robert Stephenson was frequently blamed, and Lesseps's triumph became Stephenson's failure. The Suez Canal suggested that one of England's most important engineers lacked what Lesseps had in abundance. Ironically, Stephenson lacked perseverance.

Fitzgerald had difficulty finding British characters with whom to compare Lesseps. Smiles had so thoroughly cleaned up and nationalized British engineers and projectors that Fitzgerald had to look far afield to find a British equivalent to Lesseps. Oddly enough, he draws a comparison between Lesseps and the practically unknown Thomas Waghorn, the Englishman who claimed to have established an overland route through Egypt approximately forty years earlier. According to Fitzgerald, Waghorn shares Lesseps's perseverance: "There was a certain resemblance between the persistent efforts of De Lesseps and the heroic perseverance of this projector [Waghorn]" (6). Yet Waghorn was not appreciated in his lifetime, as we have seen in *The Times'* 1846 lament that his testimonial raised a mere £70.

Fitzgerald's comparison of Lesseps to Waghorn is important because it marks the cultural valuation of Waghorn in the context of empire building. Waghorn, practically unknown during his lifetime, was celebrated upon his death in 1850 when the moving "Diorama of the Overland Route to India" was shown in Regent Street. According to Freda Harcourt, "The pictures confirmed Egypt as Britain's high road to India, and Waghorn's . . . exploits served as symbols for Britain's expanding empire" (*Oxford DNB*). Nineteen years later England, faced with the prospect of nothing to show at the international grand opening ceremony of the Suez Canal, chose to unveil a statue of Waghorn to rival the monument to Lesseps. Ironically, scholars have since demonstrated that Waghorn's claim to have discovered an overland route through Egypt was false. It was just one of many stories that Waghorn invented in order to try to raise money for his exploits. The fact that without an iota of proof and not even one eyewitness to validate Waghorn's claims, the British government built a monument to him to rival a statue of the internationally renowned Lesseps shows the importance of manufacturing national heroes in the face of empire building. Clearly Hudson, who had left thousands of miles of track behind him, had done more than Waghorn, who built not a single road in Egypt. Yet the difference seems to be in the ability to articulate a humanitarian claim. Waghorn was "opening up communication between millions of the human race" (*The Times* 23 March 1846). If Waghorn's story suggests the new importance of entrepreneurial heroes, it also reveals character itself to be a construct. That Waghorn stands memorialized next to Lesseps indicates that

Lesseps may have been of the same mettle. Few, for instance, remember that a French court found Lesseps guilty of gross mismanagement of the international project that he undertook in the 1880s, the Panama Canal, for which he was fined heavily and sentenced to lengthy imprisonment.

Waghorn, however, is ultimately no match for Lesseps, Fitzgerald admits: "He had the same energy, but unhappily, not the wonderful gift of our projectory—that of fascinating those to whom he addressed with his plans, and of inspiring them with an amazing belief in him" (11). Fitzgerald draws a further distinction between Waghorn and Lesseps at the same time that he lays British claims on Lesseps ("our projectory"). The distinction seems to be in Lesseps's vision. "Visionary" was the kind of word that could produce a smug smile in England, as Lord Clarendon knew it would when he dismissed Lesseps's project as "wholly visionary." Yet Fitzgerald made Lesseps's visionary powers into his greatest asset. Being a visionary implies an ability to see something as a whole, a quality which Smiles notes that George Stephenson lacked: "So long as he was confined to locomotive engines and iron railroads, with the minutest details . . . he felt at home . . . but when the designs of bridges and the cost of constructing them had to be gone into . . . his evidence was less satisfactory" (*Lives* 207). In addition, visionary powers depend upon the ability to articulate that whole vision to others. But not only that: visionary language can stir people to action or belief; in other words, it is performative.[32]

The success of Lesseps records a historical moment when it was fathomed that one person could match great obstacles with nothing more than a vision. Some of the most often quoted words of Lesseps are: "All of a sudden I saw a brilliant rainbow display itself and spread across the sky from west to east. I own that my heart began to beat violently, and I seem to see in this sign the true union of east and west, and a prophetic notice that the day was to be marked by the success of my scheme" (qtd. in Fitzgerald 20). In light of this it is no surprise that Lesseps became the hero entrepreneur and not Hudson, whose most often repeated words are the much more provincial "Make 'em all come to York."

Lesseps had a way of inspiring confidence—just like Doyce, who comes home and says he'll "put matters right," and he is believed. It seems that only after Doyce's imperial experiences is he able to articulate a clear vision of Britain's future business. Doyce's longest speech in the novel occurs upon his return home, (he is given twenty-four uninterrupted lines), and his language here is different as well: his words are newly persuasive and performative. They give Clennam the confidence that he needs: "You will profit by the failure," "You have it in your power" (*Little Dorrit* 686). In this final speech Doyce reveals not only that he straightened up the accounts of the firm, belying his earlier claim that he has no talent for business, but that it is on firmer footing than it has ever been. Although we know that Doyce has already done the work of reviving the business, his words have the effect of making it so (by in fact hiding the work from Clennam's and the reader's sight). Doyce also projects a vision of the future, "a new and prosperous career was opened before you and me as partners" (686). Finally, it is Doyce who predicts the Clennam/Dorrit wedding: "If this young lady will do me the honor of regarding me for four-and-twenty hours in the light of a father and will take a ride with me now towards Saint Paul's Churchyard, I dare say I know what we want to get there" (687), a prediction which is immediately followed up by the real thing on the following page. Indeed, the new Doyce seems to usurp authorial power, "putting matters right" so that this midcentury Victorian novel can close with all in order.

* * *

Hudson was brusque, he was opaque, he was bulky. Like the trains that he came to symbolize, he lacked subtlety and diplomacy. Pictures of him exaggerate his size: he is portrayed as being as big as a locomotive. Also depicted frequently was his oversized house, rumored to be the most expensive privately owned home in England. Yet Hudson's unprecedented power of material accumulation was, in the end, impotent. It could not be articulated or made sense of by him or his culture. Literal representations of his type were similarly mute and short-lived, as was the case with Dickens's Merdle.

Lesseps was different. He is depicted surrounded by people rather than objects, as in a widely circulated drawing of him amidst politicians, or another popular picture of him in the bosom of his large family—a wife and nine children. Another common cartoon of him shows him dressed as a caveman standing with one foot firmly planted in the East and the other in the West, purposefully poised between two hemispheres, his body forming a bridge. In this same picture his half-naked body ripples with muscles, and a club dangles from his waist. Similarly in another cartoon, he carries a shovel in one hand and proudly gestures to his work with the other. Lesseps is never represented with symbols of his material wealth as Hudson is; instead, he is shown carrying tools which make him appear to have a purpose. Neither is Lesseps pictured as awkward; even as he straddles two continents, he does so with strength and grace. Hudson, on the other hand, always looks out of place, possibly something Dickens picked up on when he characterized Merdle as shuffling from room to room, never quite knowing where to put himself. In one cartoon of Hudson, he stands on top of a globe but looks as if he might topple off at any moment; he is not at home in the world. Lesseps, straddling the globe with ease, represents a new comfort in the wide world. Like Doyce, he confidently slips over borders, only gaining from his movement. The pictorial representations of Lesseps, like his words, are more articulate than those of Hudson. They work to make sense of him and his type, to articulate him into the social body, to give his exploits imperial purpose and to value that purpose.

I have argued that the adoption of the idea of the "entrepreneur" enabled a positive valuation of those who crossed international frontiers to collect capital. The entrepreneur finds further acceptance because he is figured as cosmopolitan. In an age in which markets were increasingly international, projectors learned to be savvy about the world. Hudson never learned. He could not articulate the nation, let alone the world. Despite his contributions to the nation, the British perceived him to be profiting himself only. Smiles's studious avoidance of Hudson in his *Engineers* demonstrates that Smiles recognized the need to demonstrate the national value of the work of engineers and projectors. But Smiles ignored the international endeavors of his subjects.

It is no wonder that Lesseps took the nation by surprise. He represented a new character, one who could articulate a global identity. At first, however, the British could only understand him as "French." But upon the completion of his project, this "Frenchman" became English. Even so, Lesseps remained a sort of ideal. Dickens recognized the value of such an ideal, for he saw the solution to the nation's economic stagnation in its characters. Struggling to create an acceptable projector to fill Merdle's place, Dickens exploited the nineteenth-century novel's conventional nuptial ending to unite an odd couple: the domesticated businessman and the visionary engineer/projector. But this marriage, just as any other in the period, also created a productive division of labor within the partnership. Prior to partnering with Clennam, Doyce *was* a businessman, despite his insistence that he was not. The partnership allowed him to deny his past. Moreover, it enabled him to concentrate solely on the entrepreneurial role—to practice his "unerring market sense." Doyce stepped out of the role of humble engineer and thwarted projector and into the role of visionary entrepreneur who could articulate a nation with his international experience and capital. By partnering with Doyce, Clennam could distance himself from the taint of such international enterprises, and the guilty conscience that plagued him throughout the novel could be cleared at last. The newly sanctified division of labor ensured that the internationalist/French/visionary would not contaminate the newly domesticated and reeducated businessman. Doyce is no "world-famed capitalist" as was Merdle, whom he and Clennam jointly replaced, but Doyce's union with Clennam frees Doyce to exploit his international endeavors as never before.

Doyce is also no Ferdinand de Lesseps. Doyce uses his worldly knowledge to infuse the nation with new ideas. He articulates the entrepreneur into the fabric of the nation to bring about a new business outlook that is motivated by the ideology of national good rather than private gain. Lesseps, more world-wise than Doyce, uses his entrepreneurial skills to suture together Europe, articulating a vision of international cooperation that will ultimately smooth the way for European nations to economically conquer the globe. Together they make that global conquest possible. Lesseps enables Doyce, for without Lesseps's righteous ideology and the international unity that it fosters the Doycian figure would be impotent.

Chapter Two

English Exports

Romantic Investments, Novel Technologies, and Disraeli's *Tancred*

Half a century after the death of Benjamin Disraeli, Prime Minister in 1868 and again from 1874 to 1880, Hollywood came out with a movie celebrating his role in the making of the British Empire. Alfred Green's 1929 film *Disraeli* is a romantic comedy about Disraeli's purchase of the Suez Canal in 1875 and his conferment of the title "Empress of India" upon the Queen the following year. In the movie an avuncular Disraeli, played by George Arliss, overcomes all obstacles to purchase the Canal from Ismail Pasha, the Egyptian Khedive whose regime totters on the edge of bankruptcy. The movie shows that by purchasing this direct route to India, Disraeli spared Egypt from bankruptcy, saved England from the rapacious Russia, and ushered in a new age of imperialism.

Disraeli's role in Green's movie is peculiarly Lesseps-like. While everyone around him questions his desire to spend four million pounds on an "Egyptian ditch," he moves forward with visionary resolve. First he asks the Governor of the Bank of England to loan him the funds, but this stodgy representative of William Gladstone's "little England" adamantly refuses, saying, "Your scheme is harebrained, unconstitutional, and the bank will be no party to it." Adding insult to injury, he continues: "You have the eastern imagination. Because this canal runs through a desert, you see it in a dream—a mirage." Undaunted, Disraeli moves ahead and attempts to secure a loan elsewhere. As Disraeli courts bank after bank, a pair of Russian spies lurk about his office attempting to thwart his plans by stealing correspondence, spreading gossip, and sinking a ship of Argentinean bullion heading Disraeli's way. But Disraeli outwits the sly duo at every turn.

While Disraeli is busy circumventing the Bank of England and outmaneuvering the Russian spies, he also becomes involved in plotting a marriage. He takes an interest in the career and love life of a certain underling, a young and handsome minister without much initiative. Clarissa, a beautiful girl of nineteen, and a daughter-figure for Disraeli, has just refused a marriage proposal from this man, claiming that he'll never make anything of himself. Disraeli turns matchmaker and decides that the way to get the couple together is to make the young man into a hero. He therefore sends him on a "dangerous" mission to Egypt where he is instructed to give Ismail a check to pay for the Suez Canal. Disraeli's plot works. The minister hands the check to the ruler, and he returns to England a hero. Such heroism not only secures the Canal; it secures his marriage.

In a quiet moment of this busy movie, Disraeli's wife compliments her husband saying, "Ah Dizzy, always dreaming a romance." It is not clear whether it is his matchmaking skills or his canal dream that earns him this accolade. But it is clear that the movie valorizes and conflates Disraeli the romantic, Disraeli the visionary, and Disraeli the imperialist. In the crowning scene of *Disraeli,* which takes place at a royal fete, a marriage is proposed, the Suez Canal is purchased, and the title of empress is conferred upon the Queen—all brought about by the hand of the enterprising Disraeli.[1]

Conflating domestic happiness with imperial success, the movie reveals a popular ideology of empire from a prior period. It was Disraeli who fifty years earlier popularized the idea that imperialism abroad would bring status and prestige to the domestic realm. Up until Disraeli's 1874–1880 ministry, "imperialism" was a word applied exclusively to foreign despots. It was first used in the 1840s to describe the desire of *le parti imperialiste* in France to revive the glories of the Napoleonic era. During the next two decades, it was commonly associated with those who practice despotic rule at home and aggressive policies overseas. It wasn't employed in British domestic politics until 1876 during the acrimonious debates on Disraeli's Royal Titles Bill that made the Queen "Empress of India." *The Times* stigmatized the new title as "threatening the Crown with the degradation of a tawdry Imperialism" (qtd. in Eldridge 26). And the *Fortnightly Review,* the *Spectator,* and *Punch* followed suit. Thus the word "imperialism" was linked to Disraeli in the press. For the next four years Disraeli's political opponent, Gladstone, and the Liberal Party accused Disraeli not only of practicing imperialism abroad but also argued that Disraeli would bring despotic rule home to England. Imperialism became a smear-word used by Gladstone and the Whigs against Disraeli and the Conservative Party (Eldridge 26–27).

But Gladstone's plan backfired. Disraeli preached that imperialism would bring England prestige, power, and status. He called for a more active foreign policy, emphasizing the role that Great Britain could play on the world stage. In his Crystal Palace speech of 1872, famous for its forceful call for empire, Disraeli trumpeted,

> It [the issue] is whether you will be content to be a comfortable England, modeled and moulded upon Continental principles and meeting in due course an inevitable fate, or whether you will be a great country,—an Imperial country,—a country where your sons, when they rise, rise to paramount positions, and obtain not merely the esteem of their countrymen, but command the respect of the world. (qtd. in Eldridge 89)

Disraeli's appeal for empire became increasingly attractive to a public that was at first leery of the idea. In 1880, *The Times* noted that the Liberals' attempts to injure Disraeli by portraying him as an imperialist had failed:[2]

> "Imperialism" was a word invented to stamp Lord Beaconsfield's supposed designs with popular reprobation. But the weapon wounded the hand that wielded it, and a suspicion was engendered, which seriously injured the Liberal cause, that Liberalism was in some sort an antithesis of Imperialism. It will cost Lord Hartington and his associates not a little pain to eradicate this popular belief. (11 March 1880)

By the end of Disraeli's ministry "imperialism," a word that hitherto held negative connotations, glittered. *Disraeli,* the movie, captures the brief glory days of British imperialism and the long-lived nostalgia for empire that followed. It captures a romantic, visionary, and thoroughly imperialist Disraeli.

Although it is clear that during Disraeli's 1874–80 ministry imperialism became a popular ideology for the first time, Disraeli's precise relation to imperialism is still contested. Disraeli's ministry coincides with the rise of the "New Imperialism," a term used to describe the aggressive accumulation of territories by European nations in the last quarter of the century.[3] Although Britain's numerous territorial acquisitions during Disraeli's ministry is un-debatable, historians question just how responsible Disraeli was for Britain's expansion. In *Disraeli and the Rise of the New Imperialism,* C.C. Eldridge seeks to answer the question, "Was Disraeli the prophet of the New Imperialism?" and concludes that he was not. Rather, the territorial acquisitions of his 1874–80 ministry occurred in an unplanned and haphazard manner. Eldridge writes, "Disraeli was not the expansionist he is so frequently alleged to have been" (50). Disraeli lacked a plan and a theory of imperialism. He was not interested in administrative details, and he made no legislative reforms. Advancements into the tropics were not a part of a new expansionist Conservative philosophy of empire; instead, Eldridge argues, they resulted from Disraeli's failure to oversee ministers and control men.[4]

Eldridge searches for material evidence of Disraeli's imperialism by tracing his involvement in wars and acquisitions in places such as the Fiji Islands, the Gold Coast, the western Malay states, the Transvaal Republic, and Cyprus. He concludes that although Disraeli's imperialism cannot be located in his relation to any of these physical spaces, it still cannot be altogether denied. Eldridge suggests that Disraeli provided England with a "concept of a powerful England, strengthened by the resources and peoples of a far-flung empire playing a decisive role in world affairs" (73). For Eldridge, Disraeli's contribution to empire lies in an idea: "Colonial administration had never been of deep concern to Disraeli. It was the idea of empire, India and the East which fired his imagination" (Eldridge 46). In his final analysis, though, Eldridge gestures in another direction: "It was the grandeur and the romance of it all that captured him" (65). Thus, Eldridge concludes by suggesting that one might locate Disraeli's imperialism not only in his ideas but in his sense of romance.[5]

Disraeli, who is infamously difficult to pin down, becomes only more so in Eldridge's conclusion. For many scholars, Disraeli's "slipperiness" is related to his outsider status. Of Jewish descent, he was constantly in the need of "self-fashioning" for his own survival in an anti-Semitic nation.[6] But Eldridge also seems to suggest that Disraeli's indecipherability is a generic problem: "He delighted in creating an air of romance and mystery" (66). And in Eldridge's final paragraph, he asserts: "He loved romance and mystery" (73). Because Eldridge cannot fully unveil Disraeli as a prophet of the New Imperialism or debunk this long-held belief, he suggests rather that what motivates Disraeli is romance. And he intimates further that we might also find Disraeli's imperialism in the genre that Disraeli was so fond of writing. In Hollywood's *Disraeli,* when Disraeli's wife compliments, "Ah Dizzy, always dreaming a romance," she also hints that her husband's imperial dreams are related to his literary ones. Thus, I follow Eldridge's and Green's leads and take a generic turn in the explication of Disraeli's imperialism. I turn to what was reportedly Disraeli's favorite novel and one of his most perplexing romances about the Middle East, *Tancred* (1847). And I suggest that we begin looking here, in the complex form of this novel and romance about a young man's quest for religious and political truth in the Middle East, for clues to Britain's renewed imperialism.

The point here is to move away from the type of analysis that blames one man for a policy that was clearly bigger than any individual. At the same time, the preoccupation with Disraeli as the author of British imperialism should not be entirely dismissed, for it reveals the way that such an abstraction as imperialism was comprehended by many. It was associated with an "amusing" and highly "original" character.[7] Even fifty years after the fact, Disraeli was still remembered as the avuncular face of British imperialism, as the award-winning *Disraeli* shows. But it has been noted that Disraeli first dreamt up his imperial plots, not in his heated Crystal Palace speech of 1872, but twenty-five years earlier, in his novel *Tancred.* I take these observations as a cue to move away from the type of history that singles out a lone agent and focus instead on the much more social institution of genre. Based on an understanding of genre as a historical and social production, as argued by Michael McKeon, Fredric Jameson, and Franco Moretti, I query the relation of genre to imperial practices. McKeon and Jameson have shown how romance emerges during periods of rapid change and social instability. And McKeon and Moretti intimate the novel's capacity to mediate, resolve, or domesticate change. All of these theorists conceive of the historical changes recorded by romance and the novel within a national or European context. I am, however, interested in what happens when these forms' capacity to articulate, contain, or integrate change is considered outside of the European context. The question, then, is not as Eldridge conceives it, "Does Disraeli advance England's first popular theory of imperialism?," but rather, "Why does Disraeli first theorize imperialism in the novel?"

JOINT VENTURES: THE ROMANCE AND THE *BILDUNGSROMAN* IN THE MIDDLE EAST

Much of the contemporary criticism of *Tancred* focuses on its content as opposed to its form. *Tancred* is a novel of ideas. In it the young and idealistic Tancred, disgusted with the ways of the West, travels to the East to "penetrate the mysteries of Asia." He seeks ways to rejuvenate a Europe that is obsessed with progress and not enough concerned with prophesy. "Christendom," he declares, "cares nothing for that tomb [the Holy Sepulcher] now, has, indeed forgotten its own name, and calls itself enlightenment Europe. But enlightened Europe is not happy. Its existence is a fever, which it calls progress. Progress to what?" (231). Tancred believes that in the East he will find the spiritual model for a necessary revival of the West. Instead, he becomes embroiled in political battles and falls in love with a young Jewish woman, Eva. At the end of the novel, Eva states that all of Tancred's hopes have been disappointed and that he no longer believes in Arabia.

Nineteenth-century reviewers praised *Tancred* for its grand ideas: "The great merit of the work is the grandeur of its conceptions; it always suggests the supremacy of the spiritual over the material; one principal pervades the whole which may be briefly stated—'Asia thinks and lives; Europe works and perishes'" (Taylor 389). But not all reviewers were so enthusiastic about what they understood as Disraeli's denigration of the West: "All that has been done by the Reformation, by the English and French revolutions, by American Independence—is here proclaimed an entire delusion and failure; and we are taught that we can now only hope to improve our future by utterly renouncing our past" (Monckton 141). Moreover, many critics were taken aback by Disraeli's desire to revive a dying Europe with ideas culled from the East, specifically from Judaism. Although some praised Disraeli for his propensity to hold out Judaism as the source of a European renewal ("He holds with a fervour in every way honourable, a belief in the marvelous endowments of his race" (Stephen 430)), most did not. Some critics were outraged at what they considered Disraeli's audacity in desiring "to make Europe don the graceful and variegated costume of the nations of the East, and—hear it, hall of Exeter!—to convert the whole world, converted Jews and all, back to Judaism!" (*The Times* 2 April 1847).

It is difficult to find a piece of contemporary criticism that does not limit its analysis of *Tancred* to the ideas that it contains. The same is true of modern criticism. Edward Said revived critical interest in *Tancred* in 1978 when he used Disraeli's novel to illustrate orientalism:

> His novel *Tancred* is steeped in racial and geographical platitudes; everything is a matter of race, Sidonia states, so much so that salvation can only be found in the Orient and among its races. There, as a case in point, Druzes, Christians, Muslims, and Jews hobnob easily because—someone quips—Arabs are simply Jews on horseback, and all are Orientals at heart. The unisons are made between general categories, not between categories and what they contain. An Oriental lives in the Orient, he lives a life of Oriental ease, in a state of Oriental despotism and sensuality, imbued with a feeling of Oriental fatalism. (102)[8]

Said and other postcolonial critics discuss *Tancred*'s content in detail, but write little about *Tancred*'s perplexing form. Genre critics have left *Tancred* relatively untouched. However, studying *Tancred*'s generic split can yield a fuller understanding of genre's relation to imperialist practices. Thus, in this chapter I examine the two dominant genres which undergird *Tancred,* the romance and the *Bildungsroman,* and argue that it is through the combination of these forms, and then their imaginative "exportation" to the Middle East, that *Tancred* does its political work.

Tancred is made up of a variety of forms—from the romance, born in the twelfth century, to the political novel, of which it was in the vanguard.

Some critics credit Disraeli with inventing the political novel, and *Tancred,* following *Coningsby* (1844) and *Sybil* (1845), was his third novel of this kind.[9] But *Tancred* can also be considered a travelogue, and a few contemporary critics felt that one of its strongest features was its evocations of the East: "It contains brilliant and beautiful descriptions of eastern scenery" (Waller 266). Indeed whole sections of Disraeli's diary recording his 1830–31 trip to the East can be found in the pages of *Tancred.* But Disraeli was also interested in local scenery, and he spent the first third of his novel describing English country estates and the festivities of aristocrats. The first two books of *Tancred* are written in the style of the Silver Fork novel, a form which Disraeli had never quite given up since the publication of his first Silver Fork novel, *Vivian Grey,* in 1826.[10]

Most importantly, *Tancred* is also a romance, as Daniel R. Schwarz notes:

> *Tancred* reflects Disraeli's continued admiration of romance plots. Like Byron's heroes, Childe Harold and Don Juan, or Scott's hero in his historical romances, Tancred inhabits an imagined world where diurnal details rarely intrude in his quest. An imaginary voyage, *Tancred* is loosely held together by the hero's physical journey which introduces him to incredible people and fantastic places. (61)

Schwarz's claim rests on commonly held critical notions about the type of scenery, action, and character romance contains. Scenery in *Tancred* is unreal: Tancred inhabits "an imagined world" full of "fantastic places." And the novel lacks "diurnal details" or the everydayness that is often associated with the nineteenth-century realist novel form. The action of *Tancred,* too, is like the action found in romance; the hero heads out on an "imaginary voyage" organized by a "quest." Schwarz implies that *Tancred*'s characters are rather "incredible people," reflecting the common understanding that romance lacks character development.

Schwarz describes *Tancred* accurately, in part. But there is another reality to *Tancred,* as one contemporary reviewer notes: "It will be read again and again with renewed pleasure, and with equally renewed perplexity, for it is at once the most brilliant of dreams, and the most sober of realities" (Taylor 385). As much as *Tancred* could be said to be marked by its imaginary settings, it also could be said to be characterized by its "sober realities." *Tancred* also participates in the conventions of the *Bildungsroman.* We can see this by considering the shape of the novel as a whole, for although *Tancred* contains novelistic elements throughout, it demonstrably veers from the romance form towards the end, as Disraeli attempts a conclusion. Unlike the ending of the typical plot of the romance, where the hero returns home after a series of adventures, Tancred stays in the Middle East. Both his declaration of love to Eva, and the arrival of his parents in the very last line of the text, suggest that Tancred will not return to England and that the Middle East is now his new "home." What appeared to be a romance plot as defined by Northrop Frye—a series of adventures only stopped by the achievement of the final quest—turns out to be more like a classical *Bildungsroman* plot as defined by Franco Moretti—a form that aims for the integration of the protagonist into a "homeland." Tancred's "integration" into the Middle East, I shall argue, is the project of this novel.

Tancred is thus poised between romance and novel. *Tancred's* ambiguous stance towards genre allows us to see how these two technologies—romance and novel—work together to turn the Middle East into an imaginative zone for the British public. Through analysis of *Tancred* we can see how space becomes activated to incorporate new prose technologies. These technologies in turn circulate notions of investment, occupation, and ownership. Most importantly, the production of ownership is an imaginative cultural practice that happens through prose structures. For example, romance encourages an imaginative investment in an unknown world. It organizes the symbolic investments needed for a "novel" way of knowing. On the other hand, the novel, with its technologies of settlement—quotidian concerns, particularization, and everydayness—stakes out claims of home. The particular nature of the *Bildungsroman*—a form with a teleology of integration—has further implications to the newly novelized world.

Railways, Telegraphs, and the Rise of the Egyptian Novel

Although I am primarily concerned with the way that genre is used to turn the Middle East into an imaginative zone of investment and development for the British public, I shall briefly place *Tancred* within the context of the exportation of capital to the Middle East, for it is within this historical context that we can best understand *Tancred*'s generic construction. Railway construction began in Britain during the 1820s, and by the 1840s the British were building railways in France and Germany. In the following decade, they began to export railways, telegraphs, and their financing structures beyond Europe, jump-starting what would become an intensive investment in transport and communication technologies around the globe. In the process the British public's identity as investors began to change. As I have indicated in Chapter 1, a new relation was being forged between Britain and its peripheral investments. An important place to view this change is in Egypt, for it was there that the British invested in the 1850s, building the railways and telegraph lines that would ultimately aid in tightening England's grip on India.[11] As a result, during the 1850s a new culture of investing and national ownership begins, one that dreams of expansion. And Britain's expansive dreams are incorporated not only in material exports but also in newly exported romance and novel technologies. *Tancred,* with its undiscriminating setting in Syria, Lebanon, Palestine, and Egypt, represents an imaginary exportation of the romance and novel to the Middle East.

But there are also very real links between the exportation of railroads, telegraphs, and steamships and the exportation of novel technologies. The printing press arrived in Egypt in 1798 with Napoleon's expedition. For the next fifty years, it was used mainly in official and military capacities until it fell into disrepair in the 1850s. When Ismail came to power in 1863, however, he revived the press as a part of his wider campaign to modernize Egyptian culture as well as to assert independence from both Ottoman rule and his European creditors (Kelidar 2). The press flourished under Ismail and its role in the Arab cultural revival of the period cannot be underestimated.[12] Three reasons for the vitality of the press were Ismail's support of it, a political situation that sparked much discussion and debate, and an influx of new ideas from Middle Easterners who flocked to Egypt to escape Ottoman oppression and take advantage of Ismail's new openness.[13] Abbas Kelidar emphasizes the dynamic nature of newspapers during Ismail's reign: "Different political notions were taken up, discussed, supported, advocated and rejected, praised and condemned, and finally compromised over and adapted by a multiplicity of political groups and their publicists" (15). Newspapers fostered a healthy public sphere where political debate thrived, but politics was not the only topic of the new media. Short stories also flourished, first as translations from European languages, but soon as "experiments composed in Arabic" (Allen 24–25). In addition, the press played a major role in the development of the novel, "firstly by making the works available to a wider public through serialization, and secondly . . . by offering a variety of positions as editors in cultural journal and magazines, thus providing a regular source of income in an area not too far removed from their real sphere of interest" (Allen 25).

Many critics consider Muhammad Husayn Haykal's *Zaynab* (1913) to be the first Egyptian novel. As can be expected, there is some controversy over this determination. Those who make this claim rely on Ian Watt's identification of the novel with "formal realism." Roger Allen, for example, writes that Haykal is the first writer to place "genuine Egyptian people into an authentic local environment" (31). He does not, however, consider the serialized, novel-length works that proliferated during the final four decades of the century to be novels because they lack characterization, narrative thread, real people in real settings, and coherence. They are too pedagogical, too heavily intruded upon by authors, too historical, too much like travel narratives, or too action oriented (Allen 26–31). In short, they share many attributes with seventeenth-century British romances.

Michael McKeon's theory of the origins of the British novel is of use here because it articulates the common historical roots of the romance and novel forms. In Britain during the period from 1600 to 1740, the spread of print, science, and new ways of thinking about history all contributed to the creation of a profound crisis in the way that truth was told in narrative. Romance cohered as a genre at this moment in order to reflect this generic crisis. At the same time, social categories became unstable, "registering a cultural crisis in attitudes toward how the external social order is related to the internal, moral state of its members" (McKeon 20). This instability in generic and social categories, what McKeon calls questions of truth and virtue, is what the novel was born to resolve.

Borrowing Marx's terminology, McKeon calls seventeenth-century romance and the novel "simple abstractions," or "deceptively monolithic structures that enclose a complex historical process" (20). Romance thus keeps in play the dialectical processes of the epistemological crisis of the early modern period. It records the dialectal nature of the pursuit of truth in narrative, as "truth" was received, negated, and then counter-critiqued.[14] The novel continues this work. The difference is that whereas romance "reflects and internalizes this modestly historicizing self critique," the novel, in addition, "resolves" and "mediates" categorical instability. The novel is born to mediate between the new divisions in the realms of truth and virtue. The work of the novel in subsequent generations, according to McKeon, is to mediate division: "The very ground of the novel . . . is the fact of division—the division of labor, the division of knowledge—and the technical powers of the novel as a literary form are augmented in proportion to the impassability of the gulfs it now undertakes to subtend" (420).

McKeon's understanding of the romance and novel as embodying complex historical processes enables him to counter both Watt's and Mikhail Bakhtin's influential theories of the novel. McKeon challenges Watt's notion of "formal realism" by proposing a theory that explains the persistence of romance in the novel genre. He contests Bakhtin's understanding of romance as a "rigid" and "fixed" form by demonstrating its openness and ability to incorporate modernity. Whereas Bakhtin believes that only the novel is flexible enough to represent the modern world, McKeon argues that romance was the first form to embody the full dialectical complexity of modern thought.[15] McKeon's theory enables us to make sense of the development of the novel in Egypt because it points to the ways that print helped to generate an epistemological crisis which romance reflected and the novel resolved. And it also helps to demonstrate how both romance and the novel were instruments of modernization.

If McKeon demonstrates how the romance and novel work together to represent the modern world, Timothy Mitchell points to the devastation that such representation caused in Egypt. He argues that the Europeans colonized Egypt precisely by representing their own world there in the form of the Western military, Lancaster schools, French cities, and the British transport system. Modern writing technologies were just one of the many representational tools that were used to colonize Egypt.

Mitchell theorizes a direct link between the introduction of communications technologies into Egypt and the creation of a different kind of prose in the following decades. At first, the spread of newspapers and journals in the 1860s evoked discussion over the role of print in creating political authority. Many Egyptian nationalists saw it as their most effective tool for challenging British, French, and Ottoman presence and creating and spreading their own political programs. Others argued that print could only be destructive of political authority because it severed the author from his or her meaning (Mitchell 131–137). Although the latter argument did not gain many supporters, it does accurately describe what eventually happened in Egypt, Mitchell argues. Print proved to be a destabilizing force that broke up traditional forms of governance and local ways of knowing, primarily because it introduced new ways of thinking about language. Arabic was a highly literary language and Arabic words proliferated meanings rather than fixing them. But print began to threaten Arabic's literary capabilities, and with the arrival of the wireless telegraph in 1895, words lost their ability to proliferate meanings and became merely signs with only one goal—to communicate a message (Mitchell 140). The imported prose style, like the trains and telegraphs that paved its way, was faster, more direct, and more capable of incorporating modernizing practices than what it replaced.[16]

I swerved from the main argument of this chapter to reflect on how new forms of writing such as romance and the novel joined forces in colonizing Egypt. I shall now investigate the dual generic structure of *Tancred* and its implications for the construction of the imperial imagination. I begin by rehearsing Fredric Jameson's historicization of romance in response to its de-historicization by structural critics. By taking what may be a familiar Marxist argument into the unfamiliar setting of the Middle East, I aim to de-familiarize common critical notions about how genre works. I continue this work of de-familiarization by considering the *Bildungsroman* on new territory. What gets accomplished by performing the *Bildungsroman* plot in the Middle East? If genre is a geographical affair and space shapes form, as Franco Moretti argues in *Atlas of the European Novel,* then what does it mean to set a Western form in the East?

ROMANTIC INVESTMENTS: TANCRED IN THE MIDDLE EAST

I. Romance Worlds, or Why does Tancred go to the Middle East?

Tancred comes home from college to find waiting for him everything a young man could want. His wealthy parents have prepared for him a banquet of royal proportions. They have procured him a seat in parliament, and have found him a rich, aristocratic, beautiful young wife. He need only say the word, and all this would be his. But the words that Tancred says are not the ones that his parents expect to hear. He tells them that he will leave England and go to the Middle East, for he wants to see the Holy Sepulcher and "penetrate the great Asian mystery" (128).

Why does Tancred go to the Middle East? I am not only asking why the titular character chooses to leave England and travel to the East, but mainly why the dual generic structures of *Tancred* are "exported" there as well. What is the purpose of constructing a romance and a *Bildungsroman* in the Middle East? And what is the importance of place in these generic choices? It is a historical question as well as a geopolitical one. Why export romance in a period in which domestically produced romance had long been on the wane?[17] And why send the *Bildungsroman* abroad when it was experiencing its heyday at home?

When Tancred leaves England at the end of Book II, he steps out of a comfortable world into an unknown one. Similarly, *Tancred* shifts from the indigenous style of a Silver Fork novel to the foreign-born one of romance. That the portion of the novel that deals with the Middle East is largely a romance sheds light on Edward Said's accusation that *Tancred* is an orientalist novel. As we have seen, in Disraeli's Middle East a vast range of peoples including "Druzes, Jews, Christians and Muslims" blurs together, and "all are Orientals at heart" (Said 102). Landscapes too are largely undifferentiated, and it is often difficult to know whether one is reading about Palestine, Syria, or Lebanon.

Disraeli uses the conventions of the Silver Fork novel for the same reasons he relies on the conventions of romance. He can create worlds that are strange and wonderful to the majority of his readers. But upper-class readers complained that Disraeli knew nothing about their world and depicted it unrealistically.[18] The same could be said of his depictions of the Middle East. These distortions are part of the romance genre. One way to understand the resulting obfuscation is through Frye's concept of the romance "world," in which he sees three operative elements: the world, its twin protagonists (the hero and the villain), and their semic organization (high and low, good and evil, spring and winter). Outlining these three elements, Frye writes:

> The hero of romance is analogous to the mythical Messiah or deliverer who comes from an upper world, and his enemy is analogous to the demonic powers of a lower world. The conflict however takes place in, or at any rate primarily concerns, our world, which is in the middle, and which is characterized by the cyclical movements of nature. (187–188)

According to Jameson, the world that matters in romance is "our world"—the middle world in which the conflict takes place. Jameson is determined that this world, characterized by "cyclical movements of nature," not be naturalized. He therefore historicizes Frye's romance "world." Although the romance world often consists of nature, the "bower of bliss" or the "enchanted wood," Jameson argues that this world should not be accepted as natural without examination of its socio-historical formation: "What is misleading is the implication that this 'nature' is in any sense itself 'natural' rather than a very peculiar and specialized social and historical phenomenon" (112). Jameson amplifies the importance of "world" in romance, drawing on Heidegger to make the world the defining element of the genre: "Romance is precisely that form in which the *worldness of world* reveals or manifests itself, in which, in other words, *world* in the technical sense of the transcendental horizon of our experience becomes visible in an inner worldly sense" (112). Jameson's revision of Frye's "world" as the defining element of romance is useful in understanding *Tancred*'s "world" of the Middle East. Or more precisely, it will help answer the original question of this section, "Why does Tancred go to the Middle East?"

The spatial move from England to the Middle East is accompanied by a representational shift from the everyday life of the rich and powerful to the exotic world of romance. Upon arrival in the East, Tancred heads straight to see his banker, but on the way he falls asleep in a garden. Thus, his attempt to maintain the normalcy of his daily routine is thwarted, and he drops right into the "natural" world of romance:

> Like a prince in a fairy tale, who has broken the mystic boundary of some enchanted pleasaunce, Tancred traversed the alleys which were

> formed by the lemon and pomegranate tree, and sometimes the myrtle and the rose. His ear caught the sound of falling water, bubbling with a gentle noise; more distinct and more forcible every step that he advanced. The walk in which he now found himself ended in an open space covered with roses; beyond them a gentle acclivity, clothed so thickly with a small bright blue flower that it seemed a bank of turquoise, and on its top was a kiosk of white marble, gilt and painted. . . . His hat had dropped from his head; his rich curls fell on his outstretched arm that served as a pillow for a countenance which in the sweet dignity of its blended beauty and stillness might have become an archangel; and, lying on one of the mats, in an attitude of unconscious gracefulness, which a painter might have transferred to his portfolio, Tancred sank into a deep and dreamless repose. (190–192)

Tancred awakens to his romance plot. He finds Eva, who will become his love interest and one of the objects of his quest. And he learns of her adopted brother Fakredeen, his nemesis, and the villain whom he will have to overcome to fulfill his quest. Here Frye's three operative elements of romance are introduced: the world (the Middle East), its twin protagonists (Tancred and Fakredeen), and their semic organization (high/low, good/evil).

Tancred also awakens to what Frye considers to be the core of the romance plot: adventure. First Tancred fights a battle against a cabal of kidnappers, organized by Fakredeen, then struggles for his liberation from them, then leads a band of Arabs into a bloody battle in the name of their liberation from the Turks and a united Arabia, and finally charges on to try to "conquer the world." It is this ongoing sequence of kidnappings, struggles, and battles only stopped by the achievement of the quest that further defines *Tancred* as romance.

In the action-packed world in which Tancred finds himself an agent, the battle scene comes to figure the "world" itself. In one instance, when a band of Arabs surround, him, the Arabs actually become the landscape: "They [Tancred and his supporters] looked up, they looked around; the crest of every steep was covered with armed Arabs, each man with his musket leveled" (239). This anthropomorphized landscape then rushes Tancred, surrounding him and carting him off: "There was a continuous volley, however, from every part of the defile, and the scene was so involved in smoke that it was impossible for Tancred to see a yard around him" (241–242). The smoke engulfs Tancred and he is stabbed and dragged away to the kidnappers' mountain hideaway.

Worlds overwhelm Tancred: the paradisal world lulls him to sleep; the battlefield engulfs him. In England Tancred was free to come and go as he pleased, but in the Middle East, he is a prisoner to his setting. The activated landscape of the battlefield literally surrounds him and carries him away. This liveliness of the "world" in *Tancred* may be the key to understanding why Tancred himself seems so lifeless. Typical of the romance hero, Tancred is a difficult character to get hold of—his desires are abstractions to us. He wants to "penetrate the mysteries of the East," to visit the holy sepulcher, to "conquer the world." He is misunderstood by his parents who cannot fathom his motives for traveling to the Middle East, and by the Christians, Jews, Muslims, and Animists that he meets there. They mistakenly refer to him as the "brother of the Queen of England" and think of him only as a source of money or a Christian fanatic. In spite of his energetic campaigns, Tancred is a flatter character than one usually finds in a novel.

Jameson shows that there is a connection between the flatness of character in romance and the fullness of the "world," and he demonstrates that this connection is the function of the romance genre. In Frye's conception the world is the middle ground, the space in which the meaning of the hero/villain conflict can be realized. Jameson's most potent analogy in discussing Frye's "world" is to compare it to the great ocean of Stanislaw Lem's *Solaris,* which absorbs all of the meaning around it, literally sucking out the meaning of the hero's life. The relation of the characters to the world in romance is that their semic organization provides the world with its meaning. Coming from opposed worlds, they meet in the "middle," and the organization of their opposition is what gives that middle its worldliness.

Using this configuration, we can begin to see how intricately connected are "world" and character in *Tancred.* Knowing the "world" in the novel depends upon understanding the semic organization of its twin protagonists. Tancred, the Messiah-like figure searching for spiritual origins in the East, comes from the cartographically organized "upper" world of England; Fakredeen, the shifty, double-dealing, clever and even charming figure, comes from some vague "below." His active obfuscation of his origins and his chronic shape-shifting, claiming to be Moslem, Christian, Jewish, and Animist at different moments, echo traits of Mephistopheles. The meeting of these two types in the middle gives the world meaning and that meaning will define *Tancred*'s Middle East.

Tancred's character was first revealed in his two explicit reasons for leaving England: he wants to penetrate the mysteries of Asia, a motive familiar to those found in scientific travel accounts, and he wants to visit the Holy Sepulcher, a desire that became increasingly popular in the 1840s for the sightseer to the Holy Land. In one sense, then, Tancred is a traveler/tourist to the Middle East. But his itinerary differs from the traveler/tourist's when he forsakes his journey home. At the end of *Tancred,* we find our hero sitting comfortably in the house of his banker, professing his love for his daughter, Eva. A return to England is not in his plans. This then suggests that we not only consider his motives in the light of travel/tourism, but also in the related context of colonialism/imperialism.

Tancred has a third unstated reason for leaving England that motivates him more than the other two. When Tancred's parents learned that their only son was bent on heading east, they enacted a plan to dissuade him: they offered him money to buy a yacht so that he would become so caught up in the time-consuming task of yacht shopping that his trip would be delayed indefinitely. Their plan almost worked. While tracking down a suitable yacht, Tancred located a lovely soul mate. She too was an aficionado of the East, and she had a yacht for sale. They spend hours discussing their mutual interest, until Tancred considers staying in England. But she then drops these fateful words: "If Jerusalem were only a place one could get at, something might be done; if there were a railroad to it for example" (167). Tancred responds with disgust—"'A Railroad!' exclaimed Tancred, with a look of horror. 'A railroad to Jerusalem!'" (167)—and flees the country upon discovering that his soul mate has been speculating in railways abroad.

Tancred's horrified response shows what really activated his travels. Tancred wants his Middle East "underdeveloped"—without railroads, telegraphs, canals, and ports. Therefore he flees England and the type of character that his soul mate represents, the railway speculator who became notorious for his headlong participation in the railway booms of the thirties and forties. But as his soul mate's words suggest, the space between England and Jerusalem, for so long an immutable entity, could now be altered. This alteration in both physical distance and cultural remoteness is the very process that Tancred fears and *Tancred* anticipates. The placement of telegraph lines, the development of more efficient steamship routes, and the building of railways that will begin to happen in the 1850s will alter the Middle East's physical and cultural distance from England forever.[19] When Ismail came to power in 1863 only six telegraph lines existed, but by 1876 there were 36 lines spanning 5,500 miles, and Egypt was linked by wire to Europe, India, Australia, and the Far East. The length of Egypt's railway tracks increased from 245 to 1,085 during the same period (Russell 24). *Tancred* is on the cusp of dizzying technological changes in Egypt that will revolutionize that country and bring "India to England's doorstep" by the end of the decade. As *Tancred* is being written, the idea of having the colonies next door is not yet current. *Tancred* as a result can open up an imaginative space for a re-visioning of the colonies.

Ironically, then, Tancred's soul mate is his nemesis. He flees an "inveterate woman gambler" in England, who it turns out has been investing heavily in foreign railways, only to encounter an ever-scheming and speculating Fakredeen in Syria whose plots include igniting civil wars, arms trading, intriguing between Turkey, France, and England, and playing them off each other so he can carve up a little piece of the action himself. Most importantly, Fakredeen's plots involve investments in technology. His most burning desire is to buy 5,000 British muskets. And he has other investment plans: "We might improve the condition of the people; we might establish manufactures, stimulate agriculture, extend commerce, get an appalto of the silk, buy it all up at sixty piastres per oke, and sell it at Marseilles at two hundred" (280). Fakredeen is the kind of person that Tancred is running from. With his political scheming and his plans for improvements, Fakredeen is a sure candidate for bringing a railway to the Middle East.

The "world" in *Tancred* thus emerges as a battleground of modernization. Important to Frye's theory of romance, Jameson asserts, is that the world is in the midst of becoming, a world in transformation: "Romance, therefore, does not involve the substitution of some more ideal realm for ordinary reality . . . but rather a process of *transforming* ordinary reality" (110). Nicholas Daly similarly understands romance to be a "narrative theory of social change" (5) that "absorbs, reflects upon, and codifies facets of modernization" (24). The Middle East in *Tancred* emerges as a world that cannot escape the expansion of capital—a world that is to be incorporated into that ever-expanding system. Fakredeen/Tancred represent the competing forces in this new world that give it its meaning under Frye's reading. They expose its transitional state and the conflicts that the process of transformation will cause. For this reason, the romance hero does not need to win his final battle; Tancred does not expel the Turks, unite Arabia, and conquer the world. Nor does he, as a true romance hero would, return home. Instead, he loses the battle and stays in the Middle East, marking a deviation from the romance trajectory. But this deviation, I suggest, should not be understood as a failure of the hero or as a generic failure. Instead, it should be recognized as a sign that romance ultimately is not an adequate form for the completion of this story of colonization, for the final triumph of the romance hero would only convey that the hard work of conquest was done when in reality it had only just begun. The *Bildungsroman* would prove to be a form better suited to continue the battle that romance had begun. Thus Disraeli concludes his romance by adapting a *Bildungsroman* conclusion.

II. The "Donor Function" in Romance, or Who is Tancred?

The relation between the twin protagonists, Tancred/Fakredeen, can be formulated in another way. Tancred arrives in the Middle East with two letters—a letter of introduction and a letter of credit. The first establishes him as one who is searching for the great Asian mystery, and the second promises him unlimited credit with the only banker in the region, Besso. It is the second letter that firmly marks Tancred's difference from Fakredeen. In it Besso is told to loan Tancred all of the money that he needs: "Let him have as much gold as would make the right-hand lion on the first step of the throne of Solomon the king; and if he wants more, let him have as much as would form the lion that is left; and so on, through every stair of the royal seat" (171). Conversely, Fakredeen cannot get a loan, and he is deeply in debt. Here is yet another formulation of the semic organization of the twin protagonists: infinite credit/profound debt.

Fakredeen needs Tancred to complete his various capital-intensive projects; Tancred has just what Fakredeen lacks. Yet, if we consider *Tancred* as romance, it is the *hero*'s lack that matters according to Jameson, who argues that it is through the identification of the hero's lack that the genre of romance can be historcized. Vladimir Propp, in seeking to locate the deep structure of Russian folktales, reduces all tales to a sequence of actions that happen in a specific order. Naming these actions "functions," he suggests that they are all equally important and occur independent of the nature of the actor who carries them out. Jameson, however, disagrees, arguing that the "donor function" is the most important one precisely because it exposes a relation between the function of the donor and the surface character of the hero, a relation that is born of the hero's lack:

> In the beginning the hero is never strong enough to conquer himself. He suffers from some initial lack of being: either he is simply not strong enough or not courageous enough, or else he is too naïve and simple-minded to know what to do with his strength. The donor is the complement, the reverse of this basic ontological weakness. (*The Prison-House of Language* 67)

The function of the donor directly identifies the hero's lack because it is the donor who materializes in order to fill it, usually with something magical such as a weapon, a mighty bow or a steel sword. Jameson strategically focuses on the donor function because he sees the possibility of re-establishing the historicity of romance through it. He quarrels with Propp's theory because it leaves no place for character; what is important to Propp is what gets performed, not who performs it. Jameson wants to realign surface character with its deep structure of function, and he does this by invoking A.J. Greimas's work to demonstrate that if a rupture is shown between the function of the surface character and the surface character, then there exists a wedge into the historicity of the surface character.[20] Such a rupture occurs in *Tancred*. Considering the function of the donor in *Tancred* will make Tancred's flat character available as a historical production. It will also let us see the historical contours of the romance terrain of the Middle East.

The need for a donor is established after Tancred is kidnapped. After he is imprisoned in a mountain village, his adventures stop as the payment of his ransom is awaited. Fakredeen, who has had Tancred kidnapped, expects the ransom will be paid without difficulties, for Tancred is believed to be the "brother of the Queen of England." However, fulfilling the donor function turns out to be more difficult than Fakredeen had assumed, for an unexpected donor steps forward. Fakredeen's adoptive father, Besso, wants to pay the ransom, but Fakredeen declines the offer because he is embarrassed to accept the money from family. As a result, Tancred's ransom remains unpaid, forcing Fakredeen to come up with another plan. That plan is so complex that it calls attention to the primary difficulty of *Tancred*'s romance plot—locating a character to fulfill the donor function.

Fakredeen's plan involves trading arms for the release of Tancred. Fakredeen unfolds his scheme to Eva: "The great Sheikh wants arms; well, I will give him five hundred muskets for the ransom" (309). Yet the problem of how Fakredeen, infamously in debt, is to pay for the weapons is yet to be solved, as Eva points out, "But how are we to get these arms?" Fakredeen plots on: "Why, Scheriff Effendi, to be sure. You know I am to meet him at Gaza the day after to-morrow, and receive his five thousand muskets. Well, five hundred for the great Sheikh will make them four thousand five hundred; no great difference" (309). Still, the original problem remains as Eva points out: "But who is to pay for them?" Fakredeen then reveals how he will get Tancred to pay for the muskets, thus paying his own ransom: "Why, if men want to head the Asian movement, they must have muskets . . . and, after all, as we are going to save the English prince two millions of piastres, I do not think he can object to paying Scheriff Effendi for his goods; particularly as he will have the muskets for his money" (309).

Fakredeen's plan is circuitous. Moreover, it does not invoke a simple romance solution, in which a donor, whose sole function is to supply the hero with what he needs, steps forward with his magical weapon, enabling the hero to continue on his quest. Instead, the solution to the donor problem involves a combination of characters and character traits; only Fakredeen's resourcefulness and Tancred's unlimited credit can set Tancred free. A rupture exists between the donor function and the surface character, for the donor cannot be the hero or the villain, according to Propp. As Jameson suggests, such a rupture points to the historicity of the surface character.

That Fakredeen and Tancred are historical figures should come as no surprise. Yet cloaking these characters' actions in the romance trope of ransom obscures *Tancred*'s own historic contribution. "Ransom," it turns out, is just another term for "loan" in Fakredeen's lexicon, and his elaborate plan to hold Tancred hostage is simply the easiest way to get a loan. *Tancred* both proposes the historical problem of getting a loan in the Middle East and suggests a solution. The problem is twofold: first, Fakredeen can't get a loan, and second, Tancred can't give a loan, as Fakredeen makes clear when he raises the issue with Tancred: "'If I could only raise a loan,' said the Emir [Fakredeen], 'I could do without France and England' 'A loan!' exclaimed Tancred; 'I see the poison of modern liberalism has penetrated even the Desert. Believe me, national redemption is not an affair of usury'" (259). As Fakredeen's claim suggests, getting a loan in the region was not easy, so he must look elsewhere—to France and England—to obtain financing. But Tancred's impassioned reply shows that British shame and moralism surrounding lending practices stood in the way of Fakredeen's desires. *Tancred* discovers a way to solve both historic problems.

One reason that Fakredeen has difficulty obtaining a loan in the region has to do with the exorbitant rates of interest charged by local money lenders: "I am paying sixty percent at Beiroot, Tripoli, Latakia, and every accursed town of the coast at this moment" (303). Hence, Fakredeen tries to persuade Eva to convince her father, Besso, to lower his rates from sixty to thirty percent. According to the historian, David S. Landes, high local rates of interest in the Middle East were chronic: "There were few banks but many money-lenders, little investment but much hoarding, no credit but much usury" (57). Fakredeen's solution to the high interest rates is to turn outside of the local economy, refusing the loan/ransom from Besso, the "only" local money-lender, and attempting to get it from abroad. *Tancred* anticipates this historical turning away from local sources of capital, in favor of cheaper money from abroad.

But it is not enough for Fakredeen to look outside of the region to obtain a loan, if those outside sources are not willing to lend him the money. Tancred blushes every time money is mentioned, and he tells Eva, "My cheek burns while I say it; but I think, in Europe, what is most valued is money" (199). Tancred must learn to think about money in a different manner if he is going to become an investor in Fakredeen's projects. Yet it is only outside of England that Tancred unlearns his shame about investing, and Fakredeen is his teacher. When Eva asks Fakredeen how he will get Tancred to pay for Fakredeen's British muskets, Fakredeen comes up with a project, as we have seen: "Why, if men want to head the Asian movement, they must have muskets" (309). Fakredeen convinces Tancred that he, Tancred, wants to head the Asian movement, to unite the Arabs and throw out the Turks. Fakredeen teaches Tancred to invest in the name of a higher good. He instills in Tancred a belief in investing for the sake of "world-conquering" and "empire."

Tancred shows that empire is the key to Fakredeen's getting a loan and Tancred's giving one. In the 1850s the employment of the joint-stock company in foreign adventures encouraged large-scale investments in the Middle East. In addition, high local rates of interest made it not just possible, but profitable for foreigners to loan at slightly lower rates. Desperately trying to modernize, governments took advantage of the new sources of funds. Western lenders too took advantage of the situation. Because local interest rates were so high, they could charge lower rates and be guaranteed a profit, for rates were still higher than they were in their home countries. Consequently, investing in the Middle East was always a profitable business. Such a situation was a recipe for what Landes calls "economic imperialism": the production of unmanageable debts and the subsequent foreign "solution" to the debt problem. Landes's primary example of economic imperialism in the region is the situation that led to the British purchase of the Suez Canal. Ismail borrowed heavily from the West to build the Canal, and in the 1870s could no longer afford to pay off his loans. Overwhelming debts forced him to sell the Canal to the British in 1875. Egypt went bankrupt the following year.

Trying to understand the gross double standard that Western investors in the Middle East engaged in, loaning money at exorbitant rates while knowing that such rates would never be considered fair at home, Landes comes to the conclusion that investors believed that what they were doing was for the good. He argues that Westerners who loaned within the Middle East believed that they gave more than they received. I am arguing that *Tancred* shows that it is through the production of belief in the imperial project that the British unlearned their shame about the market and learned to feel good about investing. Guaranteed profits only helped. Distance helped even more, for there were no examples of ruin next door. And when economic ruin clearly did happen, as in the case of Egypt, it was reinterpreted in a new framework: national triumph. So when Disraeli purchased the Suez Canal from the nearly bankrupt regime in 1875, the British thought nothing of Egypt's tragedy, but unanimously cheered England's success.[21]

Debts have a special place in *Tancred.* Whereas Landes argues that in the Middle East debts come to be a major tool of economic imperialism, in *Tancred* they produce the energy and energetic characters necessary for a romance plot. They not only provide Fakredeen with purpose, ("I should be incapable of anything, if it were not for my debts" (303)), but they lead him into his fantastic plot:

> He was perpetually in masquerade; a merchant, a Mamlouk, a soldier of fortune, a Tartar messenger, sometimes a pilgrim, sometimes a dervish, always in pursuit of some improbable but ingenious object, or lost in the mazes of some fantastic plot. . . . he was perpetually in Egypt, Baghdad, Cyprus, Smyrna, and the Syrian cities. He sauntered away a good deal of his time indeed in the ports and towns of the coast, looking after his creditors; but this was not the annoyance to him which it would be to most men. Fakredeen was fond of his debts; they were the source indeed of his only real excitement, and he was grateful to them for their stirring powers. (381)

Chasing his creditors and hiding from them, Fakredeen is constantly in motion and incognito. "I have the two greatest stimulants in the world to action," he says, "Youth and Debt!" (213) Debts, indeed, author this fantastic character and his action-packed romance plot.[22]

Fakredeen also ushers Tancred into his romance plot, kidnapping him and providing him with a quest in which to invest. But Fakredeen enables Tancred in yet another way. The fictionalization of the scheming promoter figure, and the projection of him onto a space far away, makes the fiction of Tancred's fair lending practices all the more possible. Nineteenth-century readers considered Fakredeen's character to be original: "Fakredeen, a sort of prurient graft of eastern subtlety on western politics, is quite original, and very amusing" (Monckton 153). Yet his originality lay not so much in his character, but in Disraeli's geographical projection of it: "Almost the only character which has any pretensions to originality and novelty is that of Fakredeen, the ambitious chieftain of Lebanon, and his prototype we are inclined to believe must be sought nearer home" (Taylor 389). Although contemporaries pointed to the originality of Fakredeen's political behavior, I suggest that what was really new was Disraeli's positive spin on Fakredeen's financial prowess. Disraeli's originality lay in taking the promoter figure, whom, as we have seen in Chapter 1, was not well liked at home, and by the trick of geography making him loveable, as Lady Blessington points out: "I consider Fakredeen one of the finest conceptions ever painted, and how painted! Never was there so true a portrait of a misapplied Genius, and an unprincipled mind. With what wonderful skill have you managed this character forcing your readers to love, while they cannot esteem him" (238).

In England Fakredeen would just have been another schemer, like George Hudson the "Railway King," but by being projected outward and into romance Fakredeen does not have to meet the fate of his British contemporary. Abroad, he is a sensation. Fakredeen makes way for Tancred, whose development is stunted in England. He gives Tancred purpose, and belief in something worth investing in. Fakredeen can propose empire to Tancred and make it palatable, coloring it foreign, at the moment that it is most English. Fakredeen's originality, then is much like Disraeli's—he can embody empire, creating the fiction that it is "other" at the moment when it is most at home.

NOVEL TECHNOLOGIES: THE *BILDUNGSROMAN* ABROAD

Novel Worlds, or Why Does Tancred Stay in the Middle East?

It is telling that Northrop Frye begins his analysis of the genre of romance by discussing its ending. He does so because romance threatens to go on forever. Romance "is an endless form in which a central character who never develops or ages goes through one adventure after another until the author himself collapses" (Frye 186). He cites comic strips, where the main characters persist for years in a state of "refrigerated deathlessness" as an example of the rudimentary form (Frye 186). Only the end can stop romance and provide it with its literary form:

> As soon as romance achieves a literary form, it tends to limit itself to a sequence of minor adventures leading up to a major or climacteric adventure, usually announced from the beginning, the completion of which rounds off the story. We may call this major adventure, the element that gives literary form to the romance, the quest. (Frye 186–187)

According to Frye, "the complete form of the romance is clearly the successful quest" (187), and such a completed form has three stages: the *agon,* the perilous journey along with its minor adventures; the *pathos,* the critical struggle which may end in death for the hero or his opponent; and the *anagnorisis,* the exaltation and recognition of the hero.

Tancred's romance plot follows the pattern that Frye outlines. Initially Tancred roams throughout the desert, fighting various battles; he then escapes near death at the hands of the Ansarey; and finally, he is exalted as the hero, over and above the only other character who contends for that slot, his friend and rival, Fakredeen. However, after Tancred is revealed as the hero, the story does not end, and the novel does not finish with the conclusion of its romance plot. Instead, I shall argue, the romance plot is shed in order to conclude on more familiar territory. *Tancred,* a novel that conforms in many ways to the romance tradition, resorts to a *Bildungsroman* conclusion.

Contemporary critics did not like *Tancred*'s ending. One, who otherwise marveled at the novel, wrote: "It is impossible to give any idea within a moderate space, of the poetry and the beauty that lingers on the steps of the crusader. Pity that this effect is marred by an abrupt and somewhat frivolous conclusion . . . and which is not for the time being, in keeping with the tone that pervades the rest of the work" (Taylor 526). Indeed, the ending is abrupt. On the last page of the novel, with no warning, Tancred's parents come to visit. The very last line of the text introduces the pair who have not been mentioned for over three hundred pages: "The Duke and the Duchess of Bellamont had arrived at Jerusalem" (501). Disconcerting as it may have been for Tancred and his critics to have his parents arrive unannounced, I believe that critics who were not happy with the ending were responding to a rupture in form that happens before the arrival of the Duke and the Duchess.

A review of Tancred's final adventure, leading up to his *anagnorisis* and what follows, will show the disjuncture in form with which the novel concludes. In the crowning adventure of the novel, Tancred and Fakredeen set out to "conquer the world," a phrase that they use to describe their plan to unite Syria by convincing two tribes to join together to fight the region's occupiers, the Ottoman Empire. On their world-conquering mission, Tancred and Fakradeen visit the Ansarey, a mysterious mountain tribe ruled by the brave and beautiful Queen Astarte. As soon as the queen sets eyes upon Tancred, she falls in love with him, but Fakredeen has fallen in love with her. Astutely detecting the situation, Fakredeen takes revenge upon Tancred by telling the queen the truth: Tancred is in love with another, Fakredeen's half-sister Eva. In a fit of jealous rage Astarte kidnaps Eva (who just happens to be passing through the desert) and then plots with Fakredeen to have her murdered. But Fakredeen reveals to Eva what mischief he has caused, and they flee, leaving Tancred behind to fend for himself. Tancred is indeed left in a troubled spot, for he must contend with the jealous queen.

It is partly Tancred's ability to work his way out of this precarious situation, calming the furious queen and securing his release, that makes him a hero. More important, though, is what happens next. As Tancred is about to leave the Ansarey, it is announced that five thousand Turkish troops are on their way to invade the land of the Ansarey. Astarte tells Tancred to flee for his life, but he bravely chooses to stay, saying: "I cannot leave it in the hour of peril. . . . This invasion of the Ottomans may lead to results of which none dream. I will meet them at the head of your warriors!" (480). With these words Tancred's mettle is revealed. He will fight the empire, and he will do it alone, without Fakredeen, his partner in "world conquering." With few soldiers and even fewer weapons, Tancred fights until he and his men are cut off and surrounded. Outnumbered by more than ten to one, they make their getaway into the desert.

Tancred arrives at the desert "on the third day, before sunset." Drawing from biblical tradition, Disraeli makes the desert the site of Tancred's *anagnorisis.* There he is finally recognized by the locals, not as the "son of the Queen of England" for which they mistakenly had taken him all along, but for the brave warrior that he has proven himself to be. In a celebration for him "sheep were killed, bread baked, coffee pounded, and the pipe of honour was placed in the hands of Tancred" (490). A long and rather elaborate "Arabian revel" ensues. In addition to the biblical connotations of the desert, Disraeli draws on nineteenth-century meanings as well. In a period when roads were increasingly being built in the most out-of-the-way places and the new tourist industry was depositing tourists in all corners of the globe, the desert held out the promise of something else: the escape from civilization, unbounded freedom, and a space for man to return to nature, in a manly way. The traveler and explorer Sir Richard F. Burton writes of his 1853 trip to the desert: "Nature returns to man in the desert," where he says, "there is a keen enjoyment in mere animal existence" (150–151).

In the desert Tancred escapes civilization and returns to his natural manliness. Yet even more important, Tancred enjoys the sense of boundlessness that the desert landscape offers. Surveying the desert from above, Tancred sees unbounded space: "When Tancred had gained an undulating height, and was capable of taking a more extensive survey of the land, it presented, especially towards the south, the same features through an illimitable space" (488). When Tancred's attendant Baroni cries, "The Syrian Desert!" Tancred responds, "My heart responds to it. . . . What is Damascus, with all its sumptuousness, to this sweet liberty!" (488) In the final scene of Tancred's romance, when Tancred is discovered as the hero, he himself discovers "sweet liberty." But this liberty proves to be too much for him, and he falls asleep. The last words of the chapter freeze Tancred in his sleep: "'Indeed, great Sheikh, the longer I live and the more I think'—and here the chibouque dropped gently from Tancred's mouth, and he himself sunk upon the carpet" (491). With Tancred fast asleep on an Arabian carpet, the final chapter of this romance closes.

Tancred wakes up to a novel world. New bodies, new objects, and an entirely new set of energies inhabit the text. We learn secondhand that Tancred has just returned from Egypt: "He has been absent six months; he has been in Egypt" (493). The text offers no explanation for the temporal disjunction. Yet it might be understood as a way to distance Tancred from the moment when he was closest to "going native" in the desert. There he ate, drank, smoked, and reveled with the natives. The only other reference to Egypt in the text supports this reading. Earlier, when Tancred is asked if he will visit Egypt, he answers: "I should not be sorry to visit Egypt. It is a country that rather perplexes us in Europe. It has undergone great changes" (407). Egypt, one of the oldest civilizations in the world, now in the midst of modern development, can provide a buffer zone between Tancred's "native" lapse and the rest of the novel.

Yet Tancred's trip to Egypt provides another function. Tancred goes there in order to come home. In other words, he goes to Egypt to establish Jerusalem as home. Tancred's return from Egypt makes his home visible for the first time: "Tancred dismounted and entered for the first time his house at Jerusalem, of which he had been the nominal tenant for half a year" (494). Up to this point, Tancred's "house" has never been mentioned. The reader can surmise that Tancred bought this house at the end of his final adventure, just before he left for Egypt. But the house only became visible upon his return. It is typical of the romance hero to return home, rounding off the romance plot, but Tancred is establishing a new home, right in the center of what used to be his romance world.

Tancred's new home is more familiar, more like home than what we've seen thus far. His attendant, we are told, was "quite at home" in it (494). Tancred comes home to a whole new cast of characters, who seem to be ushered into the novel as so much furniture. They are simply referred to as Tancred's "friends": Colonel Bruce, the British Consul, the Reverend Mr. Bernard, and Dr. Roby. These men's presence in the novel remains unexplained. They just materialize along with the new house. The only time that they are wanted, they are absent: when Tancred expects them to welcome him home, they are all busy. The men are there in name only. Yet that is saying something: next to other names that populate the text, Barizy of the Tower, Pasqualigo, Scheriff Effendi, and Besso, these names are distinctively familiar. Along with these names an entire professional and colonial structure is imported into the novel: a colonel, a consul, a reverend, and a doctor.

In *The Way of the World* Franco Moretti argues that it is "essential to build a 'homeland' for the individual" in the *Bildungsroman* (26). And this is precisely what the *Bildungsroman* conclusion to Tancred's romance accomplishes. *Tancred* builds a homeland in the Middle East for its long-wandering titular character. Further, Moretti says that the *Bildungsroman* is a form that evolved in order to convince the modern individual, confronted with an explosion of new freedoms symbolized by the French Revolution, to willingly give up his freedoms in exchange for happiness in his homeland. "Home," then, is an aesthetic category with the production of "happiness" at its core. The *Bildungsroman* seeks to both make the individual give up his new found freedoms and feel at home with his decision. Thus, the freedom of revolution is exchanged for happiness of the hearth. The *Bildungsroman* solves the problem of how individuality can be made to coexist with "normality" by teaching the individual to coexist with "normality" by internalizing it. "Normality" must be internalized so that one can believe the statement, "I *desire* to do what I in any case *should* have done" (*The Way of the World* 21). Marriage becomes the best way to accomplish this statement; therefore, Moretti asserts, "the classical *Bildungsroman* 'must' always conclude with marriages" (22).[23]

Moretti describes the *Bildungsroman* as plotted in Germany, France, and England. But what would it mean to export the *Bildungsroman* plot to the Middle East? Because the *Bildungsroman* conclusion of *Tancred* is overlooked by critics, the ending of *Tancred* is often understood only in the context of Tancred's loss, as pronounced by Eva: "You no longer believe in Arabia" (500). Indeed, Tancred has lost his faith. But if we consider the novel in terms of its *Bildungsroman* conclusion, Tancred has also gained something: he has learned to internalize something of the world. Tancred now accepts modernization and the forces that make it possible. He no longer believes in the total corruption of the market. Consequently, the force that binds him and his twin protagonist in polar opposition can no longer hold, and the fiction that Fakredeen is his evil twin cannot be maintained. With Tancred's proposal to Eva, he and Fakredeen become brothers—with equal access to Besso's capital.[24] The romance "world," then, that derives its meaning from the semic organization of the twin protagonists as outlined by Frye, dissolves. It is replaced by a newly domestic world.

Disraeli embellishes the two final chapters of his novel with domestic objects. Whereas previously attention was paid to the description of exotic landscapes, dress, or customs, Disraeli now turns his attention to the placement of mundane articles: a book, hot water, and even plum pudding, which is described at length:

> Colonel Bruce was dining with the English Consul on an experimental plum-pudding, preliminary to the authentic compound, which was to appear in a few days. It was supposed to be the first time that a Christmas pudding had been concocted in Jerusalem, and the excitement in the circle was considerable. The Colonel had undertaken to supervise the preparation, and had been for several days instilling the due instructions into a Syrian cook, who had hitherto only succeeded in producing a result which combined the specific gravity of lead with the general flavour and appearance of a mass of kneaded dates, in a state of fermentation after a long voyage. (495)

This passage reminds us of what one critic disliked so much about *Tancred:* It "is marred by an abrupt and somewhat frivolous conclusion" (Taylor 526). In comparison to the "world conquering" that occurred earlier in the novel, the preparation of plum pudding indeed seems trivial. But the accusation of having a "frivolous conclusion" only holds in comparison to earlier events. Plum pudding would be at home in any novel.

Tancred's "frivolous" conclusion signals the resolution of romance into the "everyday" world of the novel, where events are indeed frivolous. For Moretti the "everyday" is the space "to the side of" the world of work in which the *Bildungsroman* hero can become fully himself.[25] The "everyday" is a space that purposely does not present the workings of capital. It is curious, then, that once Tancred's reservations about the market are resolved, attention shifts "to the side of" this bustling world. I argue that this is because the *Bildungsroman* is the form best suited to hide the pains of development and colonization, for according to Moretti, the *Bildungsroman* shows how pleasing life can be in a small world. It does not show the havoc that modernization is to wreak on the Middle East. But the *Bildungsroman* does not just cloak the battles of development; it continues them by other means.

Tancred acts differently in his everyday world. He is newly fidgety, anxious, and sad. He seems bored: "Tancred roamed about the house, surveyed his court and garden, sighed, while Baroni rewarded and dismissed their escort. 'I know how it is,' he at length said to his intendant, 'but I never could have supposed that I could have felt so sad and spiritless at Jerusalem'" (495). His vocabulary has changed. This man who wanted to "conquer the world" and "unite Arabia" now says "I feel unstrung," and he uses words like "disappointed" and "anxious." But if Tancred is different, he is also familiar in a way that he has not been before. The readers can now relate to his activities: "Tancred passed the day alone in reading, or walking about his room with an agitated and moody step" (496). Tancred's unease in the world is familiar to the reader of the *Bildungsroman*. Like Jane Eyre, Dorothea Brookes, Wilhelm Meister, and Frédéric Moreau, he is out of sync with the world. In George Lukacs's formulation, his soul is too big for the world. In Moretti's, he is beginning to develop a personality. His moods and anxieties create interiority not apparent in his prior actions of charging through the desert.

Moretti argues that "modern personality lodges at the center of everyday life" (*The Way of the World* 40), saving it from its humdrumness. He states the relationship between the everyday life and personality as such: "Everyday life: an anthropocentric space where all social activities lose their exacting objectivity and converge in the domain of 'personality'" (12). Because the world of work is not likely to encourage complex personality, the everyday world arises to exhibit the individual's multiplicity.[26] Tancred's personality is exhibited through his disenchantment with his everyday world: "I wish the battle of Gindarics had never ceased, but that, like some hero of enchantment, I had gone on for ever fighting" (496). Baroni answers, "Ah! There is nothing like action" (496). Tancred's response gives away just how much he has changed: "But what action is there in this world? . . . The most energetic men in Europe are mere busybodies. Empires are now governed like parishes, and a great statesman is only a select vestryman" (496). But it is Eva in the final scene of the novel who best describes Tancred's change: "'I have a vague impression . . . that there have been heroic aspirations wasted, and noble energies thrown away; and yet, perhaps,' she added, in a faltering tone, 'there is no one to blame. Perhaps, all this time, we have been dreaming over an unattainable end, and the only source of deception is our own imagination'" (499). Eva internalizes the change, suggesting that "imagination" is to account for it. She continues:

> Your feelings cannot be what they were before all this happened; when you thought only of a divine cause, of stars, of angels, and of our peculiar and gifted land. No, no; now it is all mixed up with intrigue, and politics, and management, and baffled schemes, and cunning arts of men. You may be, you are, free from all this, but your faith is not the same. You no longer believe in Arabia. (500)

The newly faithless Tancred does not rush home at the onset of his change, as we might expect. Instead, he learns to desire something else:

> "Why, thou to me art Arabia," said Tancred, advancing and kneeling at her side. "The angel of Arabia, and of my life and spirit! Talk not to me of faltering faith: mine is intense. Talk not to me of leaving a divine cause: why, thou art my cause, and thou art most divine! O Eva! Deign to accept the tribute of my long agitated heart! Yes, I too, like thee, am sometimes full of despair; but it is only when I remember that I love, and love perhaps, in vain!" (500)

With this declaration Tancred rids himself of the desires, hopes, and dreams that have been his life's ambition—beliefs that stirred him to leave his family, a promised wife, and a place in Parliament. He has given up the dreams that have generated a five-hundred page novel. And he has done it all in exchange for a woman. Textually this is represented without energy loss: "Arabia" is exchanged for "Arabia."

This elegant equation, in which all of what an individual hopes and desires is given up and replaced with a bundle of equal value, with no loss to the individual, represents what Moretti believes the classical *Bildungsroman* does best. It teaches the individual to give up freedom by convincing him that what he will get in return is happiness. "How is it possible to convince the modern—'free'—individual to willingly limit his freedom?" (*The Way of the World* 22). Precisely through marriage. The classical *Bildungsroman* "must" end with a marriage.

In the exchange of "Arabia" for "Arabia" no energy is lost. Romance energies are exchanged for novelistic ones. Building a homeland relies on energies that only the novel can provide—energies that domesticate. By substituting one "Arabia" for another, Tancred can shed his despair of the modern world. Nevertheless, we must take seriously his prior claim that "the most energetic men in Europe are mere busybodies," for in it, the forceful but sporadic energy of Napoleonic empire is exchanged for the persistent energy of the busybody. E.P. Thompson too notes a new type of energy in the century, one that he relates to the way that time came to discipline work: "By the 1830s and 1840s it was commonly observed that the English industrial worker was marked off from his fellow Irish worker, not by a greater capacity for hard work, but by his regularity, his methodical paying-out of energy" (399). He notes, "Without time discipline we could not have the insistent energies of industrial man" (399). Moretti also discovers evidence of the century's new energy, not in work, but in that aesthetic space "to the side of" work—the everyday world of the *Bildungsroman*. This world is characterized by a protagonist who exercises his personality through the way that he directs his energies: "What is important is to be able to dispose of one's energies at every moment and to employ them for the countless occasions or opportunities that life, little by little, takes upon itself to offer" (*The Way of the World* 45). It is the protagonist's ability to pick and choose amongst the clutter of diurnal details and events that the everyday world lets loose into the novel that shapes his personality. Events only become meaningful because he gives them meaning. Accordingly, the everyday world offers up a space in which the protagonist's personality is defined by its power to distinguish and choose. Whereas Thompson makes visible the new productive energies of the century—organized by time, Moretti highlights the new consumptive ones—as an ordering of space.

The *Bildungsroman* creates appetites and habits of consumption. It is important that of the four new British characters that are imported into the novel's ending, the colonel is the only one shown doing something. Tellingly, he is not leading men into battle. Instead, he is instructing a Syrian in the fine art of cooking plum pudding, "instilling the due instructions into a Syrian cook" (495). He is introducing national traditions—the first "Christmas pudding" to be made in Jerusalem—and creating habits of consumption.[27] Romance conquers by force, but the novel's conquest is economic. As early as 1847 Disraeli conceives of empire as a system that depends upon instilling appetites, habits, and traditions. In an age that understood empire in relation to physical conquest, Disraeli imagined the power of consumption.

It is interesting then that the novel both begins and ends with the inculcation of tastes. It opens with the story of a French cook who worked in the "Imperial kitchen" of Napoleon, and is hired to "form the tastes" of the British aristocracy, represented by Tancred's family and friends, and the novel ends with a colonel trying to teach a Syrian to cook a traditional English meal. The appetite for empire, it seems, is being constructed on both ends—in England and in the colonies. By way of conclusion, I offer one thought on Disraeli's preoccupation with the production of taste and patterns of consumption.

Just before *Tancred* resorts to its *Bildungsroman* conclusion, as we have seen, Tancred is feted in the desert. There he feasts on bread and dates and coffee. There he experiences illimitable space and unbounded freedoms. It is in this space that the novel flirts with the possibility of Tancred's "going native." But the risk is alleviated when Tancred falls asleep and wakes up in an aesthetic form that can hold him firm. He participates in the domesticating energies of the novel, moving into a house, finding a wife. In Moretti's terms, Tancred sacrifices his freedom for happiness. As we have seen, Moretti argues that the *Bildungsroman* teaches the bourgeoisie how the French revolution could have been avoided. But what does it teach in the context of colonization? Similarly, it teaches how to avoid revolution. But the revolution is of a different nature. In the desert, Tancred enjoys local appetites and he consumes local products. He does not eat plum pudding. Therein lies the threat of "going native": it teaches the Western subject a habitual resistance to consumption. The subject who "goes native" learns to consume (and prefer) local products. "Going native" ensures that one does not develop an appetite for empire. And the *Bildungsroman* ensures that nobody "goes native."

The *Bildungsroman* addresses what could only have been a symbolic threat in the century, for fictional accounts of "going native" far out-number real ones. And this may suggest a final reason that Disraeli chose the classical *Bildungsroman* to contain his story. In Moretti's reading, the classical *Bildungsroman* only spans a short period in the history of the novel—the two decades immediately following the French Revolution, with *Wilhelm Meister* and *Pride and Prejudice* being his prime examples. One wonders why Disraeli would prefer such an outmoded strategy. Yet understood in the context of the new exportation of capital, and all that that would come to involve—a new valuation of the market and investments, an extended desire for exotic consumer goods—the classical *Bildungsroman* makes sense because it encourages habits of consumption and gives those habits aesthetic value.

Similarly, one wonders why most of *Tancred* is written as a romance. According to Jameson, romance emerges in transitional moments in history in which "two distinct modes of production, or moments of socioeconomic development coexist" (*The Political Unconscious* 148). It occurs at the beginning of the century as a result of "the new and unglamorous social institutions emerging from the political triumph of the bourgeoisie and the setting in place of the market system" (148). And it occurs again at the end of the century as a symbolic reaction to the "stepped-up pace of social change" (148). The construction of a romance in the middle of the century is then odd, unless considered in terms of space. Both the "setting in place of the market system" and the "stepped-up pace of social change" were features of the Middle East by midcentury.

The full title of Disraeli's novel, *Tancred, or The New Crusade,* should be considered not only in its religious connotations, but in its financial ones as well. With that in mind, the claim of *Tancred's* peripheral character, Sidonia, becomes prophetic: "Well, the crusades were of vast advantage to Europe. . . . It seems to wane at present, but it is only the decrease that precedes the new development" (127). This new imperialist development, I have argued, was theorized by Disraeli in the romance/novel form long before it was articulated in his famous Crystal Palace speech of 1872 or put into practice with his 1875 purchase of the Suez Canal. The romance form provided Disraeli with a technology for divesting the British of their reticence about investing in the colonial project, while the novel enabled him to create a comfortable space in which readers could feel at home in the new world. The novel proved to be an ideal form through which to domesticate imperialism.

Chapter Three

Domesticating Egypt

Women's Writing, Space, and Everyday Living Abroad

In the previous chapter I have argued that romance is a technology that encourages readers to invest in an unknown world and prepares the way for the domesticating energies of the novel. Although romance conventions were incorporated into the novel at the beginning and end of the century, romance was a much more integral part of various other genres up until midcentury. Writers whose projects differed from one another's as widely as Lord Byron's romantic epics and John Murray's mass tourism guides made use of romance conventions, such as presenting space, or what Northrop Frye called the "world," as natural and outside of history. Romance was especially popular among travel writers. The social reformer Harriet Martineau, for example, relied upon romance conventions for her 1848 account of her trip to the Middle East, *Eastern Life, Present and Past,* as did Florence Nightingale in her narrative of her Nile journey, *Letters from Egypt 1849–1850.*

Travel writers, though, began to break with romance conventions at midcentury. Instead of recording natural landscapes from afar, nineteenth-century travelers increasingly ventured indoors to describe in minute detail what they saw. For their purposes, they adopted a convention of writing often associated with the novel, what theorists such as Sigmund Freud, Henri Lefebvre, and Michel Foucault have called the everyday. By incorporating this novelistic practice into their travelogues, they were better able to pry into the private lives of the Egyptians. But their interest in Egyptian life was not simply voyeuristic. During the nineteenth century, I argue, writers employed strategies of the everyday in order to modernize the lives of those about whom they wrote.

Describing Egyptian domestic interiors was not only a new practice of the nineteenth-century travelogue. The insides of private and secular buildings of Cairo were also made the subject of European art for the first time at midcentury. Before that, mosques and tombs were the common subject of many works, but particularized views of private homes were rare.[1] The history of the entry of Europeans into Egyptian interiors has been documented by Lisa Pollard, who traces a trajectory that begins with Napoleon's 1798 landing in Egypt. Employing more than 150 scholars and technicians, Napoleon ordered the documentation of every form of animal and plant life, all monuments and buildings, and all types of rocks and minerals, which resulted in the *Description de l'Egypte.* Pollard claims that "a more thorough catalogue of things Egyptian has never been written by a European" (54). Napoleon's *Description,* Pollard argues, initiated the idea that the documentation of Egypt's interior spaces was a way to gain knowledge about Egypt. Europeans were further encouraged to penetrate Egypt's monuments and decipher their secret hieroglyphs with Champollion's discovery of the Rosetta Stone in 1822 and the cracking of its linguistic code. And the private lives of the Egyptian upper classes were first opened up to Europeans with the publication of Edward Lane's 1836 ethnography, *Manners and Customs of the Modern Egyptians* (54–59).

American Presbyterian missionaries who started schools in Egypt during the 1850s took the next steps into the Egyptian home. According to Pollard, they entered homes in order to clean them up, so that their owners would be better prepared for conversion. Reform of the inner realm of their homes was necessary before any religious education could take place (Pollard 106–114). The final phase of entry into Egyptian domestic spaces happened during the last three decades of the century when British colonialists as well as Egyptian nationalists peeped into the Khedival interiors in order to discover evidence there that would justify a regime change. Such evidence was found in the sumptuous decor and polygamous lifestyle, indicative of financial frivolity and moral decay, discovered inside of Ismail's palaces. Indeed, Pollard claims that moral outrage over Ismail's family life led to his deposal by the British in 1879 (94–97).[2]

Pollard's chronology of the penetration of Egyptian interiors points to a certain continuity throughout the century. The entry into Egyptian interiors, whether public or private—tomb, mosque, church, or private home—all grew out of the desire to produce knowledge about Egypt in the manner of the *Description de l'Egypte.* She argues that the British searched for similarities between ancient and modern Egyptians' domiciles and characters. But it is also true that the British repeatedly drew unflattering comparisons between the two in order to prove that the modern Egyptians were inferior to their ancestors. Such inferiority was one of many excuses used to justify British rule.

In this chapter, I argue that the British enter Egyptian domestic spaces not only to gain knowledge, but also to alter what they find. Throughout the eighteenth century Europeans documented the interiors of Egypt's ancient buildings, borrowing much of their descriptive techniques from the Grand Tour. Although nineteenth-century travelers used some of these same techniques, they increasingly borrowed their methods from the novel. At mid-century travel narratives about Egypt began to incorporate more scenes from everyday life. But instead of just documenting what they saw, writers attempted to change what they observed through the documentation process. They no longer describe solely for the purposes of knowledge production; they remodel houses and remake families in order to modernize and colonize Egypt.[3]

I consider two examples of this genre written by women who lived in Egypt during the 1860s: Emmeline Lott, who traveled to Egypt in 1864, and Lucy Duff Gordon, who landed in Alexandria in 1862. These works register a change in generic presentations of Egypt—from a portrayal of Egypt as mysterious and otherworldly to one of it as familiar and domestic; from a representation that sees only the outside world—monuments, ruins, and sunsets—to one that ventures inside the Egyptian house and accounts the everyday life therein.[4] Lott's work, *The English Governess in Egypt: Harem Life in Egypt and Constantinople* (1867), long out of print and not well received in its day, portrays life in the harem of the Turkish viceroy of Egypt, Ismail Pasha, in a cruelly "realistic" and unsympathetic manner.[5] Lott went to Egypt to work as a governess for the Grand Pasha Ibrahim, the five-year-old son of the new viceroy, and lived in Ismail's Cairo harem for five months. Duff Gordon's *Letters from Egypt, 1862–1869,* published first in 1865 and then expanded and republished in 1875, was hailed in contemporary journals as a success for its unprecedented realism and sympathetic portrayal of the Egyptian people. At the age of forty-one, Duff Gordon went to Egypt to recover from tuberculosis, and lived there for seven years until her death in 1869, all of the time writing letters to her mother, children, and husband in England. Living in Egypt, as opposed to just visiting, and accounting that life on a daily basis prompted these women to reach for new methods to tell their stories.[6] Prevailing generic conventions were not appropriate for the portrayal of their daily lives, nor could those conventions contain the quickly modernizing world in which Lott and Duff Gordon found themselves.

FROM ROMANCE EXTERIORS TO EVERYDAY INTERIORS: GENRE AT WORK IN THE MIDDLE EAST

Although British women first started to visit Egypt in numbers in the 1840s when the burgeoning travel industry laid the infrastructure for more comfortable travel, many women still felt a decade later that living in

Egypt was not possible.[7] Nightingale, for instance, wrote in midcentury: "Let no one live in the East, who can find a corner in the ugliest, coldest hole in Europe" (176). Nightingale spent five months in Egypt and passed much of that time floating up the Nile in a dahabieh, refusing to go anywhere by steam. She represents Egypt as a natural world, unaffected by time.[8] Her account is dominated by descriptions of landscapes, usually bathed in the light of the setting sun or rising moon: "The moon rising behind the trees on the Nile bank, and shining through them and the tall bulrushes, on the lonely waters, was the most striking thing I have seen" (41). Her belief that Egypt was not habitable has as much to do with her inability to see Egypt outside of the confines of romance landscape as it does with her never having lived there. For her, Egypt only existed as landscape. Describing a church, for instance, Nightingale writes:

> Fancy a church in the middle of alleys and tangles of palms, loaded with bunches of golden fruit, stretching every way in the forest, so that you *lose* the *enclosure;* daturas, bignonias, oleanders, cactuses, and bananas making the underwood; a great well in the midst, upon the edge of which sat the most beautiful group of Egyptian and Smyrniot women, and the radiant sunset behind. (my emphasis 23)

The church, the women, and the well are not depicted as distinct objects, but only as part of the verdure that engulfs them. Landscapes threaten to "lose" all "enclosures," leaving interiors unduly exposed: "One rides out to see the sunset, but between you and the sun you see, crouching in a ditch, lumps of low huts, not even *pretending* to keep out the weather; the bulrushes which grow in the swamps round them droop over them" (Nightingale 39–40). Nightingale cannot imagine Egyptian abodes as having an interior.

Martineau, like Nightingale, floated up the Nile in a dahabieh. She too depicts the countryside in the soft, rich shades of a setting sun, but she prefers to render her landscapes in what she calls the "afterglow," a mysterious light that appears after the sun has set: "Everything begins to brighten again in twenty minutes;—the hills are again purple or golden,—the sands orange,—the palms verdant,—the moonlight on the water, a pale green ripple on a lilac surface" (18). Egypt appears in silhouette backlit by afterglow: "The effects of palm clumps standing up before these yellow backgrounds, which are themselves bounded by a line of purple hills, with silver stars hanging above them, and mysterious heavenly lights gushing up from behind all, exceeds in rich softness any colouring that sunshine can show" (Martineau 125).

Duff Gordon was critical of the kind of vision exemplified by the works of Martineau and Nightingale that could not distinguish people from the scenery. Of Martineau's book she wrote: "It is true as far as it goes, but there is the usual defect—the people are not real people, only *part of the scenery* to her, as to most Europeans" (*my emphasis* 120). People in Martineau's account slip quietly in and out of the landscape, but their presence is never fully felt. For example, she treats a party that she meets in the desert much like a mirage: "We met a party of three men, a boy and a donkey,—one of them carrying a spear. They returned our greeting courteously, but stopped to look after us in surprise. Their tread and ours was noiseless in the wind; and the only sound within that wide horizon was of a barking dog,—far away on the opposite shore" (135).

Duff Gordon and Lott desired to exhibit Egypt in a new light. Duff Gordon expressed disgust with the unnaturalness of depictions of the Middle East in art. Quoting her friend, Shaikh Yussuf, with whom she agreed, she wrote, "'If the painter could not go to Es-Sham (Syria) to see how the Beduin really look . . . why did he not paint a well in England with girls like English peasants? At least it would have looked natural to English people'" (142). She continues, "Fancy pictures of Eastern things are hopelessly absurd, and fancy poems too. I have got a hold of a stray copy of Victor Hugo's '*Orientales,*' and I think I never laughed more in my life" (142). Whereas Duff Gordon felt that Europeans who depicted the East had little familiarity with their subject matter, Lott believed that Europeans who depicted harems had never spent time in one:

> Pray, kind reader, just picture yourself surrounded by such a motley group of beings, gabbling, chattering to me in their unknown tongues, and making grimaces like monkeys from four o'clock in the morning until ten at night incessantly; and then you may form some idea of life in the Harem—that myth-like Elysium of the fertile imagination of both Western and Eastern poets. (107)

Both women aspired to photographic accounts: "How much did I regret that I had not been taught the art of taking photographs, for then I could have daguerreotyped the whole of the inmates of the Harems of Egypt and Constantinople" (Lott 45).[9] Duff Gordon, conversely, was sure that she had achieved the photographic ideal: "At Geneva I sat next to one Arnaud Bey at dinner. He has been twenty-seven years in Egypt and says, like Hekekian, that my letters are a photograph and he will endorse every opinion I have expressed" (234). I will argue, however, that their writings produced a different sort of realism, one inspired much more by the everyday life of the novel than by the detailed and timeless precision of the daguerreotype. It is through the adoption of the conventions of the everyday that women participate in the domestication of Egypt.

Whereas Nightingale and Martineau wax poetical about sunsets, Lott never once looks up at the sky. Instead, she presents a realistic and claustrophobic image of being trapped in a house with a spoiled child. During her entire stay, she only tells of leaving the harem three times, and then avoids all description of landscapes. She does, however, describe everything inside of the palace, wandering from room to room, meticulously detailing all she sees, from wall hangings to floor coverings, from mirrors to bedsteads. Duff Gordon, on the other hand, describes landscapes, but she is far more interested in detailing the daily lives of those around her. And she documents domestic practices—what goes on in her kitchen, in the market, and in her neighbors' homes with unprecedented attention.

Lott and Duff Gordon rely upon a different sort of lighting than their predecessors. So accustomed to outdoor lighting is Nightingale that when she peeps into a "hut," she sees none of its contours: "I saw a door about three feet high, of a mud hut, and peeping in, saw in the darkness nothing but a white-horned sheep, and a white hen. But something else was moving, and presently crawled out four human beings, three women and a child" (44). Lott, on the other hand, is accustomed to domestic lighting: by candlelight she views the whole of the interior of Ismail's palace. And Duff Gordon, living above the Luxor ruins in spacious and open rooms also relies upon indoor lighting. Natural light filters through her kitchen window, as she sits near it recording the everyday life of her household in letters to be sent home to her family.

"EVERYDAY WAR"[10]

In the lighting of everyday life, details emerge that hitherto went undetected. Whereas Nightingale writes that "at Thebes one feels that detail matters little—it is the grave of a world that one has come to see" (133), Duff Gordon, also writing at Thebes, makes details the matter of her letters. For many travelers to the East in the first half of the century, details are less important than impressions. Edward Williams Lane, however, who traveled in the 1830s is a notable exception.[11] His ethnographic study of the Egyptians is full of domestic details. Yet Lane's use of details differs from Lott's or Duff Gordon's. Describing how Egyptians eat, for example, Lane writes:

> The master of the house first begins to eat; the guests or others immediately follow his example. Neither knives nor forks are used—the thumb and two fingers of the right hand serve instead of those instruments; but the spoons are used for soup or rice . . . To pick out a delicate morsel and hand it to a friend is esteemed polite . . . Each person breaks off a small piece of bread, dips it in the dish, and then conveys it to his mouth, together with a small portion of the meat, or other contents of the dish. The piece of bread is generally doubled together, so as to enclose the morsel of meat, etc.; and only the thumb and first and second fingers are commonly used. (11)

Lane's intermittent use of the passive voice has the effect of naturalizing Egyptian practices, voiding all agency, while his persistent use of the present tense removes his objects from the flow of history by making their actions ever present. Words like "generally" and "commonly," sprinkled throughout his account, further promote the sense of timelessness. Any behavior that runs counter to the general rule, such as handing food to a neighbor, can be subsumed under the code of politeness; thus, personality is also written out of his account. Duff Gordon's description of a similar scene differs significantly:

> So I joined a party of five round a little wooden tray, tucked up my sleeve and ate—dipping the bread into the *Melocheea* which is like very sloppy spinach but much nicer. Then came the master and his servants to deal the pieces of meat out of a great basket—sodden meat—and like Benjamin my piece was the largest, so I tore off a bit and handed it to each of my companions, who said "God take these safe and happy to thy place and thy children and bring thee back to us in safety to eat the meat of the festival together once more." (230)

Whereas Lane naturalizes Egyptian eating practices, Duff Gordon introduces agency, mostly her own, but also that of the Egyptians. As Duff Gordon inserts her own personality into her account, she also alters the pattern established by Lane, for she represents the Egyptians' reactions to her actions. Her use of the past tense situates the event in time and as a result makes room for her subjects in history. Her choice of active verbs, "joined," "tucked," and "tore," demonstrate that she is in charge, but it also shows her as wholeheartedly taking part in a meal with Egyptian fellaheen.

Duff Gordon's representation, which stresses the action of doing on a regular basis, is what Michel de Certeau calls "everyday practice," or "ways of operating." She describes eating not just as a system of practices reducible to a set of rules, as does Lane, but as a system that is flexible for its users. She herself uses the system to her own end: to humanize the Egyptian peasants for her British audience. Here she is interfering with not only the Egyptian practice, but primarily her own culture's unwritten prohibitions against eating with the other. By way of contrast, Lott establishes British propriety by always showing herself refusing to eat with a German maid who works at the harem, even though this means taking her daily meals alone. De Certeau shows the way that a daily practice, such as shopping, reading, or cooking, can become a political act by ascribing agency, or what he calls "tactics," to everyday actions. A "tactic" is "a calculus which cannot count on a 'proper' (a spatial or institutional localization), nor thus on a borderline distinguishing the other as a visible totality" (de Certeau xix). The place of a tactic, according to de Certeau, belongs to the other: "A tactic insinuates itself into the other's place, fragmentarily, without taking it over in its entirety, without being able to keep it at a distance" (xix). Duff Gordon's tactic is to show herself to her British audience as eating with all Egyptians, even the poorest; thus, she presents herself as a woman using her agency to contest British race, class, and gender prejudices. She is using the space of the other to comment upon her own cultural practices. In the meantime, she allows her readers to see Egyptians' tactics, but only in the background.

Lott also represents herself as having agency within the harem. She does this by presenting herself as schooling the harem in European tastes. Lott, however, has no intention of presenting the Egyptians in a positive light. Her everyday practices yield another result. In Franco Moretti's understanding of the everyday, the politics of the everyday are of "creeping comfort." He argues that the everyday within the nineteenth-century novel is used to celebrate the protagonist's aesthetic choices, or what he calls the "comforts of civilization," that is making oneself comfortable in a small world. The *Bildungsroman* hero's "personality" emerges from his practice of distinguishing amongst the everyday objects that surround him. Personality, then, is not a function of heroic action, as it is in epic or romance, but of distinguishing amongst stuff on a daily basis. When Lott arrives in the harem, she applies these everyday conventions to her text, giving herself a novelistic personality, showing herself to be the heroine of the harem by presenting herself as ably distinguishing amongst the many objects that surround her. Lott quickly turns aesthetic judgment into her daily work in the harem.

These two very different interpretations of the everyday may be brought together by considering the observations of Mary A. Favret, who argues that the "everyday is a wartime" (606). She suggests that from its "philosophical and aesthetic roots in Romanticism into twentieth-century critical theory" it has been "informed by the language, the features, and the preoccupations of wartime" (606). The most prominent conceptualizations of the everyday, including those of Freud, Lefebvre, Foucault, and de Certeau, have been made in the shadow of war. Under the veneer of peace, the everyday sustains the work of war even after it has formally ended. It is, as Foucault states, "a war by other means" (608). Favret's argument that the everyday is a "critical practice that relies upon, elaborates, and promotes the logic of war" (609) is useful in thinking about what it might mean to incorporate the everyday into the travel narrative form.

One question that arises, then, when dealing with the everyday is, "whose war is it?" De Certeau and Moretti offer different answers to that question. For de Certeau, everyday acts such as shopping, reading, and walking serve as war-like tactics waged by the oppressed against the oppressors. The everyday thus becomes a position from which the conquered can do battle. For Moretti, everyday acts such as shopping, distinguishing, and decorating are taken up by the bourgeoisie in order to erect a buffer zone of sorts against a menacing world. The everyday then enables the creation of a safe space in which bourgeois ideologies can flourish. This space is the novel. Here the protagonist asserts her individuality and forges a personality by way of her everyday choices.

Moretti's understanding of the everyday borrows much from Henri Lefebvre's, who wrote about the everyday at the close of World War II. Lefebvre conceives of the everyday as an ideology by which the bourgeoisie assert control over the vanquished. He shows how the French peasants' everyday life is sodden with bourgeois ideologies, especially that of private property. Lefebvre believes that it is the critic's task to study everyday life and through a dialectic process reveal the mechanics of class oppression. Since the critique of everyday life exposes how ordinary people's lives are impoverished by bourgeois ideologies, the ultimate goal of such critique is to change the economic system. Practicing everyday critique means to plot the overthrow of capitalism.

If "the everyday is a wartime," it is a war on many fronts. The bourgeoisie fight to control the peasants' lives and to justify their own power; the oppressed struggle against their oppressors to maintain their own life rituals; and the critic battles lies, misperceptions, and deeply held "truths" in order to uncover the "real" everyday life. Keeping this in mind, we might better understand why Duff Gordon and Lott turned to the everyday. On the one hand, Duff Gordon, like a good Lefebvrian critic, wanted to expose British presence in Egypt for what it really was—a lot of hypocrisy, racism, and chauvinism. On the other hand, Duff Gordon could not shed her own ideologies. As an aristocrat, she had her own class politics. As a liberal, she carried with her a complex ideology of the necessity of imperial rule.[12]

At first sight, Lott seems to be a completely different animal. She, and the more famous Florence Nightingale, distinguish themselves as being the most hateful of the nineteenth-century women travelers to Egypt.[13] Lott, however, is a far more complicated subject than Nightingale, or at least a more modern one. Unlike Nightingale, Lott sees a future for the Egyptian people. She is there to usher in that future. Her discontent with what she sees is wrapped up in her desire to change it for what she considers to be the better. For just a moment, I would like to consider two very odd bedfellows in order to make a point about the everyday: Lott and Lefebvre. What these two share is a desire to use the everyday as a means to alter the economic base. As we have seen, Lefebvre wants to root out private property and the alienation that it engenders. Lott is no Marxist. However, like Marx, she is profoundly modern.[14] She represents everyday life in order to change the way that capital flows throughout the harem, seeking to connect domestic flows to world-wide rhythms.

It is no wonder, then, that she shapes her travelogue to read like a novel. According to Mikhail Bakhtin, the novel is in the process of becoming. As such, it is the generic form best adapted to incorporate change. The romance tradition that had dominated Egyptian travel narratives was more appropriate for British views of Egypt as a static repository of the past. Many travelers saw Egypt in terms of the past. Some could not conceive of Egypt otherwise: "Without the past, I conceive of Egypt to be utterly uninhabitable" (Nightingale 139). The static nature of Lane's 1836 text is revealed by Jon Manchip White, writing only twenty-five years after *Modern Egyptians* was published:

> Mr. Lane wrote his account of the "Modern Egyptians," when they could, for the last time be described. Twenty-five years of steam-communication with Egypt have more altered its inhabitants than had the preceding five centuries. They then retained the habits and manners of their remote ancestors: they now are yearly straying from old paths into the new ways of European civilization. Scholars will ever regard it as most fortunate that Mr. Lane seized his opportunity, and described so remarkable a people while yet they were unchanged. (xxii)

Lott and Duff Gordon, on the other hand, purposely break with the past to represent Egypt in the process of becoming. Lott portrays Egypt as "wonderfully improving," while Duff Gordon records the life of Egyptians in the act of responding to those improvements.

Women were well placed to view modernization's affects on daily life. After comparing two separate Nile voyages taken by Nightingale and Gustave Flaubert in 1849–50, Derek Gregory concludes that only Flaubert was able to engage with Egyptians. He attributes Nightingale's inability to do so to the limits imposed upon her by her gender (48). Although this may have been true at the time, I am arguing that by the 1860s, when women were more likely to live in Egypt, they were as able to engage with Egyptians as men. Moreover, they were as involved in plotting Egypt's future as their male counterparts. I have argued in Chapter 2 that the romance and the novel together provided the techniques with which to colonize the Middle East: romance encouraged investments in an unknown world, and the novel fostered the aesthetic commitments that would be necessary to make oneself feel at home in that world. Romance transforms, and the novel domesticates. Romance conventions, however, transform in a slightly different manner when they are adapted to the travel narrative form, especially when authored by women because they could not fulfill the adventurous role of the romance hero. Women were better equipped to fight battles on the home front. Even though women portray Egypt as exceedingly static in their travel romances, these depictions of Egypt as frozen in time also promote change, for they provide the impetus for development and heighten the call for action—even if that action is performed by a woman.

Mary Louise Pratt writes that women's spatial restrictions when traveling make them more likely than men to record political change within a country. According to Pratt, men travel through space while women stay in one place, making that place a home base for their ventures out. Pratt's claim sheds light on Duff Gordon's account, which was prescient in its recording of Egyptian nationalist movements. Whereas British newspapers failed to report on these incipient movements, Duff Gordon records them regularly. Pratt believes that the key to women's ability to see politics is their staying in place long enough to record the multiple voices of a region, or its heteroglossia. I am suggesting, however, that it is the adoption of another novelistic convention—the everyday—that enables Duff Gordon to record political activity. On the one hand, the employment of the everyday allows Duff Gordon to capture the daily reality of Egyptians. On the other hand, Duff Gordon's and Lott's everyday accounting promotes changes that were not always in the best interest of their subjects, demonstrating the roles that women played in imperialism. Women's most potent tools, however, were not guns, treaties, or loans, but the everyday practices of writing, decorating, and shopping.

HAREM FURNITURE: EMMELINE LOTT IN THE BEDROOM

Lott prefaces her account by invoking the memory of Lady Mary Wortley Montagu, the English traveler who distinguished herself in the eighteenth century by being the first European woman to describe the Turkish harem. Writing that Montagu's account was superficial ("The interior of those Harems were to her Ladyship a *terra incognita,* and even although she passed through those gaudy halls like a beautiful meteor, all was *coleur de rose,* and not the slightest opportunity was permitted her to study the daily life of the Odalisques" (vi)), Lott claims that Montagu failed to describe the "social manners, habits, and customs" of the harem. Therefore, Lott sets as her own task the study of "daily life" therein. Lott states that her study depends upon doing what no European had done to date, "domiciling" in a harem. Lott's new job as governess to Ismail's son, Ibrahim, suits her purpose.

Lott sets a fast-paced tempo for her narrative: she whizzes into Alexandria on "one of the fleetest steamers," jumps upon an "express train," and is "whirled away by the iron king *en route* for the capital" (2). She represents Alexandria as "wonderfully improving," attributing that improvement to one man, the "*billionaire* Eastern merchant prince," the "richest man in the world," Ismail Pasha. She, like many Europeans, came to take advantage of the new order, characterized by an increase in foreign investments. In the train on the way to Cairo she meets two businessmen, one brought to Egypt by the cotton boom, and the other by the burgeoning financial industries. They discuss the current influx of foreigners to Egypt, but their conversation is interrupted when their train is stopped so that a private dispatch train full of pretty girls can rush past. One of the men explains that the women are "fair damsels who may chance to come on *flying* visits to Ismael Pasha" (3). Trainloads of girls fly by while well-meaning businessmen are shunted off the tracks. Lott begins her tale by suggesting that not only the flow in conversation, but the circulation of goods, is at risk in modern Egypt.

When the businessmen discover that Lott will be entering Ismail's harem, they warn her about what they call his "abode of bliss": "I would have you, Madam, alive to the well-established fact, that the whole *coterie* into which you will be introduced is the very hot-bed of intrigue, jealousy, and corruption" (6). Such a description mimics commonly held Western views about the harem;[15] however, the men update these views to comment upon the current economic boom by adding that Arabs "bury their gains in their

Harems, instead of putting them out to interest" (11). With this comment, Lott introduces her account with a theme which will be repeated throughout her text: the harem is a symbol of economic stagnation; in it capital is hoarded rather than reinvested. Lott takes an interest in the everyday life of the harem because she wants to restructure its economy.

Lott's role as governess promises her certain privileges within the household. Like many of the *Bildungsroman* heroines with whom she shares the title of governess, Lott is privileged with a certain authority and mobility. Also like her fictional counterparts, Lott is charged with the education, not only of herself, but of those who are closest to her. Jane Eyre, as Nancy Armstrong argues in *Desire and Domestic Fiction,* educates not only her charge but her employer, Rochester, indoctrinating him into middle-class values. But it can also be observed that she schools him in middle-class living: after his mansion burns down, Jane habituates Rochester to his smaller abode, as she leads him around it and physically accustoms him to it by touch. Similarly, Lott reorders Ismail's domestic space, schooling his household in Western living practices.

Soon after her arrival to the Cairo harem, Lott claims that all of her efforts to do her job have been thwarted because the prince is impossibly cruel and greedy, and she is not permitted to establish a regular schedule. She portrays her charge as a sadistic boy who throws hot coals into the face of one slave, tosses another off his father's yacht into crocodile-infested water for amusement, and brutally beats a third, tearing her cheeks apart "until the blood streamed down her chin like water" (80). Further complicating her educational efforts, Ismail refuses to let her use books. She, however, is most critical of the irregularity of the daily schedule: "The irregularity which prevailed in the domestic arrangements of the Harem had totally frustrated all my endeavours to carry out any regular system" (102). Ultimately, Lott gives up altogether saying, "I abandoned all idea of educational training" (102). I argue, however, that she does not abandon her work as an educator, but rather adopts a different audience and novel methods.

I. Decorating the Harem

Lott quickly turns her attention away from educating the boy and towards describing the harem, making daily pilgrimages through its rooms, inventorying their contents.[16] It is through these daily descriptions that Lott does her educational work. She uses the congested space of the harem to teach her readers the necessity of the flow of goods and services, and she uses her copious descriptions of stuff to justify an aesthetic ordering of those items. Most importantly, she uses her self-appointed position as diarist to claim aesthetic authority, putting herself in charge of making aesthetic judgments upon the daily life of the harem inhabitants, and then using her authority to teach them the art of consumption.

Lott crafts her descriptions to show the sumptuousness of the harem rooms. Here she describes the princesses' apartments:

> [They] consisted of two large saloons, covered with magnificent Brussels carpet, but completely besprinkled, as it were, with spots of white wax, which had been suffered to fall from the candles which the slaves carry about in their fingers. Around them were placed divans covered with red satan damask; the windows and door hangings of the same materials: a very large mirror, reaching down from the ceiling, which was painted with flowers and fruits, with the crescent, and numerous war-like instruments, and music placed in each corner, to the top of a marble table supported on gilded legs, on each of which stood a silver chandelier containing eight wax candles, with red-coloured glass shades covered with painted flowers. (40)

Missing in this description are the harem women, yet their traces are embedded in Lott's descriptions of the décor. Through the wax drippings on the carpet, the everyday actions of harem slaves who carry the candles "in their fingers" get narrated.

Similarly, when Lott documents the interior of the royal yacht, she elaborately details the furnishings: "The floor was covered with matting, over which was placed a rich-looking drab-ground carpet, interspersed with rose and large blue convolvuluses. The divan in which His Highness sat is covered with red and white silk and gold thread, which gives it a most gorgeous appearance" (94). She continues in the same manner for five pages, using up to four modifiers for each noun. Yet in spite of the adjectival abundance and fullness of her account, Lott complains that the viceregal spaces are bare. She realizes this bareness when she arrives to her own room:

> I gazed at the accommodation assigned to me with surprise; and yet, what could I have expected, as every apartment which I had passed through was totally destitute of everything that ought to have been placed therein? Not a footstool, no pianos, nor music-stools; not a picture adorned the walls. . . . In short, not any of the splendid rooms of the Enchanted Palace of the Croesus of the nineteenth century contained anything, either for ornament or use, except the bare decorations. (41)

Lott's complaint about the harem furnishings is that they contain nothing "for ornament or use"; they merely decorate. In other words, they are not integrated into an economy of use or pleasure. If they do afford pleasure, then that pleasure is not circulated, but perversely hoarded. When Lott describes her own bedroom, she singles out what's missing:

> The furniture consisted of a plain green painted iron bedstead, the bars of which had never been fastened, and pieces of wood, like the handles of brooms, and an iron bar, were placed across, to support the two thin cotton mattresses that were laid upon it. There were neither pillows, bolsters, nor any bed-linen; but as substitutes were placed three thin flat cushions; not a blanket, but two old worn-out wadded coverlets lay upon the bed. Not the sign of a dressing-table or a chair of any description, and a total absence of all the appendages necessary for a lady's bedroom—*not even a vase.* (my emphasis, 41)

Pillows, bolsters, and blankets are missing from her room, yet it is the absence of a vase that most disturbs her. Lott's fixation on this item reveals the aesthetic nature of her concerns.

A vase, like the eight candles in the chandelier, has a function, and akin to the wax drippings on the carpet, bears the mark of an everyday action. Lott laments her missing vase because it signals that nobody is serving her, that her room is cut off from the circulation of the harem. Its presence would connote daily service, somebody arranging objects for her aesthetic pleasure. One day as she makes her harem rounds, she spots "several beautifully-painted Sèvres and Japan china vases, filled with mostly lovely nosegays!" (43) In an uncharacteristic joyful outburst, she describes the vases' contents:

> Ah! gentle reader! They were bouquets such as the hand of no European court florist could possibly have arranged; they were, in fact, mosaics of petalled gems, works of art, touches of genius, brilliant gewgaws, toy-like bouquets, which would outvie the far-famed taste of the flower-girls of lovely Florence, with all nature's fair charms at their command to construct, which only the fingers of the ladies of the Harem (for that is one of the special duties they perform) could possibly mingle together. The harmonious blending of brilliant colours, the amalgamation of the delicious fragrance of their powerful perfumes produced nosegays which, while they charmed the eye, emitted forth a fragrance that quite intoxicated the senses. (44)

At first it is difficult to determine if the flowers are real, for by using the words "mosaics," "works," and "gewgaws," Lott stresses their made quality. It is not until she reveals that they emit a fragrance that we know for sure. Lott's emphasis on artifice calls attention to the everyday practice of the harem dwellers, whose "special duty" it is to arrange flowers. She enthuses about the vase because it gives her the opportunity to represent an object *as it should be:* integrated into an economy of use or pleasure, and it allows her to imagine the harem dwellers busily at work.

Lott often, however, depicts the residents as slothful, nicknaming their home the "Castle of Indolence." Of the harem slaves, she writes: "Their occupation during the best portion of the day consisted in lolling or rolling about the divans and mattresses which lay upon the ground, or squatting upon all fours, doubling themselves up like snips upon their boards, or clasped knives, which *pose plastique* I was for ever doomed to behold" (106). She opposes the laziness of the harem to her own busy self, yet since she cannot represent herself at work because she has abandoned her job, she must reinvent her work. She decides to be a writer, which, she makes clear, can only be done by first rearranging her bedroom furniture, itself an arduous task:

> I resolved to keep a diary. But how was that to be accomplished, since I had no table in my chamber upon which I could arrange my writing materials? The top of my French chest of drawers had already been turned into a toilet-table, and even if I had removed my dressing-case and all the appendages thereon, even then I had no chair. Thinking that the slave who had arranged my chamber might, in the hurry of the moment, have forgotten both the necessary articles of furniture . . . I resolved to appropriate some to my own use; but, when attempting to do so, I was point-blank told by the eunuchs that I must not touch or take anything which had not been expressly given me. Thus I was checkmated, and powerless even to move a chair for my own accommodation. This was a kind of domestic tyranny I could not endure . . . So, placing two of my largest square trunks upon one another, for a table, which I covered with my traveling-rug, and for a chair laying my traveling-cloak upon another box, and turning a larger one upright, I placed it at the back; which gave me a support for my back; and thus did I begin to jot down these incidents of my experience of Harem life in Egypt. (71)

Lott reveals her genesis as a diarist to be in her skills as a decorator. Indeed, she redecorates her bedroom, checks "domestic tyranny," and becomes a writer in the same move. And she authorizes herself—spatially—to take charge of the aesthetic process, articulating the relations between space, authority, and taste.

Lott records the description of interiors in her diary so that she can assert her own taste and habits over space. By discovering objects and distinguishing them from other objects, Lott shows herself at work, as author and as tastemaker. Similarly, she demonstrates her good taste by locating hideous furniture. One day, for instance, Lott spots a bunch of English cane-bottom chairs and cries out in despair: "But, oh! horror of horrors!" (44).

II. The Art of Consumption

When Lott first came to the harem, she was thoroughly disliked. She explains that she was hated because she "insisted on receiving proper respect" (104). It is not hard to imagine why her haughtiness went unappreciated by the harem women: she complains incessantly about their "filthy manners," "barbarous customs," and "disgusting habits." However, immediately after Lott spots the ugly chairs, she represents a change in her reputation. On that day, the harem surrounds her:

> All of a sudden I was electrified at hearing upwards of fifty voices exclaiming simultaneously, "*Koneiis! Qui-yis! Koneiis!*" "Pretty! Pretty!" While a whole chorus shouted forth, "*Gurzel! Gurzel!*" "Beautiful! Beautiful!" Some of them took up the black straw-hat which I had taken off and laid down upon the divan at my side. This they passed from hand to hand, gazing with pleasure and delight at that specimen of English manufacture. From that they examined the whole of my costume from head to foot. (47)

Lott's aesthetic judgments appear to give her a new role in the harem. They also supply her with a new role in her narrative: she becomes its heroine. In Moretti's terms, Lott develops a novelistic personality, which emerges out of the practice of distinguishing amongst the everyday objects. The everyday within the novel, according to Moretti, is used to celebrate the protagonist's aesthetic choices. The harem women visit her bedroom daily, seeking out her opinion about their new clothes: "It was often quite ludicrous to behold their Highnesses the Princesses, who could neither read nor write, the Ladies of the Harem, and slaves, as they came shuffling into my small room, and which was frequently crammed full of them, to ask my opinion of nearly everything they received" (131). Lott represents herself as the ultimate arbitrator of taste. Whenever the princesses got anything new:

> they handed them to me, at the same time appealing to my taste to decide whether they were *quiyis,* "pretty," or *batal,* "ugly," and my verdict was final. The instant that any of the slaves received presents from their Highnesses, they came and showed them to me, almost stunning me with the same interrogatories. If, as frequently happened, I examined the dresses and found them damaged (for many of the boxes contained last year's fashions), some of the pieces soiled, and others deficient in quality (for having been purchased in that condition they had been obtained at cheap rates), I condemned them, then the recipients returned them to the Princesses, who bestowed others upon them. (131)

She keeps the harem in fashion, or more importantly, in a consumptive loop, teaching the women to attune themselves to fashion's rhythms, accepting only this year's fashions, and scoffing at the rest. In this way she gains their respect and earns her keep. But Lott does not only influence their habits of dress; she gains sway over their living habits as well:

> In short, the whole of the inmates of the Harem soon began thouroughly to appreciate my European ways and habits in many respects. If they were taken ill they consulted me, followed my remedies, and did their best, poor ignorant, deluded, and neglected creatures, to abandon any habits which I explained to them were repugnant to delicacy, especially when I told them that such were not *a la Franca,* "European." (131)

During one of her harem strolls, Lott discovers, to her delight, a "secret chamber" full of Western furniture. She and the prince proceed to "take an inventory of the miscellaneous articles which were huddled up together in that 'Old Antique and Modern Curiosity Shop'" (141). They find a Broadwood's grand piano, spring-easy chairs, sofas, ornaments for mantelpieces, clocks with birds that sing, and others with fish swimming around lakes. Ultimately, her inventory of the "curiosity shop" grows so long that she gives up, saying that a "catalogue would take twenty pages to enumerate" (154). Lott's response to this "curiosity shop" is itself curious:

> I then determined to ask the Viceroy . . . to allow me to have the furniture which was in it (for therein I had found everything that even a European lady of rank could desire to make her rooms comfortable) placed in the rooms above it, which would have enabled me to keep the Prince apart from the host of slaves, whose disgusting ways tended to counteract my best endeavours to bring him up in European habits and manners. (155)

For Lott, the problem is that the "secret chamber" is not at all like a "curiosity shop" to which she analogizes it. Though filled with curiosities, it is nothing like a shop, where goods are bought and sold; instead the furniture is locked away and kept out of circulation. Lott's solution is to move the furniture upstairs, putting it to use and into circulation. Lott draws a connection between rearranging the furniture and educating her charge, demonstrating the relation between her taste and her work.

On another one of Lott's harem sojourns she discovers a room filled with life-sized mechanical animals: polar bears, tigers, and cranes. Imagining a purpose for this furniture, she writes: "It is a well-known fact that Ibrahim Pasha was of a cruel and brutal disposition, and it is most probable that he had these animals collected together and set in motion whenever he had commanded the attendance of any Turkish or Arab dignitary from whom he desired to extort money, for avarice was one of his predominant vices" (57). She imagines the Prince's grandfather hoarding these technological toys and then using them for perverse ends—setting the toys into motion and scaring his victim into submission. Similarly, when she encounters a young eunuch crying, she explains that he had been frightened by the prince who had ground the horns of a "snow-white mechanical lamb" into his groin. Both stories suggest that easterners don't know what to do with technology, contributing to the narrative that was emerging at the time that technology belongs to the West because only Westerners know how to use it.

One day the prince initiates a game of banking with her by cutting up pieces of cardboard and pretending like they are bills of exchange. During the game, she demands more change, claiming that he charged her too much. When he refuses, she writes, "He looked the impersonation of a usurer; his close resemblance at the moment to the portrait of his grandfather [Ibrahim Pasha] . . . was very striking. There sat the prototype of that Viceregal usurer who so thoroughly understood the art of making money to yield its best value, a gift which has descended to his descendents" (142). She then quits in protest, and he throws a tantrum, which ushers his father into the room. Ismail takes her place, saying, "Allow me to take possession of your stock-in-trade," speaking in a "tone of voice that was of a professional money lender" (141). In this scene, she creates a family tableau of usurers—three generations who disrupt the flow of capital by their hoarding habits. When Ismail leaves the room, she complains, "I had flattered myself that when he rose up from the banking department, the Viceroy would have left some packets of golden *paras* on the cushion. None, however, were deposited there; for, like his son, he was reported . . . to be fond of accumulating treasure as a means to happiness, and, by a common but morbid association, he continued to accumulate it as an end" (144). What disappoints her most is that none of the viceroy's money finds its way into her pockets.

Lott extends her critique to the entire harem. One afternoon she finds the prince's nurse hunched over a pot of money: "She opened her *sarat,* 'trunk,' and, guess my surprise, when she took out an English workbox . . . and I saw it was full as ever it could hold of napoleons, half-napoleons, gold five-franc pieces, Turkish, Egyptian, and English sovereigns; in short, she had the greatest difficulty in lifting it out of the trunk" (137). She then learns how the nurse acquired the hoard: she picks the prince's pockets who "had been accustomed, as soon as he could talk and toddle about, to have his pockets filled with *paras,* 'silver coins,' by the Viceroy" (141). The nurse then "doled out miles of them . . . to the undernurses" (141), who created their own hoards, so that the entire household was filled with "uncirculated buried treasures." Lott inquires about what happens to the hoards after the death of the servants, and is horrified when she finds out that they are spent on extravagant funerals—her most literal proof that the harem is burying their treasures.

Lott discovers an entire system of everyday practices that she claims result in the Prince's miseducation. She had been forewarned by the two men whom she met on the train who claimed that the Arabs "bury their gains in their Harem instead of putting them out at interest" (11). Documenting their charge, she records a system of practices that stop the flow of capital: the viceroy's misuse of the railway, the stoppage in the circulation of useful objects and aesthetic pleasure within the harem, the practice of extortion and usury, the hoarding of coins and the mismanagement of their circulation, and most significant, the hoarding of women and their productive (and consumptive) labor. To remedy the problem she introduces into their daily life a system of consumption practices, organized by her own writing practice. Aesthetic in nature, her practices encourage a desire to make meaning and create pleasure out of everyday life; she introduces into the harem what Moretti calls the "comforts of civilization." Simultaneously her practices validate an economic system based on flow and circulation.

HAREM FURNITURE: LUCIE DUFF GORDON IN THE KITCHEN

The *Edinburgh Review* received Lucie Duff Gordon's 1865 *Letters from Egypt* enthusiastically, stating that her account of Egypt was a vast improvement upon her predecessors'. She alone had succeeded in depicting "the true aspect of the people" ("Lady Duff Gordon's Letters" 109). Even Lane, whose 1836

Modern Egyptians was considered the most authoritative source on the Egyptian people to date, had not accomplished this: "True, Mr. Lane may be said to have done all that can be done in the way of describing that people; but the 'Modern Egyptians' is not intended to give us *every-day* experience of life in Egypt—rather the results of that experience" (my emphasis, "Lady Duff Gordon's Letters" 109). Distinguishing between "everyday experience" and its "results," the *Edinburgh Review* points out what was markedly different about Duff Gordon's text. In her letters she is able to perceive change as it happens at the micro-level of the everyday occurrence. The *Edinburgh Review* further distinguishes Duff Gordon's work by suggesting that only she sees the "inner life" of her subjects:

> Even the brilliant pages of *Eothen,* of Miss Martineau, and those of two or three other writers, afford us little insight into the *inner life* of the Egyptian. Nor is the cause far to seek. A foreign people cannot be understood in a short, and generally hurried, visit; nor indeed can they be appreciated by the oldest resident, unless he will consent to waive all prejudice and *live among them as one of themselves.* (109)

It is unclear what the *Review* means by "inner life" since such a phrase could refer to anything from emotional life to intellectual life, but since the *Review* emphasizes Duff Gordon's domestic arrangements as her advantage over her predecessors, we might also consider these words literally: "inner life" means life indoors. In this reading, what distinguishes her is that she records the daily domestic life of Egyptians. Duff Gordon's predecessors, as we have seen, cared little about the household, and she is most critical of them when they come the closest to writing about it in their accounts of Middle Eastern harems. Of Martineau, she writes, "Her attack upon harems are outrageous; she implies that they are brothels" (121), and she dismisses Lott's work because her account of harems was mean-spirited and unjust. As a corrective, Duff Gordon writes that the harem "is just like a tea-party at Hampton court, only handsomer, not as to the ladies, but the clothes, furniture and jewels, and not a bit like the description in Mrs. Lott's most extraordinary book" (269). By analogizing a harem to a "tea-party" Duff Gordon suggests the ordinariness of the social gathering. Throughout her text Duff Gordon demystifies the harem, making it less exotic and more mundane, redefining it for her Western audience: "Harem is used here just like the German *frauenzimmer* [womenfolk], to mean a respectable woman" (55). She even points out more than once that she is considered part of her servant Omar's harem. In her letters Duff Gordon uses harem to mean both a respectable woman and womenfolk. She also uses it to connote a space where women gather to socialize, and more often than not, to do their daily household work.

Duff Gordon represents the Egyptian house differently than her predecessors. Romance conventions made houses indivisible from the landscape, and thus invisible. Kinglake, Martineau, Nightingale, and Herbert describe neither the outside nor the inside of a house, and Lott, who does describe three viceregal harems' interiors in detail, never turns her eye to a common house. But Duff Gordon visits the houses of all Egyptians. In one surprising passage, Duff Gordon attempts to convince her readers that houses actually do exist:

> The best houses have neither paint, whitewash, plaster, bricks nor windows, nor any visible roofs. They don't give one the notion of human dwellings at all at first, but soon the eye gets used to the absence of all that constitutes a house in Europe, the impression of wretchedness wears off, and one sees how picturesque they are, with palm-trees and tall pigeon-houses, and here and there the dome over a saint's tomb. (56)

In order to see these houses, Duff Gordon asks her readers to erase all of their notions of what constitutes a house. Interestingly, the houses are not described, but rather differentiated by their context; their placement amongst palm trees and pigeon houses is what gives them their "houseness." Her ultimate invocation of the picturesque indicates how difficult her task is: because she can rely on no existing conventions for describing an Egyptian house, she falls back upon the domestic convention of the picturesque.

When Duff Gordon attempts to describe the interior of a house, she again defines the house by what is missing. Like Lott, she records the lack of furniture:

> In each [room] were as many bits of carpet, mat and patchwork as the poor owner could collect, and a small chest and a little brick cooking-place in one corner of the room with three earthen pipkins for I don't know how many people—that was all—they possess no sort of furniture, but all was scrupulously clean and had no bad smell whatever. (50)

We can see that Duff Gordon's idea of an Egyptian house is a clean, sparsely decorated room. If furniture exists at all, it is a mat, a carpet, or a chest. She does perceive distinctions amongst Turkish, Arab, and Coptic houses, with the Turkish houses being the best decorated and the Coptic houses the worst. Here she describes an Arab house: "I stooped low under the door, and several women crowded in. This was still poorer, for there were no mats or rags of carpet, a still worse cooking-place, a sort of dog-kennel piled up of loose stones to sleep in, which contained a small chest of the print of human forms on the stone floor" (50). Although this Arab house lacked standard furniture, it did contain a cooking place. Duff Gordon makes a stove the common denominator of an Egyptian house, and places the kitchen at the center of her understanding of that term: "Can you imagine a house without beds, chairs, tables, cups, glasses, knives—in short, with nothing but an oven, a few pipkins and waterjars, and a couple of wooden spoons, and some mats to sleep on?" (153). Essential to her understanding of the Egyptian house is the kitchen.

Duff Gordon places the kitchen at the center of the household, the harem, and her story, and in doing so she brings consumption to the center of Egyptian life. Consequently, women, who were previously conceived of in the context of production (in the bedroom), become active agents of consumption. In addition, the Egyptian family gets defined by the work it does in the kitchen. Duff Gordon's focus on kitchen consumption allows her to extend her story beyond the harem, as they do their daily shopping in local markets that are much affected by fluctuating prices. She incorporates into her story a wide array of causes that explain the steady rise in prices, including taxes, debt, greed, conscription, epidemics, and modernization. She shows the connection between micro- and macro-economic principles, demonstrating the interrelatedness of these two spheres—a concept that was well before her time. And she goes one step further, portraying the encroachment of global systems on the economy of Egypt, demonstrating how people there begin to question the relation between foreign occupation—by the Turks and Europeans—and their own "daily oppressions."

Duff Gordon's unique contribution to Egyptian travel literature, her deliberate synthesis of micro- and macro-economic activity, accomplishes two things. First, she creates empathy for the Egyptian people by showing how individual families suffer because of national projects that squeeze labor and financial resources out of them. She reports that one Egyptian told her that he detected a new wave of kindness towards Egyptians from American travelers and attributed this change in attitude to her book. While Duff Gordon's book favorably influenced travelers' opinions about Egyptians, it also propagated an imperial logic of consumption practices. Her emphasis on her own harem's economizing—pinching pennies, watching prices carefully, haggling for the lowest price—puts her consumption practices at the center of her text. Her actions stand in for the behavior of Egyptians who must do the same, on an even tighter budget;

thus, through her penny-pinching, she creates empathy for the everyday living practices of the Egyptians. Similarly, her economizing behavior causes her readers to feel for her, as she tries to make ends meet so far from home. Second, it shows her readers how inexpensively things can be done in another country—how cheaply a household can be run outside of England. Ultimately she demonstrates how cheaply domestic work can be performed abroad. Lucie Duff Gordon is one of the few Europeans in her day who attempts to create understanding for Egyptians by describing their daily activities in a sympathetic manner. Yet, no matter how well-intentioned her liberal attitudes, her lifestyle created a justification for the consumerist habits of imperialism.

I. Conscription in the Kitchen

On the surface, Duff Gordon's interest in the harem does not resemble Lott's in the least.[17] While Lott plotted to fill her bedroom with European furniture, Duff Gordon had no interest in adapting Western apparatuses to the Egyptian kitchen. For Duff Gordon, modernization is a problem, and Ismail's rampant modernization of the country is a major object of her critique. Duff Gordon reacts to Ismail's reconstruction of parts of Cairo to look like Paris with disgust, showing how this reconstruction affected Egyptians far from the city:[18]

> My grocer [in Luxor] is half ruined by the 'improvements' made *a l'instar de Paris*—long military straight roads cut through the heart of Cairo. The owners expropriated, and there is an end of it. Only those who have half a house left are to be pitied, because they are forced to build a new front to the street on a Frankish model, which renders it uninhabitable to them and unsaleable. (329)

Duff Gordon's attention to the habitability of the improved abodes is singular in the period. Most commentators dwell on the widened streets and changed facades, but Duff Gordon shifts the focus indoors, imagining how Cairo's Haussmannification will affect its inhabitants. She uniquely focuses modernity through habitation.

Duff Gordon's explicit critique of modernization has to do with its reliance upon forced labor:

> Of course half these acts [conscription] are done under the pretext of improving and civilizing, and the Europeans applaud and say, 'Oh, but nothing could be done without forced labour,' and the poor fellaheen

> are marched off in gangs like convicts, and their families starve, and (who'd have thought it) the population keeps diminishing. No wonder the cry is, 'Let the English queen come and take us.' (85)

She criticizes the common European belief that forced labor (in the colonies) was a necessary evil and then absents the British from the social implications of modernity by hinting at England's oppositional role. This is only to say that Duff Gordon's relation to modernization was complex.[19] Duff Gordon's depictions of technology are noteworthy, for while descriptions of actual ports, canals, railways, sugar refineries, irrigation systems, and cotton improvements are absent from her text, these "improvements" are still represented indirectly through her portrayal of the household economy.

Her techniques for representing improvements differ from other visitors', such as those of her daughter, Janet Ross, who describes the Suez Canal construction site in 1862: "You may imagine what a hole has to be made in the sand when I tell you that the canal is to be 189 feet broad and 28 feet deep" (126). Ross begins by citing depth and width, measuring out the canal in the sand and firmly anchoring her object in its place. Ross's description never extends beyond the borders with which she began. Ross's mother, on the other hand, omits measurements from her descriptions and does not delineate borders. Instead, she represents projects as they relate to local peoples and households, as she does when she spies workers through her own window in Luxor on their way to one of the Ismail's works:

> From my window now I see men limping about among the poor camels that are waiting from the Pasha's boats to take them, and the great heaps of maize which they are forced to bring for their food. I can tell you the tears such a sight brings to one's eyes are hot and bitter. These are no sentimental grievances; hunger, and pain, and labour without hope and without reward, and the constant bitterness of impotent resentment. (202)

Striving to represent this scenario outside of the conventions of sentimentality, which often isolate its subjects through the use of the vignette, she seeks rather to root this scene in its home environment, showing how the conscripted men do not only take with them the fruits of their labor but also the food that would be consumed by their families. She says, "I grieve still more over the daily anguish of the poor fellaheen, who are forced to take the bread from the mouths of their starving families and to eat it while toiling for the private profit of one man" (201). And of her "donkey-boys," she writes: "The father of one, and the two brothers of the other, were gone to work on the railway for sixty days' forced labour, taking their own bread, and the poor little fellows were left alone to take care of the hareem" (240). Modernization, seen through the harem window, is uniquely related to domestic production and household consumption, as development projects are shown to be the cause of fields lying fallow and families starving.

Duff Gordon represents the workers who harvested the cotton, and built the railways, canals, and ports, as bodies in transit. Whether she sees them "limping" about the village awaiting orders to leave, floating up the Nile on a barge, or being herded along the banks of the river, Duff Gordon shows the conscripts moving through space, traversing Egypt. Conversely, Ross keeps them penned within the boundaries which she so nicely drew, representing them confined within the borders of the object which they make. In her account, they are walled in by the banks of the canal: "I pitied the poor fellaheen their treadmill labour. Up and down the sliding sandbanks from sunrise to sunset, and a lick over the back when they did not go fast enough" (57). Further, Ross depicts them as a mass, never differentiating the workers from each other, and when she does it is only to racialize their labor: "Eight thousand of the men came from the upper Nile between Philae and Khartum, a far finer race than the lower Egyptians and better and faster workers. There was more animation in their section, much talking and some laughter, while the Behere looked dispirited and melancholy" (57). Duff Gordon's strategy is different; she breaks up the stereotypical clumping of bodies, individuating them, as she does in this passage where she shifts her focus from a mass of laborers to one individual:

> The other day four huge barges passed us towed by a steamer and crammed with hundreds of the poor souls torn from their homes to work at the Isthmus of Suez, or some place of the Pasha's, for a nominal piaster a day, and find their own bread and water and cloak. One of my crew, Andrasool, a black savage whose function is always to jump overboard whenever a rope gets entangled or anything is wanted, recognized some relations of his from a village close to Aswan. There was much shouting and poor Andrasool looked very mournful all day. It may be his turn next. (57)

"Hundreds" of conscripts are focused through "one" crew member, whom she individuates by assigning assets of character, a name and a "function." She depicts Andrasool as a member of her household, living on a boat with her for four months. Through her everyday accounting, she opens up a space in this tale for the future, as she warns that it "may be his turn next."

The strict borders that Ross draws around the Suez Canal serve to disconnect this project and its workers, who are contained within its machinery, from their surroundings; Ross is invoking a sense of "technology"—as an object divorced from the social system that organized it—that did not emerge until the concept of technology developed in the beginning of the twentieth century, according to Leo Marx. Whereas Marx sees the concept of technology emerging out of the complex arrangements necessitated by the building of Western railways, I have argued in the introduction to this book that we must also consider how technological projects built in the colonies shaped the concept, for if, as Marx argues, technology developed to obscure the agency of those involved in its making, then to recognize the colonial roots of such an antidemocratic concept shows how imperial projects chip away at the rights of those on both sides of the colonial divide.

In the context of the development of the concept of technology, Duff Gordon's techniques of depicting technological improvements are especially noteworthy. Unlike her daughter, Duff Gordon draws no borders around the Canal. Instead, she connects this massive project to its social making, and in doing so unveils "technology" to be a means of social organization brought about by a reorganization of production and consumption at the level of the household. Further, she nationalizes the process by scattering her citings of transported bodies throughout Egypt, "200 from Luxor, 400 from Karnac, 310 from Zenia, 320 from Byadyeh, and 380 from Salamieh—a good deal more than half the adult men to go for sixty days leaving their fields uncultivated and their hareem and children hungry—for they have to take all the food for themselves" (230). Duff Gordon shows the way that modernization projects draw from and draw out the entire nation. And in the process she reveals just what the concept of technology came about to obscure.

In order to further drive home the reality of conscription to her family and wider audience, Duff Gordon translates the issue into a domestic problem:

> To you all this must sound remote and almost fabulous. But try to imagine Farmer Smith's team driven off by the police and himself beaten till he delivered his hay, his oats and his farm-servant for the use of the Lord Lieutenant, and his two sons dragged in chains to work at railway embankments. (202)

Thus she translates the "remote" and "fabulous" scene to a local and real one, invoking the domestic genre of the picturesque, only to destroy its complacency.

Conscription, however, was not a domestic problem. England had outlawed slavery in the colonies thirty years earlier. For the British, forced labor belonged to France or Turkey: "Everyone is cursing the French here. Forty thousand men always at work at the Suez Canal at starvation-point, does not endear them to the Arabs" (66). By conceiving the Suez Canal as the pinnacle of modernization in Egypt, the British were enabled to believe that they themselves had nothing to do with forced labor, for they could loudly protest the use of forced labor without implicating themselves. Yet British railways throughout Egypt were being built by conscripted labor, and the many British companies that came to Egypt in the sixties invested in improvement projects that profited from conscription. Duff Gordon's own daughter was in Egypt because her husband directed such a company.[20] In a very rare indulgence in gossip, Duff Gordon tells a story of Ferdinand de Lesseps that acts as an allegory for modernization: "A Frenchman told me he was on board a Pashas's steamer under M. de Lesseps' command, and they passed a flooded village where two hundred or so people stood on their roofs crying for help. Could you believe it: they passed on and left them to drown? None but an eye-witness could have made me believe such villainy" (93). Poised on their rooftops, clinging to the last of their domestic security, Egyptian villagers are swept away in a flood of change, while Ferdinand de Lesseps, the symbol of that change, callously stands by. The Suez Canal was one of the few modernization projects in Egypt at that time that used no British monies. By attacking it on the grounds of the use of forced labor, the British could be sure that they were attacking something in which they had little investment. British investments lay elsewhere.

II. Investing in Saving

The British felt proud of their laws that banned the slave trade in 1807 and slavery in the colonies in 1834. In Egypt, where slavery was all but outlawed by Said Pasha in 1855, they smugly pointed their fingers at the French who had tens of thousands of Egyptians conscripted to build the Suez Canal. Yet Duff Gordon, who was adamantly opposed to conscription, kept house slaves. During her seven years of living in Egypt she acquired seven slaves, buying and selling them without expressing any compunction. How does a woman who was clearly conscious of the domestic ills of slavery justify keeping slaves at home? Duff Gordon's justification is written into the practices of her everyday life. Reading her domestic habits will not only help us understand how a liberal woman like herself could so easily keep slaves, but it will also aid us in seeing how a liberal nation, that had little interest in imperialism in midcentury, grew proud of its acquisitions by the last quarter of the century.

Duff Gordon lived cheaply. And she turned her living habits into the subject of many of her letters. Even so, her letters do not detail what it is that she lived without in order to meet her budgetary constraints; instead, they detail what she purchased for that very purpose. That is to say, she invested her energies in consuming, and she consumed in order to save money. Such behavior is usually associated with the British a decade later in the 1870s, when consumer goods from the colonies first flooded the domestic market, but Duff Gordon's fixation on consumption a decade earlier reveals the connection between consumption practices and colonial living. Even so, she seems to be an odd choice to study in order to understand the change in consumption practices in the last quarter of the century because she consumed so little. Moreover, she took great pride in how little she consumed, frequently describing her Luxor apartment as being equipped with only the bare necessities. Her letters to her husband gloat about how little she spends, often listing her purchases alongside of how much she paid in comparison to how much she could have paid or how much her neighbor paid. Her prolonged stay in Egypt due to her illness, and the necessity of keeping two separate households—one in England and one in Egypt—is the stated cause for her thriftiness. Yet her attention to her spending is so constant that it emerges as the most persistent theme of her letters, and it becomes clear that she is doing much more than justifying her spending to her husband. She is exposing a way of living that calls upon a set of skills that encourage her to use consumption as a way to save, and it is those skills that justify her continued stay.

Duff Gordon's description of her arrival to Egypt is singular. While her contemporaries describe the architecture or landscapes, she dotes on the prices. Egypt is simply too expensive. Her immediate response to the high costs of living is to get a servant, her logic being to spend a little in order to save a lot. A servant will help her get things for less: "I am frightened of the dearness of everything here. I found it quite impossible to get on without a servant able to speak English. The janissary of Mr. Thayer, the American Consul-General, recommended to me a youth called Omar . . . whom I have taken. . . . He will do all I ask for £3 a month and a greatcoat" (41). When Omar at first mistook his duties, thinking that Duff Gordon, like most Europeans, wanted to live extravagantly, she made it clear that he was hired to aid her in living cheaply: "As soon as I told him that my master was a bey who got £100 a month and no backsheesh [tips] he was careful as if for himself" (81). Duff Gordon lets her husband know that Omar is the key to her economical living, often incorporating praise for Omar into the review of her budget: "Thanks very much to Omar's good management I have spent little more than £250." With Omar's help, she eats well and pays less than other Europeans:

> Omar performs wonders of marketing and cookery. I have not spent above ten shillings a day for the four of us and have excellent dinners—soup, fish, a petit plat or two and a roast every day. But butter and meat and milk are horribly dear. I never saw so good a servant as Omar and such a nice creature, so pleasant and good. When I hear and see what other people spend here in traveling and in living and what bother they have, I say, "May God favour Omar and his descendents." (98)

Omar's skill at making domestic arrangements is a factor of his success: "At Cairo . . . Omar will get a lodging and borrow a few mattresses and a table and chair, and as he says, 'keep the money in our pockets instead of giving it to the hotel'" (68).

Yet Omar's value lies not so much in that he saves her money, but in *how* he saves it. She uses Omar to demonstrate the art of consuming. Helping her to set up her household, Omar accompanies her to purchase everything from kitchenware to a houseboat, and Duff Gordon describes these shopping trips in detail. Early on, she and Omar buy a boat, and she describes the transaction, accentuating the teamwork and skill involved in getting a bargain:

> The owner of the boat, Sid Ahmad el-Berberi, asked £30, whereupon I touched my breast, mouth and eyes, and stated through Omar that I was not, like other Ingeleez, made of money, but would give £20. He then showed another boat at £20, very much worse, and I departed (with fresh civilities) and looked at others, and saw two more for £20; but neither was clean, and neither had a little boat for landing. Meanwhile Sid Ahmad came after me and explained that, if I was not like other Ingeleez in money, I likewise differed in politeness, and had refrained from abuse, etc., etc., and I should have the boat for £25. (45)

During an earlier purchase, she relies on Omar to complete the hour-long transaction, but here she and Omar cooperate; he provides the voice and she the pantomime. It is ultimately her politeness, learned from Omar, that seals the deal. Although the purchase is collaborative, she attributes it entirely to Omar: "My servant Omar turns out a jewel. He has discovered an excellent boat for the Nile voyage, and I am to be mistress of a captain, mate, eight men and a cabin boy for £25 a month. Similar boats cost people with dragomans £50 to £65. But, then, 'I shall lick the fellows,' etc., is what I hear all round. The dragoman, I conclude, pockets the difference" (45). If the dragoman [guide] pockets the difference, she makes it clear that Omar pockets none.

A year and a half later, Duff Gordon, now a seasoned veteran, buys a carpet without the help of Omar. She records the purchase at length:

> You would have laughed to hear me buying a carpet. I saw an old broker with one on his shoulder in the bazaar, and asked the price, "eight napoleons"; then it was unfolded and spread in the street, to the great inconvenience of the passers-by, just in front of a coffee-shop. I look at it superciliously, and say, "Three hundred piastres, O uncle"; the poor old broker cries out in despair to the men sitting outside the coffee-shop: "O Muslims, hear that and look at this excellent carpet. Three hundred piastres! By the faith, it is worth two thousand!" But the men take my part and one mildly says: "I wonder that an old man as thou art should tell us that this lady, who is a traveler and a person of experience, values it at three hundred—thinkest thou we will give thee more?" (103)

Duff Gordon credits her own style—her "supercilious" look, her cultural fluency demonstrated by the punctuation of her request with "oh uncle," and her language skills—with her bargain. Of course, she learned everything she knew from Omar. Yet what is most important about this passage is that Duff Gordon shows in detail the practice of consuming to save.

Not only does Omar teach her to bargain hunt, he at £3 a month *is* a bargain, which she proclaims to her husband more than once: "It is becoming quite a calamity about servants here. Arthur tells me that men, not fit to light Omar's pipe, ask him £10 a month in Cairo and would not take less, and he gives his Copt £4. I really feel as if I were cheating Omar to let him stay on for £3; but if I say anything he kisses my hand tells me 'not to be cross'" (162). One wonders why Omar works for so little, and one day while he rubs her feet, we get the answer. When she tells him that foot care is below his dignity, he sings in response: "the slave of the Turk may be set free by money, but how shall one be ransomed who has been paid for by kind actions and sweet words" (164). Just as Duff Gordon's kindness procured her a cheap boat, it also lets her keep a servant underpaid by all accounts.

If Omar works for so little because he is paid in kindness, he also does so because he is part of the family.[21] Repeatedly, she represents Omar as such: "You would be amused to see Omar bring me a letter and sit down on the floor till I tell him the family news, and then *Alhamdulillah,* we are so pleased, and he goes off to his pots and pans again" (127). Omar, she suggests, delighted to be one of family, skips off to perform his domestic labor. Incorporating Omar's laboring body into the family circle, Duff Gordon writes, "This morning I went into the kitchen and found Omar cooking with a little baby in his arms, and giving it sugar" (169). And again she draws Omar's labor into the family: "I am now writing in the kitchen, which is the coolest place where there is any light at all. Omar is diligently spelling words of six letters, with the wooden spoon in his hand and a cigarette in his mouth, and Sally [her British servant] is lying on her back on the floor" (175). Imbedded in this ordinary family portrait is a revelation of Omar's economic value. With his wooden spoon in hand, he cooks dinner and teaches Arabic, and is, of course, adequately paid for neither.

When Duff Gordon's British servant, Sally, gets pregnant with Omar's baby, Duff Gordon quickly breaks up the family which she had so sentimentally portrayed, sending Sally back to England on the first steamer and the baby out to an Egyptian woman to nurse. She has Omar cover all expenses; thus she transfers the costs of her British servant onto her Egyptian one. She then swears off English maids: "I think I will not take an English maid, but bring only Omar to Europe and get a Syrian or a black woman when I return. I find that these disasters are wonderfully common here—is it the climate or the costume I wonder that makes the English maids ravish the Arab men so continually?" (187). A year later, when Maria, her German maid, becomes "bored," "dissatisfied," and "ill" in Luxor, Duff Gordon gets rid of her too saying:

> I do so much better without a maid that I shall remain so. The difference in expense is enormous, and the peace and quiet a still greater gain; no more grumbling and "exigencies" and worry; Omar irons very fairly, and the sailor washes well enough, and I don't want toilette—anyhow, I would rather wear a sack than try the experiment again. An educated, coarse-minded European is too disturbing an element in the family life of Easterns; the sort of filial relation, at once familiar and reverential of servants to a master they like, is odious to English and still more to French servants. (265)

The real reason that Duff Gordon dismisses Maria has to do with her unruliness: "The European style of abusing me and making faces behind my back, and trying to set my household against me—in short, the vulgar servant view of the master as a natural enemy—struck absolute dismay among my hangers-on, paid and unpaid" (254). As Duff Gordon gradually rids herself of European workers, she lays out an argument for the use of Egyptian labor: they are cheaper; they will play the family part; and they are easier to control.

Duff Gordon reveals the family to be a domestic work unit, itemizing the cost of each member. Omar himself costs 1/6 to 1/8 the price of a European in food: "Omar does everything well and with pride and pleasure, and is delighted at the saving of expense in wine, beer, meat, etc. etc. One feeds six or eight Arabs well with the money for one European" (265). And he has no desire to be aided in his work: "Omar of course is hardworked—what with going to the market, cooking, cleaning, ironing, and generally keeping everything in nice order but he won't hear of a maid of any sort. No wonder!" (269).

III. Saving on Household Slaves

Some scholars have based their assertion that Duff Gordon is an imperialist on the fact that she owned slaves.[22] This is indeed the case; however, I have been arguing for an understanding of imperialism that includes a broader range of practices. In my reading her ownership of slaves is a symptom of her everyday practices of saving and consuming. Her purchase of Zeynab, then, can be seen in relation to her dismissal of Sally and Maria. Interpreted in this way, imperialism itself can be understood as a system not only based on racial distinctions but on economic ones as well.

Duff Gordon uses her need to save money to justify paying Omar so poorly. As she records the rise in prices all over Egypt, she never increases Omar's pay even though her expenses decrease because of the dismissal of her costly European maids. Duff Gordon replaces these Europeans with workers for whom she paid little—slaves from Egypt and other parts of Africa. During her stay in Egypt, she kept seven slaves; she acquired the majority of them only after Sally and Maria left. Slaves for her were a good investment; they worked for free and Duff Gordon never paid much for them, although how much she pays is unclear. Only once does she mention the transaction. This was when she said that she considered her purchase price to be the wage. Usually Duff Gordon was reticent about discussing financial transactions when it came to slaves. She announced the acquisition of her first slave, Zeynab, by simply writing, "I have a black slave—a real one" (73).

The language that she employs to discuss how she gets her slaves is familial rather than commercial. She often speaks of "adopting" or "inheriting," as when she gets a slave from her son-in-law's business: "I am to inherit another little blackie from Ross's agency at Kenneh: the funniest little chap"

(313). Or she acquires slaves as a good deed, saving them from others' brutality, as she does when a friend shows her his new slave: "He fetched me to look at her, and when I saw the terror-stricken creature being coarsely pulled about by his cook and groom, I said I would take her for the present" (74). Similarly, she gained two more slaves when a Belgian died and "his two slaves . . . got my little valet, Darfur, to coax me to take them under my protection, which I have done, as there appeared a strong probability that they would be 'annexed' by a rascally Copt who is a Consular agent at Keneh" (350).

Just as the English saw themselves as protecting the Egyptian fellaheen from the French and Turks who forced them to toil on their projects, Duff Gordon imagined herself saving Egyptian and African slaves from mean masters. She offered a safe haven for them in the bosom of her family, where they would work tirelessly without pay. If she portrayed Omar as alternatively the father, son, and wife in that family, they were the children: "What would an English respectable cook say to seeing 'two dishes and a sweet' cooked over a little old wood stove on a few bricks, by a baby in a blue shirt? And very well cooked too, and followed by incomparable coffee" (276). Duff Gordon incorporates their playful, childish bodies into her family scene: "I go on very well with my two boys. Mabrook washes very well and acts a *marmiton.* Darfur is a housemaid and waiter in his very thin way. He is only troublesome as being given to dirty his clothes in an incredibly short time" (329). Weaving together a child's role, getting dirty, and his work, waiting, Duff Gordon creates an image of productive children, and a family always at work. Omar, whom they call "uncle," is portrayed as an older sibling or father, who supervises their work while busily performing his own. If Duff Gordon portrays Omar as a father figure, she portrays herself as a mother.

Sensitive to the problem that this portrayal may cause for her biological children, Maurice and Urania, she tells them that her slaves pay homage to them: "She [Zeynab] sings a wild song of joy to Maurice's picture and about the little Sitt [Urania]" (74). Duff Gordon's children's feelings, however, may not be her only concern; she may herself fear that she is replacing her family. If this is true, then her Egyptian family is a much better deal. They, after all, work to make her comfortable: "In this large dusty house, and with errands to run, and comers and goers to look after, pipes and coffee and the like, it takes two boys to be comfortable" (303). But more to the point, everybody in her Egyptian family works. Her English family is never portrayed as laboring; to the contrary, she complains about the laziness of Maurice, her youngest son: "I wish he would work; it is a great heaviness of heart to me to know that he is so idle and unsatisfactory" (334). The only time that she entertains a family visit is when, frustrated with Maurice's indolence, she asks him to come to Egypt to learn Arabic from Omar, so that in the future he may get a job in the colonies. And when Maurice does come, Omar works wonders. He teaches him Arabic, reforms his work habits and his spending habits, prompting Duff Gordon to proclaim, "I never beheld such a change for the better in any human being. Really Omar has done good service in keeping him out of mischief and teaching him to be more careful with money" (350). Duff Gordon reverses the colonial trope of the lazy native and projects it back home. Seemingly, Duff Gordon replaces her biological family with a more productive one. She out-sources the family, making its productivity visible by showing it at work.

Her slaves only fully enter into the narrative when Omar is away. It is not until Omar spends time away from home fixing her boat that she incorporates her "boys" into her text: "I am better again now and go on very comfortably with my two little boys. Omar is from dawn till night at work at my boat, so I have only Mabrook and Ahmad, and you would wonder to see how well I am served. Ahmad cooks a very good dinner, serves it and orders Mabrook about" (276). That she fills Omar's absence with accounts of her slaves is telling, for she seemingly replaces his domestic labor with theirs,

> It is surprising how fast the boys learn, and how well they do their work. Ahmad, who is quite little, would be a perfectly sufficient servant for a man alone; he can cook, wash, clean the rooms, make the beds, and do all the table service, knife and plate cleaning, all fairly well, and I believe now *he would get along even without Omar's orders.* (my emphasis, 303)

Here, she is only one word short of omitting Omar altogether.

Work defines her Egyptian family. She can live without her European maids, but she cannot live without Omar—until she discovers how well young slaves work in his absence. The step from domestic work to household slavery is short. Duff Gordon need only redefine "wage" as "purchase price" or rewrite "family" as those who work in the household to justify the use of slaves. It should be noted that in the process, Duff Gordon excludes female labor: she gets rid of Zeynab; she fires Sally; and she dismisses Maria. It appears as though Duff Gordon wants to eliminate any threat to her role as mother in her all-male family. If Duff Gordon has discovered an ideal labor force, that does ot get paid, that does not need to gratify its own cultural desires, that doesn't stir up dissent, she has also found a gentler way to rule—an imperialism based on an economy of kindness, where people work for little or nothing because they are getting paid in other ways, as does her slave, Mabrook: "A man asked [Mabrook] the other day after his flogging, if he would not run away, to see what he would say, as he alleged; I suspect he meant to steal and sell him. 'I run away, to eat lentils like you? When *my* effendi gives me meat and bread every day, and *I eat such a lot.*' Is not that a delicious practical view of liberty" (282).

Duff Gordon is a conundrum. On the one hand, she lives with Egyptians and treats them better than any of her peers. On the other hand, she lives cheaply off of them. Viewed through the window of everyday life, Duff Gordon appears less complicated. Duff Gordon's daily, habitual ways of thinking about saving and consuming made her own misdeeds invisible to her. While she ably described large-scale injustices wrought by modernization, she could not see beyond her own domestic behavior. Similar traits in other British travelers, though, were only too apparent to her. For example, she relates a story of an Englishman to whom she recommended a dragoman. When the Englishman promised him employment and then cheated the dragoman out of £120, Duff Gordon became so incensed that she considered writing a letter to *The Times.* She was especially outraged at the reason for the behavior: "It seems that they found one or two parties who had done it cheaper, but that is no reason for breaking their word" (355). She then draws a conclusion about the Englishman that one could easily draw about her: "The English have taken to doing very odd things about paying" (355).

GENRE AND POLITICS

The result of Duff Gordon's everyday accounting of her seven-year stay in Egypt is a narrative that makes visible political movements at the same time that it motivates them. Gordon depicts various uprisings against Turks, tax collectors, and other foreigners. Her account of one such uprising, the Gau rebellion, is notable for she does not only depict the 1865 revolt against the Turks of three villages, Gau, Rayanaeh, and Bedeh, a rebellion that took form as an attack upon a boatload of Greek traders in which one person was killed, but she depicts the daily occurrences that led up to that rebellion. Further, Duff Gordon shows the way that a local revolt, headed by Ahmad et-Tayib and originally supported by almost nobody outside of the three tiny villages in which it originated, grew into a national cause supported by all: "Every Arab sympathizes with him" (226). She shows the way that the government's brutal reaction to the villagers, which included the extermination of four villages and the beheading of 1,600 people, garnered national support for the cause. More importantly, she demonstrates the way that the revolt against the Turks contained sentiments against Europeans as well because "everyone believes that the Europeans aid and abet" the government's oppression (212).

Duff Gordon was one of the very few British writers in Egypt during the 1860s who recorded the Gau rebellion and the massacre that followed. She herself was surprised when her daughter did not mention it in a letter to her. And unlike so many others who reported colonial rebellions, Duff Gordon motivates the actions of the participants in a way that makes their behavior understandable, sympathetic, and inevitable. Her account of Egypt from within—the house, the harem, the kitchen—encourages her to show what she calls the "daily oppressions" of the Egyptian people, accumulating until the point at which politics penetrate the household and "everyone is exasperated—the very harem talk of the government" (244). She demonstrates the effects of conscription, price fluctuations, and tax increases on the household, uniquely focusing modernization through habitation.

Duff Gordon's narrative gives us a fuller understanding of national movements that remained unobserved in Western accounts until it became politically convenient to tell these stories. It wasn't until the next century that a popular account of a large-scale national movement in the Middle East was articulated. T.E. Lawrence's 1926 account, *Seven Pillars of Wisdom*, of the British exploitation of the Arab national movement in order to defeat the Turks and gain sway in the Middle East could only be recounted after the British and French were firmly entrenched in the Middle East and the Arab movement was pacified.

Unwittingly, Duff Gordon reveals her own part in motivating Egyptian rebellion. In unveiling her everyday habits, she shows that even the most liberal and well-intentioned visitors to Egypt were implicated in the colonial project. I have argued that Duff Gordon's domestic habits, adopted to cut costs, have imperial implications.

Lott's world is more circumscribed than Duff Gordon's. She provides no windows in her harem walls through which we can perceive the outside world. Instead, she offers a painstakingly detailed depiction of the world from within. The harem, indeed, is her world, and Lott's role in her representation of that small world, similar to that of the protagonist in a novel according to Moretti, is to make herself comfortable there. While Moretti argues that the politics of the conventions of the everyday are of "creeping comfort" because the everyday promotes bourgeois detachment from the larger world in favor of making oneself at home in a small world, I point out how the application of the conventions of the everyday in a colonial setting reveals the imperial violence implicit in these novelistic conventions.

Chapter Four

World-Girdling Technologies

Around-the-World Travel Narratives of the 1870s

In the 1870s Europeans traveled around the world with new vigor, causing a surge in the publication of accounts of circumnavigations. Indeed, the increase in round-the-world travel introduced a new word and character type into the English language, the "globe-trotter," that sure-footed yet unambitious traveler who goes "round" rather than straight "to."[1] "Globe-trotter" entered the language in the wake of the new round-the-world travelers.[2] Narratives about global travel represent nothing new, but the circumnavigations of the 1870s were radically different than the ones that came before. In this chapter I argue that unlike earlier accounts of circumnavigations, these come about to inspire confidence in a technological fitting of the globe.

The reemergence of this travel trend in the 1870s followed on the heels of the completion of three of the largest and most innovative technological enterprises of the nineteenth century.[3] The Suez Canal, the Great Indian Peninsular Railway, and the Pacific Railway all were completed and opened for traffic by 1870. The Suez Canal and the Pacific Railway were finished in 1869, while the Indian Peninsular Railway was opened in 1870.[4] With the completion of these projects a new route around the world was born, drastically altering the way that the world would be experienced. Travelers could now cut through Egypt en route to India, instead of taking the much longer way around the Cape of Good Hope.[5] They could steam from Bombay to Calcutta without worrying about procuring a palanquin or an unwieldy coach, or from San Francisco to New York without encountering "Indians or wild animals."[6] By the 1870s travelers could more easily circle the globe, traveling with speed, agility, and relative comfort. And the Suez Canal, the Indian Peninsular Railway, and the Pacific Railway ushered in a new way of writing the world.

It is important to consider this subgenre of travel writing because it records bourgeois global re-visioning on the cusp of what is called by many the New Imperialism. Of course, there is nothing new about imperialism in the century, as many scholars have shown.[7] Still, the unprecedented accumulation of territories during the 1880s and the new popular support of imperialism do suggest changes in the way that imperialism was practiced and valued. Hannah Arendt argues that the bourgeoisie were at the center of those changes. Arendt's assertion that "imperialism must be considered the first stage in the political rule of the bourgeoisie rather than the last stage of capitalism" (135), as Vladimir Ilich Lenin had argued, is useful, for it suggests a Victorian beginning, a setting in motion of a way of seeing the world that carries into the twentieth century and beyond. Characteristic of that new bourgeois vision is the "expansion is everything" ideology, best represented by Cecil Rhodes, who famously stated that he would "annex the stars" if he could.[8] Arendt believes that it is the bourgeoisie's entry into the political realm in the late century, propelled by their discovery that a "never-ending accumulation of property must be based on a never-ending accumulation of power," that fuels their new expansionist ideology (143).[9] Only through the exportation of their new found power, she argues, can the bourgeoisie realize such limitless accumulation.

If this is so, where can we find literary evidence of the bourgeoisie's new claim to acquisitive power? I have argued in Chapter 1 that British novelists struggled with the representation of powerful financiers, especially after the speculation debacles of the 1830s and 1840s. Charles Dickens discovered a queer solution to the problem of representing what was economically necessary but morally fraught with his marriage of the projector and the businessman in his novel *Little Dorrit,* but that was only after he brutally murdered his most acquisitive character, Mr. Merdle. Nor was it any easier for Anthony Trollope, writing after the upsurge of a new round of speculative fervor in the 1860s and 1870s. He too created a grasping financier, Malmotte, in his novel *The Way We Live Now,* only to murder him. I have argued that it was due to the need to export capital beyond Europe that the entrepreneur began to be portrayed positively in literature. I have also suggested that such financially tainted figures were represented better in genres other than the novel. Percy Hetherington Fitzgerald's 1876 laudatory biography of Ferdinand de Lesseps is a prime example. Another such positive representation of acquisitive power happens in the travel narrative form. In this chapter I argue that the round-the-world travel narratives of the 1870s developed, in part, to represent what Arendt sees as the root cause of imperialism, the bourgeoisie's new belief in limitless expansion. And I suggest that this new belief is both enabled by and concealed in another new ideology of the era: technology.

If Franco Moretti is correct in his assertion that particular spaces create particular genres, then the new global highway brought forth a new type of tale (*Atlas of the European Novel* 35). Round-the-world narratives are born in the 1870s to represent to the bourgeoisie *their* technology. When the bourgeoisie circle the globe, they meet face to face with their newest imperial ways: their recently exported steel roads and their newly reconstituted steamboat industry. In writing about their global shortcuts, they write about technologies that facilitate a new relation to the colonies and the world, and they develop writing styles and narrative techniques that represent that relationship. The technology that they survey, and intimately get to know, is what enables their class to take hold of the globe more firmly.

I explore this new subgenre, both in its real-world form, and then in its most famous fictional representation. Informing my argument is David Harvey's concept of "time-space compression," of which he writes, "The history of capitalism has been characterized by speed-up in the pace of life, while so overcoming spatial barriers that the world sometimes seems to collapse inwards upon us" (240). According to Harvey, the depression that "swept out of Britain in 1846–1847 and which quickly engulfed the whole of what was then the capitalist world" so shook the "confidence of the bourgeoisie and challenged its sense of history and geography" that representation itself was imperiled (260). Thus what Harvey deems the "first unambiguous crisis of capitalist overaccumulation" sparked a crisis of representation, which "derived from a radical readjustment in the sense of time and space in economic, political, and cultural life" (260–261).

I argue that the round-the-world genre emerges to resolve that representational crisis.[10] This is so because the global technologies that enable the genre are also its main subject. As technology becomes the object of sightseeing, circling the globe becomes the project of staring at the world's newest technological sites. Monuments are made of overaccumulation when sites such as the Suez Canal and the Mont Cenis tunnel begin to appear on the tourist trail. Thus the crisis in the representation of time and space, sparked by the first crisis in overaccumlation, can now be resolved into a tourist attraction. Technology's unique ability to speed up time and break down spatial barriers can be especially appreciated in its new environment outside of Europe.

Moreover, when tourists look at these new global technologies they see more than meets the eye, for technology, in Martin Heidegger's theorization, is not just a thing to look at like a river; it is rather a way of looking at an object that calls out and reveals its reserve energy. Technology, according to Heidegger, calls us to see not the river, but the river's pent-up energy, its potential to be damned up into a power plant so that we might store its energy for future use. Technology is a way of thinking which involves conceiving of objects as "standing-reserves" that are always "on call for duty." Even if an airplane is parked in the runway, for example, we conceive of it as ready for takeoff. Similarly, technology in the round-the-world narratives calls up a certain future duty for the spaces of the globe. That it does so without any input from the peoples who inhabit these spaces is what Leo Marx calls the "hazards" of technology. Marx argues that technology is a new concept that emerges in the early twentieth century to describe large complex systems, such as railways, as opposed to single units, such as engines. With the advent of the concept, progress became redefined in technological rather than socio-political terms. Improved technology, then, became an end in itself, and democratic means of determining progress were abdicated. I suggest that it is precisely because the modern concept of technology developed within the context of rapid colonial expansion that technological progress became an end in itself. More accurately, the concept of technology develops in order to facilitate unlimited expansion.

Since my argument is that the round-the-world genre remapped the spatial and temporal way of viewing the globe, I first look at the spatial remapping of the world performed by the British writer William Simpson's 1877 account of a circumnavigation that he embarked upon in 1872. I show how the genre represents a new global aesthetic, one that involves a smoothing of geographical and political boundaries. And then I suggest how the narrative's world-flattening technology aids in real-world technology transfer across national boundaries and across the globe. I argue that the narratives represent technology only to reproduce it and scatter it about the globe. Further, they articulate a logic of world ownership in ascendance in Europe and America in the last quarter of the century, a logic that relies on systems of technology to assert its claims on the world. The "techno-logic" of these narratives is not just a British phenomenon, but transnational and Western. It relies upon the establishment of a "Western" subject position that can be mobilized to a variety of inter/nationalist projects.

The respatialization of the globe performed by this genre was accomplished by a remapping of the temporal order. In the second part of this chapter I turn to the French popular writer Jules Verne to show the way that temporal restructuring of the globe was achieved through narrative. It is Verne and his fast-paced protagonist who popularized and internationalized the temporal logic of the genre. *Around the World in 80 Days,* published in 1872, the same year that Simpson embarked on his journey, and translated into English in 1873, is the only narrative of this genre that is still widely read today, and I argue that this is because of Verne's astute ability to give story to the temporal reimagination of the globe.[11] Just as the respatialization of the globe mounted in excitement, curiosity and anxieties about the proximity of the world, the retemporalization of the globe provoked enthusiasm, but more often fear, about a new temporality. I show how Verne not only resolves these anxieties about the new fast-paced world caused by that restructuring, but also creates a hero who conquers time. Verne's tale, then, can be read as an allegory of how the bourgeois came to have time on their side. By looking at Simpson's spatial mapping and Verne's temporal interpretation, I hope to uncover a chronotopic logic of the new round-the-world journeys.[12]

FACILITATING THE GLOBE

Accounts of round-the-world voyages have been a staple of European travel writing since the 1520s when the Magellan circumnavigation was recorded. Throughout the sixteenth, seventeenth, and eighteenth centuries Europeans purposefully ventured out to discover territories and commercial routes, map coastlines, and plant coastal colonies. However, as knowledge about territories and coastlines neared completion in the nineteenth century, these purposeful round-the-world voyages waned. Instead of venturing around, people increasingly headed inwards.[13] Circumnavigations were replaced by journeys to explore continental interiors, described and theorized most notably by Mary Louise Pratt. According to Pratt, the rise of natural history and internationally sponsored scientific expeditions in the eighteenth century are responsible for the new interior travel. She argues that journeys to the interior produced and were the production of new ways of knowing, beginning in 1735 when Carl Linne published the *Systema Naturae,* and Europe launched its first major international scientific expedition.

But starting in the 1870s, travelers again took to circling the globe. Unlike their predecessors they carried no measuring instruments and drew no maps; instead, they brought games, books, and fancy dresses. They recorded their circumnavigation, but what they produced was a body of literature that is lighter, swifter, and less serious than what had come before. They took little interest in discovering and documenting; instead, these outpourings speak sporadically and unsystematically about the landscapes, peoples, flora and fauna that they encountered. They share a lack of studied interest in the conventional preoccupations of circumnavigations of old: history, geography, and science. As the travelers trot from country to country, they skip from subject to subject; and in recording it all and shaping it into a narrative pattern many of these narratives create a uniquely unengaged tone, lacking in a "serious" and scientific purpose.

It is most likely due to their largely unserious tone that the latter-day circumnavigations are overlooked by scholars.[14] The works of the celebrity explorers such as John Speke, Richard Burton, James Grant, Samuel Baker, David Livingstone and Henry Morton Stanley, who went into Africa to search for the Zembezi, Nile, and Congo rivers in the 1850s and 1860s and 1870s, attract more critical attention. Their serious projects, including the abolition of slavery and the Christianization of Africans, mark them off for study, and implicate them in the imperial project. By contrast the buoyancy and lightheartedness of many of the around-the-world voyages suggest an unimportant and even unimperial content. Many titles of the genre, such as H.J. Burlingame's *Around the World with a Magician and a Juggler* (1891) or Thomas Woodbine Hinchliff's *Over the Sea and Far Away* (1876) make light of round-the-world travel. Others, such as Ellen Walworth's *An Old World, as Seen through Young Eyes* (1877) and Emmet Carr's *All the Way Round; or What a Boy Saw and Heard on His Way Round the World* (1876) purport to be written by children. Egregious errors in these child-authored texts would cause one to think that the narratives were edited by children as well: the ten-year-old Emmit Carr's narrative brims with historical and geographical inaccuracies, the most blatant one being the placement of Cape Horn in Africa. The project, then, is not, as in the circumnavigations that came before, one of geographical accuracy, but the impression of an idea: traveling around the world is now so simple that even a child can do it.

Even adult authors take pains to exhibit the simplicity of world travel. They often do this by showing just how easy it is to begin, offering impetuous motives for travel, and making light of their journey. The German traveler Baron de Huebner lacks a serious motive and begins his 1874 account by writing: "On my road, I mean to amuse myself; that is, to see all I can which is curious and, to me, new: and every evening I shall note down in my journal what I have seen, and what has been told me during the day" (vi). Other adults demonstrate the simplicity of circumnavigation by taking pains to show just how little they know or care to know about the world. The English traveler Egerton K. Laird describes in his 1875 account why he and an American travel companion that he met en route travel so well together: "H—and I hit it off pretty well, as neither of us . . . know, I'm afraid, anything of, or take any interest in, botany, geology, entomology, or any other *ology,* and he is generally lively and in good spirits" (Laird 245).[15]

These happy-go-lucky travelers presented themselves as a conundrum to indigenous peoples, who had little context for understanding this new lot of visitors. Annie Brassey, a British woman who circled the globe in her yacht "Sunbeam" in 1878, told of this encounter with some perplexed natives in the South Seas, "'No sell brandy?'—'No.' 'No stealy men?'—'No.' 'No do what then?' Their knowledge of English was too limited to enable us to make them understand that we were *only* making a voyage of circumnavigation in a yacht" (my emphasis, 205). Imagining the sort of gestures that Brassey might have produced in her efforts to "make them understand" exposes just how unintuitive the round-the-world journeys were. She projects the purposelessness of her own project onto the South Sea Island natives, who could not understand such a venture. It is their "knowledge of English" that stands in the way, and it is also the "knowledge of English" of her home reading public that enables understanding. By summoning up a knowledgeable public, she naturalizes her project and subsumes it in a realm of innocence, "We were *only* making." Yet the project of this genre, circling the world, and the naturalization of that project were far from innocent, as we shall see.

My point is not that circling the globe was easy. World travel was still prohibitively expensive, and if not dangerous, replete with annoyances. Rather, the narratives' focus on ease propagates the idea of mobility, a new reality of the age that Marshall Berman understands as being both liberating and restrictive to the bourgeois subject. He illustrates this point by invoking the modern pedestrian. On the one hand, he is a newly liberated agent, able to move about the city as he likes. On the other hand, he is thrown into "the maelstrom of modern city traffic, a man alone contending against an agglomeration of mass and energy that is heavy, fast and lethal" (Berman 159). I shall argue that the round-the-world narratives propose a different sort of split. Rather than depicting a Western subject torn between her new found mobility and the technologically induced restrictions born of the same energies that made her freedom possible, these narratives posit a geographical division in which the Western bourgeois subject is promised unfettered mobility, while everybody else is subject to a sort of technological lockdown.

Paul Virilio's understanding of mobility is instructive here because he shows how even this split between the mobile West and the immobile East is a fallacy. He sees the rise of the "mobile public" as one of the driving forces behind Britain's conquest of the world, but it is a conquest that has its own people as its ultimate object. Coupled with speed, Virilio argues that the idea of the "mobile public" was propagated by the new transportation and communication technologies in order to incorporate the British public into its military machinery. In his reading the British public was never freed by mobility; conversely, it was forged into faster and more powerful weaponry.

In other words, this newfound mobility, only served to better incorporate the British public (and all publics) into the military machinery of the state. Although Virilio's understanding of the rise of the "mobile public" suffers from a sort of one dimensionality, it is useful to expose the ideology behind the freedom of movement that these narratives celebrate.

Nobody did more in the nineteenth century to propagate the idea of the mobile public than Thomas Cook, the British travel entrepreneur who organized the very first tour group to circle the globe in September of 1872. Cook reflected that "this going around the world business is a very easy and almost imperceptible business" (Brendon 144). Just as Cook eased the way around the world for his clients by organizing their journey, providing tents, food, guides, and coordinating the transfers from trains to steamboats, the round-the-world travel narratives projected a new sense of ease with the world to the reading public at home.[16] If Cook's travel infrastructure provided comfort and ease, it also provided "national" security. It was of major use to the British government in its various military campaigns in the Middle East, most notably the fight against the Egyptian nationalists who rose to protect their country against the British invasion in 1882, during the battle of Tel-el-Kebir.[17] Cook's travel infrastructure was also employed during Charles Gordon's expedition to the Sudan in 1884, where he went to quell a local rebellion and restore the British to power. The British organized yet another expedition to the Sudan in which "Cook was responsible for the conveyance of some 11,000 English and 7,000 Egyptian troops, 1300 tons of stores and war material and 800 whale boats" (Pudney 203). Most notably, the development of armies in the nineteenth century was influenced by the type of management and organization carried out by Thomas Cook and Thomas Mason Cook in their travel companies. Thus Susan Buck-Morss points out that "Cook's tour industry which, in utilizing an industrial infrastructure to transport, provision, and deploy people in large numbers, first developed skills of movement control which became vital to late-nineteenth century mass armies" (205).

Often it is Cook who is given credit for innovating the round-the-world journey; and he is sometimes even accredited with inspiring Jules Verne's fictional account.[18] Indeed, in 1872 he led the first guided world tour when he took eight people on a 222-day journey around the globe. Further, his company led more people around the world than any other travel company in the nineteenth century. By 1892 1,000 people had circled the globe with Cook & Son (Brendon 151). But it is inaccurate to think of Cook as the innovator of the global excursion; indeed, he just capitalized on the new travel possibilities. It is more useful to think of Cook as one of the early articulators of the new global communications network. More importantly, Cook popularized that network through advertising and articles in his journal *Cook's Excursionist.* Cook opened the globe to the participation of an increasingly mobile public through the accessibility and immediacy of advertising. Likewise, the globe-trotters wrote accessible prose, not bogged down with botany, entomology, biology, or any other of what Laird called the ology's, with the same results. The accessibility of their writings, often published first as letters home to newspapers, opened up the world to a broadening reading public at home.

ENTITLING A GENRE

The titles in this genre are important to consider because they indicate its new vision. Earlier round-the-world narratives relied on titles that advertised a mission, destination, or name of a ship. The word "voyage" often appeared in the title, as it does in Darwin's *The Voyage of the Beagle.*[19] In the 1870s travelers dropped this enterprising word from their titles. Without a mission or destination the circumnavigations of the 1870s flatly spoke their purposelessness, and were frequently called some variation of "Around the World." Put another way, the titles of these narratives baldly state a new purpose of circumnavigation, simply to get around the world, to draw a circle around it and enclose it within. Going around the world then becomes an end in itself, as Simpson suggests when he concludes his circumnavigation by writing: "When I put my foot on a certain door-step, the girdle had been put round about the earth, and there was an inward sense of satisfaction in feeling that a long journey was ended, and a task had been accomplished" (413). Thus Simpson turns the round-the-world journey into an accomplishable "task." At the same time he articulates the globe from the threshold of his own home, a common move of the globe-trotters, as seen in Ellen Walworth's account of her arrival home, "Thus, June 1874, finds us where June, 1873, left us—Uncle absorbed in the duties of his parish, I intent on my studies, and more strongly convinced than ever of these three things: that the world is round, that the finest country in the world is the United States, and that the brightest spot in the United States is Home!" (316).

An important purpose of these narratives, then, is to articulate the world as a globe, and to make that globe knowable from the familiar space of home. In this way, the globe is familiarized. But the home base functions in another way as well. As both starting and finishing point, it fosters a circular trajectory that prompts another trip, as the end point is converted into the starting point upon arrival home. As globetrotting becomes automatic in this way, the globe is roped into a predictable future based upon its newly defined present.

In titling his 1887 work *A Girdle Round the Earth: Home Letters from Foreign Lands,* D. N. Richardson emphasizes the words "home" and "girdle" to map familiarity onto the project. "Girdle," a recurring word in these works, simultaneously accomplishes a sense of familiarity and a sense of constriction, a spatial shrinkage of the globe that approaches a smug at-homeness in the world. The girdle familiarizes the globe, putting it in the same spatial framework as the body, the usual object of girdling, and calls to mind the constrictive nature of this body wrap. "Girdling" was not a new way to describe round-the-world travel; Shakespeare has Puck "girdle round about the globe in forty minutes" (qtd. in Simpson 5). Yet girdling the globe, in the restrictive sense, is a newly found reality, made possible by rail and steam technology. In the 1870s the word "girdle" was increasingly used to conjure up the world railway system, and usage such as R.H. Brown's, "50,000 miles of track in operation in 1870, enough to *girdle* the earth twice" was common (*Webster's*). Thus girdling the globe in the seventies signifies not just an innocent act of circling the world, but a technological feat that depended on the "cooperation" of global powers, England, France and America, and the submission of countries and zones, Egypt and the Red Sea, India and the Arabian Sea, and China and the Pacific. Richardson's title points out the strictures that this act imposes, a monopolistic tightening of control of the globe that Lenin associates with the New Imperialism.[20] The genre celebrates a new-found bourgeois mobility that is predicated upon tightening their grip on the globe.

The most prolific contributors to the genre of round-the-world literature were Americans, and the American C.C. Coffin was one of the first to girdle the globe in the new fashion.[21] In *Our New Way Round the World* he explains the motivation for his 1869 journey: "The last rail has been laid between the Atlantic and the Pacific, and the locomotive runs from ocean to ocean. A few months hence the waters of the Mediterranean and Red Seas will mingle together through the Suez Canal, and a new way for trade and travel will thus be completed round the world" (Preface). Here he explains the "new" of his title, but one has yet to understand what he means by "our." The use of this pronoun is puzzling because it modifies "new way" which he defines by two pieces of technology, one "American" and the other internationally held on Egyptian territory controlled by the decaying Ottoman Empire. American investment in the Canal project was negligible, and Americans had little to do with the international company.[22] Yet Coffin claims both roads as American. I suggest that Coffin is doing more than just making a national claim on the global highway. The circumnavigations of the 1870s make national and Western claims to the globe-girdling technologies and all that fall in their tracks. As Coffin uses the possessive pronoun to take hold of the new global highway, the authors of round-the-world travel narratives invoke "Western" technology to claim *all* technological enterprises and imaginings as their *own.* The genre establishes a "Western" subject position suggested by Coffin's "our" that could be mobilized to a variety of inter/nationalized projects.

MAPPING THE ROUTE: WILLIAM SIMPSON'S *MEETING THE SUN: A JOURNEY ALL ROUND THE WORLD, THROUGH EGYPT, CHINA, JAPAN AND CALIFORNIA* (1877)

In 1872 the British journalist William Simpson was dispatched by the *Daily News* to Peking (Beijing) to report on the marriage of the emperor of China. The internal policies and events of China were of increasing interest to England for a variety of reasons. First, China was the world's most sizeable empire, and England's move towards expanding her own empire made China a natural object of study and curiosity. Second, China represented a large potential market for goods and source of raw materials, not only to England, but to France, Russia, and America; thus the coming of age of its emperor offered a new hope for a change in China's isolationist policies, which had hitherto kept European traders confined only to a few treaty ports on the coast. Simpson's travel account is of note because he saw an opportunity to penetrate the most intimate spaces of China by writing about its age-old custom of marriage, and he turned the story of imperial nuptials into a circumnavigation, incorporating a local event into a global context. Thus he girdles the globe by incorporating its most recalcitrant locality. And he does it with a nonchalance typical of the genre: "As I should be so nearly halfway round the globe, it might be as well to return home by the New World, and thus put a girdle round about the whole" (Simpson 7). Simpson's ability to girdle the globe by incorporating its largest resistor makes his round-the-world narrative stand out; nevertheless, Simpson's account remains understudied by scholars. His work is important though because it articulates the way that the expansionist thrust of these narratives is justified through the language of globalization.

The "expansion is everything" mentality that Arendt associates with the imperialism of the 1870s and 1880s is portrayed by Simpson as the completion of the globe by the incorporation of countries outside of its fold, in this case China. Chinese leaders were adamantly opposed to building telegraphs and railways on their territory. Because China stood outside of the global communications network, it was the largest impediment to the smooth transfer of Western technology and goods across the surface of the globe. But the round-the-world travel narratives incorporate China into the technological imagination of the globe, and Simpson provides a roadmap for that incorporation. Simpson's work reveals the technologies of incorporation that round-the-world narratives adopt.

I. Making the Way

Simpson devotes his eight-page introduction to mapping out and justifying his route. Like many other globe-trotters, he claims to go "all" the way around the world, entitling his narrative *Meeting the Sun: A Journey All Round the World.* Yet such a claim can only be a construction since it would be impossible to encompass "all" of the world. His route then reveals the constructed nature of the geography of the circumnavigation. Simpson defines the skeletal route of the genre; beginning his travels in Europe, Simpson goes on to Egypt, Aden, Ceylon (Sri Lanka), Singapore, China, Japan, America, and then back to Europe.[23] "All" then simply means the quickest and most direct route: "What I will call the *Direct Route* will be generally chosen, *via* Egypt. Any one wishing to reach Egypt by the quickest means will go by the Mont Cenis Tunnel. Speed was my object, and so I propose to take my readers by this last route" (Simpson 6). Almost all round-the-world travelers pass through America, Europe (England, France, Italy), Egypt, Aden, Ceylon, Singapore, China, and Japan. Many see India. Some see Australia, New Zealand, and Honolulu. Travelers almost never visit Russia, Africa (excluding Egypt), or South America.[24] Simpson provides a justification for these exclusions, saying that the Siberian Overland Route from St. Petersburg to Peking is a "long and a very serious undertaking" (3). Of the globe-trotter's avoidance of South America and Africa he asserts that the "modern traveler"

> has no wish to risk his neck in attempting to go over impassable peaks, or to die of hunger and thirst in the burning deserts; painted savages with heavy clubs and poisoned arrows, or Indians with scalping-knives, are a class of society he has no desire to mix with. Jungles with tigers or venomous snakes he marks as places to be avoided. (Simpson 5)

The "modern traveler" avoids extreme landscapes, "impassable peaks," "burning deserts," and "jungles." Yet in the round-the-world travel genre, he does not just eschew, as Simpson suggests, deserts, jungles, and mountains, but he stays clear of the semi-arid, the wooded, and undulating areas as well. Globe-trotters, it seems, are averse to landscapes altogether. In this respect they are not like explorers, who exult in landscape reporting. William Burchell's 1822 text of travel in Africa is typical of this tradition: "The path soon became more steep and laborious, and the sun from behind the distant mountains of Hottentot Holland, rose upon us before we had climbed much more than half the height" (40). Packed tight into one sentence are evidence of the incline of the hill, the weather, the landscape, and the subject positioning vis-à-vis the landscape. Although hills, weather, and landscape reporting can be found in the round-the-world travel accounts, such density of landscape reporting is conspicuously absent. Again and again Simpson produces potentially dense landscape descriptions as not textured. Passing through a jungle in Penang, he writes: "There is a dense jungle all round, but a good road has been cut through to the foot of the waterfall" (88). Absent in this description is a corporal knowledge of the landscape, which in Burchell is conveyed by a report of the incline of the hill and an account of the weather. In Simpson's account the "good road" that cuts through the jungle seems to flatten out the landscape itself.

Explorers often feel the road beneath them, as John Campbell, traveling in South Africa clearly does: "The roots of the grass, which was growing in separate tufts, were so hard, that they jolted the wagons like so many stones" (134). Such literature had a way of incorporating the road, bumping around and jolting its passengers as it goes. Yet in the round-the-world travels, the road is rail smooth. At sea too one meets neither tempests nor pirates; steamships smoothly ply from shore to shore with surprisingly few storms, deck fires, or battles to check their movement. Making a twenty-six-day journey across the Pacific in a new American steamer, Simpson typically writes: "We found the Pacific not untrue to its name. There were one or two days which we might say were not quite smooth; but a storm, or a gale, or even a rough sea, we did not encounter the whole way" (340). One gets the feeling that the sea itself has been pacified by the new American steamers, whose powers and size he describes in ample detail.

During Simpson's trip he rarely indicates that he has risen above sea level. He infrequently records heat and rain, despite time spent in the tropics.[25] Instead, he records a geographically smooth world.[26] Related to the lack of geographic borders is the lack of cultural and political ones. Language, dress, or customs rarely hinder his movement, and he encounters no passport controls, customhouse hassles, or money problems.[27] Guidebooks from the period suggest that even the most pampered tourist would have no such luck; typically, tourists complained of everything from fleas and bugs to collapsing tents and grounded steamers. And tourists' logs were filled with strange encounters that suggest a very bordered world. Visiting four continents, seven countries, and thirteen cities, one would expect that Simpson might experience a few more inconveniences. Yet states hinder his movement in no way; he enters all ports and stations without interruption. Nor does Simpson encounter the mundane problems that happen when one must rely on trains and ships for conveyance. His trains are never late, and he is always prompt. A common complaint featured in the "Travel through Egypt" column of the *The Times* throughout the 1860s was of "stranded" travelers, who missed steamboat connections and were thus "stuck" for weeks at Suez. But for Simpson there are only smooth transfers from steamboat to train and train to steamboat. Nothing, it seems, gets in the way of the new technology. Technology smoothes out geographical, cultural, and political borders. People and goods flow freely over the surface of the globe, and a common problematic of modernity, traffic, is elided. Indeed, these are traffic utopias.

Traffic utopias should be unreadable. Their frictionless accounting provides no bumps or snags to give a story grip. Borders are the stuff of narrative; it would be hard to imagine a story without them.[28] Even the most fundamental narrative theories take them into account.[29] Round-the-world travel narratives practice imagining a world without borders, and they are invested in producing a narrative of a borderless world. In this way, they reflect the development of capitalism as understood by David Harvey: "Innovations dedicated to the removal of spatial barriers . . . have been of immense significance in the history of capitalism, turning that history into a very geographical affair—the railroad and the telegraph, the automobile, radio and telephone, the jet aircraft and television, and the recent telecommunications revolution are cases in point" (232).

Such world-flattening bourgeois imaginative practices found ideological impetus in the nineteenth-century visionary dream of the seamless joining of the hemispheres. Round-the-world travel narratives are globalizing technologies. They project onto the world a homogenizing smoothness that comes out of and makes apparent an imperial dream of hemispheric union. These narratives are particularly interested in the joining together of the western and eastern hemispheres, made evident by the route that they most often reproduce—a route that moves from west to east smoothly and without snares.

II. Making Technology Western

Round-the-world narratives, technologies themselves, are born out of the global transport technologies that they seek to reproduce. New global technologies—ports, tunnels, canals—provide them with the structure that they need to articulate the imperial project of global union. Thus the description of technology takes a prominent place in the narratives. Technology gives materiality to abstracted imperialist claims of global union. Prominently placed in these accounts are representations of works that are lodged between worlds: Mont Cenis Tunnel, the Suez Canal, the Great Peninsular Railway, the Pacific Railway, and various newly built ports. The most instrumental of these technologies is the Suez Canal, for it symbolizes that seamless joining of the hemispheres in its dramatic linkage of two oceans—the Mediterranean and the Red Sea, of two nations—England and India, and of two abstract concepts—West and East.

Although the Suez Canal is the symbolic center of his work, Simpson launches his narrative much closer to home, at the mouth of the Mont Cenis Tunnel on the border between France and Italy. He begins his narrative with a long description of the new technological processes used to build the tunnel. Like the Suez Canal and the Pacific and the Peninsular Railways, the tunnel was most significant in that it provided the means of communication between nations. It symbolized the reduction of what was once a three-day long crossing of the Alps to a matter of minutes.

Most interesting about Simpson's account of the tunnel is the way that he incorporates his detailed description of technology into the literary. Standing at the French end of the recently completed tunnel, he thinks back to the previous century, when no tunnel existed and the mountain was a formidable block to movement between France and Italy. Pondering the tunnelless mountain, he says that it is here that Laurence Sterne ends his travel novel *Sentimental Journey,* as if to suggest that England's most innovative novelist was himself immobilized by the mountain. Sterne therefore strands his beloved character, Yorick, in front of the formidable landscape, leaving Yorick's journey and Sterne's novel uneasily incomplete. Simpson's ruminations suggest that where technology ends, literature too must find its conclusion. He hints that the development of global technologies will fan British literary culture. At the very least, the completion of the tunnel will increase the circulation of letters, Simpson notes as he maps out their new and improved route south: "The mails which leave London on Friday evening, reach Brindisi early on Monday morning. The whole of this distance, via Mont Cenis is 1477 miles" (33).

The Mont Cenis Tunnel, then, opens up the world to British letters. And Simpson's circumnavigation maps out the road that they will follow. From England to Brindisi via the Mont Cenis Tunnel, from Brindisi to India via the Suez Canal, from India to China via the Peninsula Railway, Simpson projects English letters around the world.

This is an important function of the circumnavigations: they project across national borders self, commodity, culture, and technology. Thus they rely upon a smooth world vision so as to encourage the flow. Further, they streamline movement, gathering all roads into one, forging practical and logical connections between technologies and technological spaces around the globe. The Mont Cenis Tunnel merely connects France to Italy, an idea that is politically fraught but nothing new. The Suez Canal is different. It connects two truly abstract notions, the West and the East.

As the home of the Suez Canal, Egypt is the most symbolically active space in this narrative. Since the opening of the Canal, Egypt occupied a new space in the European geographical imaginary: "Egypt of old was the gate of the east, and now she has again got back her lost privilege" (Simpson 16). Egypt was now again the space in which East and West meet and mingle: "Port Said would in a short time be the Liverpool of Egypt; all the commerce of east and west would meet there" (Simpson 36). What enables Egypt to become a geographical space of encounter between East and West is the technology that it harbors. The Suez Canal is the active agent of East/West union: "As Vasco de Gama's discovery of the Cape of Good Hope divorced the connection with the East, so the Suez Canal is to restore it, and the Adriatic and the Indian Ocean will be more closely wedded again than ever" (Simpson 17). In round-the-world travel narratives, Egypt is synonymous with the Suez Canal, and Egypt and the Canal function symbolically as the site of East/West union. And this site of union is proclaimed to be Western.

Since round-the-world narratives claim "Western" ownership to this unique space of union, the new international transport technology gains credence as Western. The narratives assure that what might be considered an Egyptian project (for Egypt was the biggest contributor, giving lives, labor, land, technical expertise, and money) is collectively available for "Western" ownership. Simpson westernizes the canal by claiming belief in it at the same time that he distances eastern claims to its technology by portraying the Alexandrians as disbelievers in the canal project. He projects England's lack of belief in the "practicability" of the project onto the "East," by telling an elaborate tale of Alexandrian inability to believe that the canal was completed. Simpson's arrival in Alexandria in 1869 on the eve of the opening celebrations of the canal is colored by such disbelief:

> The first news received was that an impenetrable mass of rock had turned up on the canal at the Serapeum; that it would be quite impossible to cut through it in time; that the canal itself, generally speaking, was a complete failure; that Lesseps knew this all along, and that the

> rock at the Serapeum would put the inauguration out of the question. There were people from all parts of the world, including an Empress, and an Emperor, Princes, and great folks of all ranks; and so Lesseps, unable to carry on the imposture any longer, had that morning blown out his brains with a revolver. Such was the intelligence that first came on board our ship when we got into Alexandria. Of course it was of Alexandrian manufacture. (36)

By exporting British doubt to Egypt, Simpson helps to shape the notion that while Egypt and the East lack faith in technology, Britain and the West believe. Simpson continues to dislodge the ownership of the canal from "the East" by writing about the changes that the canal project produced on the environment. Noting the vast transformation of desert land into a sea, he writes:

> The transformation seemed like enchantment, as if the wizards and genii of the east had been at work,—but, on consideration, it might appear doubtful whether individuals of that kind could have wrought such transformations. Engineers and contractors are our modern wizards and genii, and not only the bitter lakes, but the whole Suez Canal, is evidence that they are far ahead of their ancient rivals. (Simpson 40)

The Suez Canal is proof that eastern "geniis" are incapable of orchestrating technological transformations and that Western engineers own that ability. Simpson represents the canal as materially and imaginatively Western. In so doing, he represents the symbolic power of the canal to "unite" East and West as a Western power. Thus the magical union between East and West is facilitated by the invention of technology as Western.

III. Making Technology Inevitable

Round-the-world travel accounts are narratives of inevitability. They rely on the production of repeatable (and knowable) spaces to make meaning of the vast world. As their project, the drawing of the whole world into a narrative, is nearly impossible, they rely on the production of repeatable (thus knowable) spaces to create continuity. The spaces that get repeated are spaces of technology, newly Westernized spaces that define the East/West union narrative. Technological spaces are repetitions of the ones that came before; thus the Suez Canal is a repetition of the Mont Cenis Tunnel; the Peninsular Railway is a repetition of the Suez Canal. As each technological space repeats one that comes before, each new space of technology anticipates one that will follow. It is this automatic process of the narrative that contains its hidden violence, for in the inevitably of its action it promises to "batter down all Chinese walls."[30] Property, thus, finds itself with a new historical role, for it becomes a "dynamic new property-producing device" (Arendt 145). Such a turn of events describes what Hannah Arendt considers to be crucial to the development of imperialism: property and wealth "were no longer considered to be the results of accumulation and acquisition but their beginnings" (145). In these narratives, I suggest, global technology becomes the site at which property's new role is revealed. In other words, the new global technologies are portrayed as spaces in which accumulation becomes inevitable. Technology then emerges to propagate acquisition on a global scale.

Spaces of technology are thus proleptic; they predict a future that is knowable in the present. Prolepsis then predicts a world in which all roads will be paved, and "Western" technology will inhabit every corner of the globe. The story of the Mont Cenis Tunnel announces the Suez Canal; the Suez Canal announces the Peninsular Railway; and the Peninsular Railway announces a Chinese railway. But herein lies the problem. There was no Chinese railway, and any "foreign" encroachment into China to build railways was strictly forbidden. China was opposed to Western ideas and technologies, and the creation of Western spaces on that territory, outside of the handful of treaty ports, was impossible. It was important, then, that a body of narratives arise which would smuggle Western technology into China. The force of the prolepsis suggests that what has happened to Egypt will happen in China. Thus the form of the narrative itself works hand in hand with Simpson's most prophetic claim about China: "If machines do not come in today, they will find admission tomorrow" (292). Simpson's words express the automatic violence of the round-the-world narratives that I have been describing. It is as if the machines themselves will set up house in China, and in a sense, they will. They will because they carry within them a record of the violent processes—the alteration of space and time—that enabled their erection. To possess these global technologies is to possess their future power to destroy. Arendt writes, "The most radical and the only secure form of possession is destruction, for only what we have destroyed is safely and forever ours" (145).

The Suez Canal, symbolically resonant in its (uniquely Western) ability to unite the East and the West, is imagined in China. Simpson reports, for example, that European missionaries published and circulated pamphlets with descriptions and pictures of the Suez Canal and the Mont Cenis Tunnel to prove to the skeptical Chinese that the Westerners were indeed a civilized people. Like the pamphlets, Simpson's text reproduces Western technology in China. Simpson, however, unlike the missionaries, has no interest in persuading the Chinese of the West's state of civilization. Instead, he imbues Westerners with a sense of themselves and a belief in their own technological inevitability. In the face of an obstinate Chinese government, who had "set their faces against railways and telegraphs" (Simpson 210), Simpson offers his readers a sense of the inevitability of Western technology in China and around the globe.

As Simpson approaches China, steaming through the Chinese seas, his narrative changes. The smooth journey that has hitherto been presented is seemingly ruffled by the contemplation of China. The rebellious seas frighten his crew, and the fear of monsoons make them worry that they "might be all thrown upon one of those desolate rocks before to-morrow morning" (Simpson 106). Bloodthirsty pirates clog the sea and doom European passage: "Their plan with a European ship is to kill the crew, as dead dogs tell no tales; then, after taking whatever they want from the vessel, they set her on fire or scuttle her" (108). Once he is on shore, rebellious natives threaten them. Simpson arrives in China two years after the "Tsiensing massacre," a rebellion in which hundreds of French missionaries and Chinese converts were killed by Chinese rumored to be angered by the kidnapping of their children by missionaries. Simpson visits the sites of the massacre, various Roman Catholic churches, and documents the atrocities. He speaks of children who took refuge in the basement of a church being suffocated, of native converts being "savagely butchered," and of corpses floating down the river for days afterwards (222). The Tsiensing massacre colors his entire visit. Tsiensing is his first stop, and his entire time there is spent visiting the sites of the massacre. Later, when he travels to Peking and the Great Wall, he continually refers back to the killings. Everywhere that he travels in China he sees frightened Europeans, whom he describes as being in a constant state of military preparedness, flying their flags and ready for an attack. His readers cannot help but be made aware of the constant threat that a Chinese rebellion, what he calls "another Tsiensing," posed. What is most interesting about the massacre is the way that it calls into account a "European" object of attack (rather than French).

Simpson's writing on China differs from his writing on the rest of the world. China represents a potential snag in his smooth journey around the world. Monsoons, pirates, and especially massacres throw up borders and threaten to disrupt the ease in which he circles the globe. Indeed, he perceives the entire Chinese landscape as uniquely bordered. Burial mounds cover the landscape and "are so thick and close that the whole country has the appearance of being one vast burial ground" (116). Simpson writes:

"In sailing up the Pei-Ho, I was struck with the infinite number of grave-mounds which were visible in every direction, and I found that this is the case in all the northern part of China" (190). The importance of the mounds to the round-the-world travelers is most bluntly announced by E.K. Laird: "The whole country is disfigured by unshapely mounds; and, worst of all, no railway can be built" (243). Coffin too makes this point:

> The empire is a graveyard. Railroads are remorseless; they cut through the cities of the living and the dead alike. A railroad running ten miles in China would disturb the whole spirit-realm. Unlike strokes from spades might sever skulls from vertebrae in some ancestral burial ground, and then there would be headless ghosts wandering through the land of darkness, and sickness, pestilence, calamity, and untold horrors would settle upon China. (343)

Yet Coffin continues by proposing that a railway is the only solution. Travelers portray these mounds (and the massacres) in order to suggest the inevitability of their leveling (and squelching). They imagine the landscape flattened and ready for the production of Western technology upon it. Simpson sees the landscape with one purpose: "The country here is perfectly flat, and a railway could be constructed with the greatest ease" (125).

Globe-trotters understood the resistance to "Western" technology as cultural.[31] By portraying the landscape as filled with mounds, they could materialize a cultural practice, so as to more easily imagine it expunged. Western technologies, they imagined, could plow through China, ridding it of its uncomfortable contours. The narratives employ technologies that make the inevitability of China's flattening apparent. They proleptically suggest that what had happened elsewhere would happen too in China. The railway had rid India of its cultural symbols: "Ten years ago five thousand images of the idol Doorga were sold at the annual festival held on the banks of the Ganges in honor of that god; but since the opening of the railroads the sale has almost wholly ceased" (Coffin 107). In India, Coffin continues, "the locomotive, like a ploughshare turning the sword of the prairies, is cutting up a faith whose roots run deep into bygone ages" (108). And China would follow suit:

> When that screeching innovator, the locomotive, begins to move across the plains of this flowery land, ploughing up old bones, breaking the chains which bind the living and the dead, there will be hope for China. . . . It will yet do for China what it is doing for India. It is a

> powerful missionary. Idols, caste, prejudices, sacred bulls, Brahmans, customs, religions, laws, governments, dynasties, pashas, mandarins, and kens are borne down by that great leveler. (Coffin 343)

The round-the-world narratives offer up a way to thread together the world, to connect the spaces of the globe through a particular spatio-temporal logic, characterized by the inevitability of the reproduction of space in time. What will happen here, they suggest, will happen there. It is only a matter of time.

TIMETABLE ANXIETIES: JULES VERNE'S *AROUND THE WORLD IN EIGHTY DAYS* (1872)

Thus far I have been describing the way that space is homogenized, reproduced, and scattered around the globe by the round-the-world traveler. I have suggested that the technology of the round-the-world narrative is the flattening out of cultural difference and the spatial reining in of the world. In *Around the World in Eighty Days* Jules Verne invents a character to whom the spaces of the globe are no matter. Phileas Fogg whisks his way around a world which is all the same to him. Aloof to the scenery that he steams by, he is the embodiment of indifference: "He made little effort to observe this Red Sea. . . . He did not come and observe the fascinating towns crowded along its banks, whose picturesque silhouettes sometimes appeared on the horizon" (Verne 39). A chapter heading can sum up his whole attitude: "Chapter 14: In which Phileas Fogg Travels the Whole Length of the Wonderful Ganges Valley without even Considering Seeing It" (68). Given a chance to learn about India from a fellow traveler, Fogg prefers not to: "He was an educated man, who would willingly have provided information about the customs, history, and political system of India if Phileas Fogg had been the sort of man to ask for it. But this gentlemen requested nothing. He wasn't traveling, he was describing a circumference" (48). Fogg is not interested in the particularities of the spaces of the globe; his task is quite literally to describe a circumference. Phileas Fogg travels around the world in eighty days and sees nothing.[32] *Around the World in Eighty Days* is almost a parody of the round-the-world genre in which a commodity-like self is projected around the globe and meets no friction along the way. But instead of thinking of it as a parody, one would do better to consider it as an improvement on the genre. As I have argued, the work of the genre is the projection across national borders of self, commodity, culture, and technology, and the streamlining of movement around the world. Verne improves upon that projection and creates a character who forges an even better route. Phileas Fogg is an entrepreneur of global travel, and Verne offers the round-the-world genre the benefit of entrepreneurship.

Verne's contribution to the round-the-world tradition is based in the second part of his masterful title, "in eighty days." No previous narrative made such a temporal promise. Although the American George Francis Train traveled around the world in eighty days two years prior to Verne's protagonist, it was still considered ill-advised to make the journey in anything less than a year. One of the first Americans to go around the world in the new fashion, Charles Coffin, explains that it would be possible to circumnavigate the globe in ninety days, but that it would not be advisable: "He who makes it in that time will have weariness of body and a confused brain" (509). Further:

> Japanese, Chinese, Hindoos, and Arabs will be so completely mixed,—there will be such indistinct recollections of joss-houses, pagodas, mosques, temples,—of junks, sampans, proas, and other queer craft,—such a snarl of streets, lanes, and alleys, filled with myriads of people, carrying baskets, bundles, chests of tea, and dressed in blue blouses, baggy trousers, flowing robes, long gowns, turbans, broad-brimmed or steeple-shaped hats,—or wearing nothing at all, except a narrow strip of cloth about the loins,—with pigtails, cures, or gaven crowns, plucked brows, painted faces, tattooed skins,—riding in sedans, palankeens, or on donkeys, elephants, and camels,—that the brain, instead of retaining distinct pictures, will be in the condition of a sportsman whose horse turns a somersault in a steeple-chase, and the unfortunate rider beholds only a whirling landscape of fields, trees, hounds, hedges, and blinking stars! (Coffin 509)

A too-quick journey around the world caused anxieties about fatigue, "weariness of body," and a fear that things would not stay in their place. Peoples, "Japanese, Chinese, Hindoos," and places, "pagodas, mosques, temples," would lose their distinction, jumbling together in a meaningless heap. Indeed, one of the biggest casualties of the quickened pace is the unit of meaning itself. The integrity of the sentence is threatened as it swells to twelve lines and is barely held together by threads of punctuation. Coffin offers a sea of words in danger of losing coherence. But Verne's narrative seeks to restore the syntax that Coffin fears will be lost in a too-swift journey around the world. He will reestablish a temporal coherence to a globe threatened by an ever-quickening pace. While Simpson worked to narrate the world as a spatial unity, Verne will succeed in authoring it as a temporal one.

Verne's proposal, an eighty-day journey around the world, was realistic enough. The advancement of international routes and technologies around the globe made necessary a newly internationalized standardization of time so that commodities could flow freely around the world. What Lenin had written about the spatial monopolization of the globe by railways and their owners was now becoming true of time.[33] Temporality had to rush to meet the needs of capital flows. Time could no longer run at its local pace. Beginning in the 1860s the international community's grip on time began to tighten. The timetable and timekeeping were at the forefront of this constrictive movement. In 1871 the first regularly-held conference to establish an agreed upon timetable for passenger services was established (Wedgwood 6, 20). And in 1884 a world standard for timekeeping was adopted when the Greenwich Meridian was established as the Prime Meridian by twenty-five countries.

One *could* get around the world in eighty days, and proof of that appeared to Verne *in Bradshaw's Continental Railway, Steam Transit and General Guide*,[34] which he uses to structure his narrative. One afternoon at the Reform Club, Fogg picks up the *Morning Chronicle* and finds this *Bradshaw*-style timetable:

London to Suez via the Mont Cenis Tunnel and Brindisi by rail and steamboats	7 days
Suez to Bombay, by steamship	13 days
Bombay to Calcutta, by railway	3 days
Calcutta to Hong Kong, by steamship	13 days
Honk Kong to Yokohama, by steamship	6 days
Yokohama to San Francisco, by steamship	22 days
San Francisco to New York, by railroad	7 days
New York to London, by steamship and railway	9 days
Total	80 days

Fogg therefore confidently claims that he can go around the world in eighty days. His friends at the club are incredulous. They worry about what the timetable has left out; it is "not allowing for unfavourable weather, head-winds, shipwrecks, derailments, etc." (19). The circle of disbelief widens when the Royal Geographical Society publishes its thoughts on the matter: "And what about breakdowns, derailments, collisions, bad weather, and snowdrifts—wasn't everything against Phileas Fogg? On the steamships would he not be at the mercy of the winter squalls and fogs?" (26). All of London is worried about headwinds and shipwrecks and snowdrifts and fogs. However, to Fogg, those unpredictable elements—promoting the confusions and miscalculations so productive of narrative—have disappeared into the confident lines of the timetable. The stops and the slowdowns that create spaces from which stories emerged are erased by Fogg's ever-forward dash. A colleague argues, "Twenty thousand pounds that you could lose through an unforeseen mishap!" To which Fogg answers, "The unforeseen does not exist" (20). In Fogg's world there are only the timely predictions of the timetable. And Fogg's timetable leaves no space for unforeseen delay and narrative flourish: it leaves out story altogether.

Verne plays with a very real nineteenth-century fear of loss of specificity, similar to but different from what Coffin had recognized and produced in his dizzying narrative. While Coffin envisions the loss of definition in the jumbling together of places and peoples caused by unprecedented haste, Verne's Londoners fear the loss of space altogether in the face of the effort to eliminate it into the precision of the international timetable. Wolfgang Schivelbusch argues that in the nineteenth century people thought that railway travel, which in its early phase was three times the speed of the usual means of conveyance, would obliterate space and time. Temporal shrinkage was projected onto space: "The temporal diminution is expressed mostly in terms of a shrinking of space" (34). People feared that those interstitial spaces between destinations would lose all distinction as they disappeared into the blur of speed. The loss of space in terms of the shrinkage of time in *Around the World* appears as such: "The Earth has shrunk because it can be covered ten times as quickly now as a hundred years ago" (18). Time has gobbled up space. *Around the World* plays with the anxiety that all space will be squeezed out by that grand organizer and symbol of compressed time, the timetable. The Londoners fear that Fogg's timetablic journey, leaping precisely from rail to steam and steam to rail with no time in between, leaves no room for story. One can hear echoes in Walter Benjamin: "Every morning brings us the news of the globe, and yet we are poor in noteworthy stories" (Benjamin 88). While Benjamin argues that it is the immediacy of information that curtails the time-bound experience of story, Verne's Londoners fear that the speedy and unhampered flow of goods and peoples will erase all trace of familiar experiences and the stories that they provoke.

But the accomplishment of *Around the World* is that Fogg circumnavigates the globe in record time *and* finds time for story. He does this by incorporating adventure into the seams of the timetable. Verne's novel is remarkable for the number of adventures that it includes, considering that its protagonist prefers staying comfortably on board playing whist to venturing out. Fogg, who is on the strictest of schedules, should not have time to get embroiled in adventures if he is to make all of his connections. But *Around the World* is replete with adventures, including twenty-one of them in its two hundred pages.[35] Mikhail Bakhtin makes visible the connection between adventure and time in his formulation of Greek adventure-time in the ancient novel. He calls adventure-time "a time of exceptional and unusual events, events determined by chance, which, moreover manifest themselves in fortuitous encounters (temporal junctures) and fortuitous nonencounters (temporal disjunctures)" (116). Verne incorporates adventure into a timetable, reinventing the globe as a temporal unity. He mixes Greek adventure-time with the newly synchronized transport time, and ultimately incorporates all temporal junctures and disjunctures (adventures) into the timetable, revising it for the better, improving its productivity and grip upon story.

IMPROVING *BRADSHAW*'S BY LEAPS AND BOUNDS

The novel begins with a wager. In England Phileas Fogg, the hero so famous for his precision and punctuality that he is called a chronometer, challenges the men of the Reform Club, of which he is a whist-playing member, to a wager. He bets twenty thousand pounds that he can go around the world in eighty days. He gathers up his servant and leaves London less than a half-hour later. Taking Simpson's "Direct Route," Europe, Egypt, Aden, Ceylon, Singapore, China, Japan, America, Europe, with a few modifications—he substitutes India for Ceylon, taking the Great Peninsular Railway from Bombay to Calcutta, and he spends less time in China, indeed he only visits Hong Kong—he and his servant travel around the world. Although they have adventures along the way, exactly eighty days from their departure, they arrive in Liverpool with nine hours to spare, the trip to London only taking six. However, upon his arrival on British territory, he is thrown in jail because he is believed to have stolen £55,000 from the Bank of England before his departure, and the wager is lost. But he has one final adventure (fortuitous temporal dis/juncture): he discovers when he tries to plan his marriage for the following day, a Sunday, that the following day is a Saturday. He arrived a day early. He had insistently kept his watch to London time, and on account of his traveling east, he had gained a day, so he really circled the globe in seventy-nine days. He weds.

This is the plot that gets remembered in summaries and films. But I would like to wind back the clock, and look at two moments that occur before what seems to be the initiating action of the text, the wager. Two actions, a hiring and a crime, predicate Fogg's famous bet that sends him hurtling around the globe, and it is important to consider these two actions because they set up the circumnavigation as a global project within a social context, disavowing the idea that Fogg represents merely an eccentric individual set in motion by a bet. These two initial actions allow us to see the social apparatus and control surrounding Fogg's seemingly idiosyncratic journey.

Around the World begins with a hiring. The ever-exacting Phileas Fogg engages a new servant because his old one "had made the mistake of bringing in his shaving-water at a temperature of 84 F, rather than the statutory 86" (10). He employs the Frenchman, Passepartout. The title of the first chapter, under which this hiring is subsumed, is, "In Which Phileas Fogg and Passepartout Accept Each Other, the One as Master, the Other as Servant." Here symbolically what is "accepted" is England's new global domination and France's diminution in global importance following the Franco-Prussian defeat in 1871. Thus the initiatory action of the novel sets in motion an international partnership, however hierarchical, suggesting that global circumnavigation will be a joint endeavor. Verne makes explicit what other round-the-world narratives state implicitly: the project of global circumnavigation will rely on international relationships and agreements if it is to succeed. Globalization, or the propelling of goods, technologies, and peoples around the globe unfettered by states or cultures, cannot be conceived of as a national project; the coordination of networks and routes relies upon international cooperation. The chapter ends with a synchronization of watches, in which an Englishman tells a Frenchman that his watch is four minutes slow. "You're four minutes slow. It is of no consequence. What matters is to note the difference" (11). The project of circumnavigation becomes one of international synchronization, in which one power creates the standards and everybody else "notes the difference."

The second event that precedes the "wager" is a bank robbery. The Bank of England is robbed of £55,000—not by a common criminal, but by a "gentleman." This robbery provides the catalyst for Fogg's circumnavigation, making it the first round-the-world journey motivated by a crime. It happens this way: the robbery becomes the subject of discussion at the Reform Club, and it is generally believed that the robber will try to escape the country, so that "detectives chosen from among the best policemen were sent to the main ports of Liverpool, Glasgow, Le Havre, Suez, Brindisi, New York" (17). In an ensuing discussion the men at Fogg's club argue about the likelihood of a getaway:

> "And where do you think he might go, then?" "I can't say," replied Stuart. "But after all, the world is big enough." "It used to be," Fogg said quietly. . . ."What d'you mean, 'used to be'? Has the Earth suddenly got smaller by some chance?" "Unquestionably it has," responded Ralph. "I share Mr. Fogg's view. The Earth has shrunk because it can be covered ten times as quickly now as a hundred years ago. And in the case we are discussing, this will make the search faster." "You must admit, Ralph, that you have a funny way of saying the Earth has shrunk! Because you can now go round it in three months." "Eighty days," interjected Fogg." (18)

Thus begins the wager. Fogg becomes Scotland Yard's primary suspect for the robbery because he fits the description "gentleman" and he appears to be escaping. The detective, Fix, sets off on his trail. This plot is not only an around-the-world narrative, it is also a prototypical-spy novel, in which two international players, of unequal power, travel the globe hand-in-hand, chased by a bumbling detective, named ironically Fix.[36] In this sense the round-the-world narrative becomes a projection of the British state not just to India and Hong Kong, where it already has a presence, but around the globe. Projecting an explicit system of control around the world is an innovation of Verne to the round-the-world narrative. He uses the detective plot to bind together his novel, giving coherence to the project of narrating the world.

Reading *Around the World* as a prototypical-spy novel opens up the apparently simple plot and its idiosyncratic hero.[37] Indeed there are no indicators that Fogg is *not* a criminal. In addition to the coincidence of his departure, just one day after the robbery, there is the source of his fortune of £20,000, which is never accounted for. He did not seem to earn it as he "was not engaged in industry, business, commerce, or agriculture" (7). And if the money were inherited, it was not public knowledge, "Was Phileas Fogg well off? Without any doubt. But how he made his fortune, even the best informed could not say" (8). His pockets are shockingly deep, as Fix notes: "He's spending money like a thief" (80). Indeed, he spends £2,000 to buy an elephant, £2,000 on bail, $8,000 for passage across the Atlantic, and $60,000 to purchase a sloop. In total he spends £55,000 on his journey, but he takes home nothing that he purchased. He gives away the elephant, and burns the sloop for fuel. Of course, his timely circumnavigation justifies all expenditures.

But Verne casts suspicion upon the round-the-world traveler. If we take Verne's claims seriously, that Fogg is a "commodity," a piece of "merchandise," and a "machine," then we must see Fogg as simultaneously passenger, commodity, and technology. He embodies every sort of thing that could and did go around the world. Fogg then represents the entire round-the-world apparatus. By linking telegraph, rail, steam, information, commodity, merchandise, passenger with Fogg, Verne succeeds in casting suspicion upon the whole global project.

Around the World holds us in a state of suspense—will he make it? did he steal it? will he get caught?—until our hero reaches home. Then, we discover, all is well. The suspicion of Fogg, that "enigmatic figure" and "mysterious gentleman," is dispelled along with suspicions about the project of circling the globe at lightning speed and all that it entails. The real robber is apprehended; Fogg wins his bet; he marries his Indian bride; and he beats the record for global circumnavigation. Order has been reestablished, but it is a more orderly order than ever before. Before Fogg embarks on his mission, one nonbeliever tells him, "But in order to do it, you'll have to mathematically jump from trains into steamships and from steamships on to trains!" And Fogg replies, "I'll jump mathematically" (20). Herein lies Verne's chronotopic formula. He subjects Greek adventure-time to the newly emerging international precision. In doing so, he advances the girdling—the constriction—of the world. *Bradshaw's* promised an eighty-day journey around the world. But Fogg increasingly supplements his *Bradshaw's* with other means of travel. He travels in every means of conveyance: steamer, railway, elephant, yacht, trading vessel, flying train, sledge, carriage, mail boat, sloop-on-fire. These unlikely adventures are undoubtedly the attraction of the novel for its readers.[38]

On the micro level each adventure slows him down. But on the macro level, misconnections and adventures actually speed up the journey. For example, in the midway point between San Francisco and New York, Fogg and his fellow travelers fall behind schedule by twenty hours after a series of adventures. If Fogg were to follow his *Bradshaw's*, he would only need to reach New York and there make a connection to a steamboat heading for Liverpool. Instead, Fogg forges an alternative route and has five adventures along the way: a sledge ride hounded by wolves, missing the *China,* hijacking a boat, burning a boat, catching a mail boat. In spite of (or because of) these adventures, Fogg arrives in Liverpool with six hours to spare.

Adventures enable him to move faster, not slower; they put him back on schedule, rather than taking him off it. Ultimately, they put him so far ahead of schedule that they create a new standard by which to move. Verne subsumes adventure to the timetable, and suggests that eighty days is not the limit, but a new frontier.[39] Thus it comes as no surprise to Fogg at the end of his seventy-nine day journey around the world that he could have done it in less time. Passepartout discovers "that we could have done the trip around the world in only 78 days" (202). Fogg answers, "Undoubtedly."

Verne has discovered a formula for improving upon *Bradshaw's* timetables: to jump mathematically. Adventure comes to service the needs of capital, quickening the pace of global circulation, and making it fun to boot. Verne unglues adventure from its lexical history—removing it from that slow-moving, road-bound mercantile "venturer," to whom adventure may result in total loss. In its place, he gives us a sure-footed, unambitious, yet willing-to-risk-it-all *entrepreneur.* Fogg can jump mathematically. He can take risks with the precision of one who knows the gain of risk.[40] Thus when Fogg risks his life to save an Indian woman from suttee, he words it as if it were an investment: "Saving this woman, Mr. Fogg?" exclaimed the Brigadier General. "I'm still twelve hours ahead. I can use them that way" (62). Fogg banks hours and invests them in adventures. This one turns out to be a particularly good investment, for he gains a wife who will make him the "happiest of men."

Fogg's famous imperturbability comes from his confidence in his ability to use all objects to his gain. Fogg illustrates Heidegger's understanding of technology perfectly, for he sees all objects as standing in reserve, waiting for him to convert into resources for his use. When caught in a storm in the Chinese Seas, "this nerveless man felt neither impatience nor annoyance. It really seemed as though the storm formed part of his schedule: that it was forseen" (92). When Fogg misses the only steamer that will get him back to Liverpool on time, he is again unperturbed. Immediately he sets out to look for a better way to cross the Atlantic. Eventually he finds a merchant "with a steamer with an iron hull, but with upper works made entirely of wood" on his way to Bordeaux (178). He coaxes Captain Speedy, despite the fact that Speedy refuses to veer from his course to Bordeaux and never carries passengers, to carry him and his three friends to Bordeaux, offering to pay him $2,000 per person, causing Speedy to remark, "passengers at $2,000 apiece are no longer passengers, but precious merchandise" (180). It is next reported that "at midday on the following day, 13 December, a man went up on a bridge to take the bearings. It will certainly be assumed that this man was Captain Speedy—but it wasn't. It was Phileas Fogg" (181). Effortlessly Fogg took over Speedy's captainship, crew, and vessel, and steered a new course to Liverpool. Fogg overthrows the single-minded merchant capitalist, unwilling to alter his route to Bordeaux, and replaces him with a much more flexible capitalist, who not only alters his route, but changes the rules of the game; the narrator compliments Fogg's ability to "maneuver." When Fogg discovers that there is not enough coal to make it to Liverpool, he decides to burn the boat for fuel. Thus he makes use of every last object, converting the upper parts of the ship to fuel and returning its steel hull to Speedy. Fogg returns home to England at the helm of a ship, fully in control of all of the resources within his reach.

GLOBAL TEXT, LOCAL DISSENT

Verne offers up a formula for global conquest that utilizes mobility, flexibility (of capital), and above all, a way of seeing the sights of the globe as "standing reserves," ready to be employed in his service. With the help of a large fortune, an international partnership, the state, and an entrepreneurial persona, Fogg facilitates global circulation. *Around the World* is a global text with worldwide appeal. The two countries to first see translations of Verne's work, England and America, were the ones that had the most to gain from it. England, soon to be in the throes of a new round of global conquest, would by the end of the century begin to be eclipsed by America, a country more accepting of Verne's lessons.[41] As Americans were the largest contributors to the round-the-world genre, it is not surprising that *Around the World* was immensely popular there. If round-the-world narratives offered their bourgeois readers a glimpse of *"our"* new road, *Around the World* offered them a formula for its improvement.

But that improvement was not without complications. Cultures resisted being improved, as Verne's Londoners demonstrated: "Even if the Indians and Red Indians tear up the rails? . . . Even if they stop the trains, plunder the carriages, and scalp the passengers?" (19). What if *these* stories get told? What if stories about peoples who tear up technology, or who flat-out refuse it, as in the case of China, get put into circulation? *Around the World* offers a particular technology to make sure that *if* circulated *these* stories will do no harm. It makes sure that these stories are interchangeable and therefore not particularly powerful. Adventure is prone to interchangeability, as Bakhtin points out: "The adventure chronotope is thus characterized by a *technical, abstract connection between space and time*, by the *reversibility* of moments in a temporal sequence, and by their *interchangeability* in space" (100). Within *Around the World* the interchangeability of adventures is made evident when Fogg and Passepartout are brought to trial in Calcutta. Neither of them knows why they are being prosecuted. Passepartout believes that they are being brought to trial for their first adventure, the pagoda melee, but it turns out that they are being held on account of their second adventure, the suttee rescue.

Verne offers his readers an onslaught of adventures, and none of the adventures seem to follow a particular order or readily adhere to their surroundings. They seem to be departicularized to the point of operating within the space of romance. Their romance quality assures their interchangeability. But if we look closer, we begin to see that adventure has a spatial component, disguised by its seeming interchangeability. In Fogg's most "benign" adventure, he saves a woman who is being sacrificed to the practice of suttee. On his way to Calcutta from Bombay, Fogg is stopped in Allahabad because fifty miles of track from Kholby to Allahabad have not been completed. He is forced to disembark from the train and travel to Allahabad by elephant. On his way he fights fanatics, halts a suttee, and steals away the bride. These adventures have the air of romance. The space, quickly moving from "great forests" to "vast arid plains," is departicularized in a way that is typical of romance. Morality too is easily bifurcated, as is typical of that genre, with the forces of good, Fogg and Passepartout, fighting the forces of evil, the fanatics with their barbaric customs.

Yet this space, flattened out and departicularized through romance and made interchangeable through adventure, has a history. Allahabad stops Fogg in his tracks. Why? Murray's 1892 *Handbook for Travelers in India & Ceylon* suggests one possibility:

> The history of the outbreak at Allahabad is one of the saddest chapters of the long list of misfortunes which marked the commencement of the great Mutiny in 1857. Fifteen officers were murdered by the Sepoys . . . anarchy reigned in the city—the jail was broken open, and the prisoners, with the irons still rattling on their limbs, murdered every Christian they met. (37)

Verne echoes this sentiment but places this scene on the road to Allahabad, instead of in Allahabad itself: "The whole northern flank of the Vindhya range is the scene of incessant murder and pillaging" (61). Allahabad had a long hold on the British imagination. Thirty-five years after the rebellion, Murray's guidebook still cites the "mutiny" as Allahabad's major point of attraction. Just as Simpson dwelled upon the "Tsiensing massacre" in his round-the-world journey, Verne cannot visit India without referencing the famous rebellion against British domination. And just like Simpson, Verne cites the rebellion in order to remedy it. Verne stages his own version of the mutiny in which Fogg squelches the mutinous "fanatics" *and* takes away booty, which becomes his bride when he reaches England. So not only has Fogg restaged the mutiny, he has fought it and won—this time with the help of a French cohort.

The day after he returns to London, Fogg marries the woman that he saved. She is the only object that Fogg brings home, and seemingly the only thing that he gained from his journey, since he spent the equivalent of his prize money during the journey, a point with which Verne ends his novel. And he finishes his text with this cheeky observation: "In truth, wouldn't anyone go around the world for less" (202). He begs the question. Would anyone? It seems unlikely that a Victorian would go around the world for an Indian bride. However, the accomplishment of such a union is another story. With this marriage, Verne elegantly achieves a restaging of the mutiny, and a final symbolic smoothing out of India's rough terrain.

Verne introduces India to us by saying that it was not fully conquered:

> British India in the strict sense only covers an area of 700,000 square miles (out of 1,400,000) and a population of 100–110 million (out of 180 million). In other words, a considerable part of the territory still escapes the Queen's authority; and, indeed, amongst certain fierce and dreaded rajahs of the interior, Indian independence continues absolute. (43)

Fogg's unscheduled journey takes us through an unconquered territory, ruled by a "dreaded rajah":

> This whole region of the Upper Bundelkhand, where travelers rarely go, is inhabited by a fanatical population inured in the most repugnant practices of Hinduism. British domination has not been able to take proper hold over a territory still under the rajahs' influence, difficult to reach in their inaccessible fastnesses of the Vindhya Range. (57)

Interestingly, Fogg does not follow the tracks of the interrupted line; instead, he goes out of his way to take the route where the English railway company dare not go. Verne willfully leads us through independent India, ruled by the "dreaded" rajahs. Railway projects were often thwarted by Britain's incomplete dominance over Indian territory; often rajahs would not grant permission to build on their land; sometimes they wanted to start their own railway companies on their lands, an act which Britain soon made illegal. Aouda's husband, it should be remembered, was "one of the independent rajahs of Bundelkhand" (61). Thus, when Fogg carries her away, he symbolically steals away a piece of Indian independence.

We can now reconsider Verne's cheeky conclusion:

> But what was the point? What had he gained from all this commotion? What had he got out of his journey? Nothing, comes the reply? Nothing, agreed were it not for a lovely wife—who however unlikely it may seem—made him the happiest of men! In truth wouldn't anyone have gone around the world for less? (202)

Clearly not. Fogg circled the globe with the British state in tow, and in the process stole away just a bit of Indian independence. Moreover, he shows the way. He not only maps out the journey but a way of journeying that incorporates improving energies in every step. Thus, for example, the "eighty days" of the title is revised to the "seventy-nine" days in which they really make it, and the "seventy-eight" days in which Passepartout discovers they could have made it. These reserve improvements are indeed what Heidegger calls the essence of modern technology. As we have seen, technology is a way of thinking that calls out the reserve energy of every object.

Not only does the text improve upon itself, it invites people to follow in its footsteps, and many real-life adventuresome souls, inspired by Fogg's journey, took up the challenge. Most notable is the American, Nellie Bly, who made it around the world in 72 days in 1890. A few years later a circumnavigation club was formed in England for this purpose, and in the twentieth century journeys proliferated as the route got better. Indeed, by midcentury the land route could be done in 32 days.[42] And advances in aviation technology made around-the-world flights possible to a wider public. In 1936 Herbert Roslyn Ekins, demonstrating the true spirit of the around-the-world narratives, wrote a how-to book of global aviation titled *Around the World in Eighteen Days and How to Do It.*[43] These globe-trotters and travel writers imitated the entrepreneurial spirit of Fogg and Verne, girdling the globe, telling their tale, and inspiring others to follow.

Most importantly, Verne's neatly concluded tale quells anxieties about this process—the kind of anxieties that were expressed in the nineteenth century by travelers like Coffin who perceived that a too-quick journey around the globe threatened meaning itself. But Verne's narrative assuages these fears by creating an excessively satisfying closure—supplying the journey with telos. The final pages of Verne's novel simultaneously wrap up a journey, a bet, and a chase; solve a mystery; set a world record; and produce a marriage.

But the true comforts of this ending are provided by its moral. The text's final lesson is that time is money. Fogg has demonstrated that he who controls time and space will profit. According to Harvey, capitalism has been characterized by "continuous efforts to shorten turnover times" (229), for "if money has no meaning independent of time and space, then it is always possible to pursue profit (or other forms of advantage) by altering the ways time and space are used and defined" (229). If, as I have argued, Fogg goes around the world in order to seize a bit more of India's territory, then his control of time is vital for that process. Ultimately, he discovers a way to conquer economically, to alter time and space in order to make money. But this novel is not simply a tale about conquest; it is a formula for conquest. It offers a way of thinking—a technology of development—that would be emulated in narratives for generations to come.

Epilogue

I have told a story of how the British came to embrace the Suez Canal—a story that reveals the alterations in the way that they perceived character, investments, and technology throughout the century. Narrative itself played a role in the process. From the incorporation of the entrepreneur to the mapping out of a global highway, nineteenth-century narratives plot a culture increasingly accepting of global technologies. By intentionally blurring the lines between narrative and what we have come to think of in the twentieth century as technology, I have argued that we register the interconnectedness of the two, for they are both cultural productions dependent upon each other for their mutual articulation. The most poignant example of their interdependence came in my final chapter, where I argued that circumnavigation narratives represented global technologies at the same time that European missionaries in China depended upon Western technology—namely the Suez Canal and the Mount Cenis Tunnel—to articulate conversion narratives to the Chinese. While in the former case narratives represent technology, in the latter technology enables narrative.

I have argued for an expansion of the ways that we think about narrative and technology. It is not an accident that my work draws upon novels, the dominant genre of the century, or that travel narratives play a large secondary role. The novel developed the ability to proliferate characters—to propose and dispose of them at will—at precisely the moment when the market itself was demanding an acceptance of diverse character types, such as the entrepreneur. In addition, the novel and travel narrative were the forms that best incorporated everyday life. While the everyday had been a convention of the novel since the beginning of the nineteenth century when the everyday itself emerged, we have seen the coincidence of the introduction of everyday life into the travel narrative form at midcentury when Egypt was becoming a colony. It was through the incorporation of the everyday, I argue in Chapters 2 and 3, that novels and travel narratives asserted their own spatial practices abroad—organizing habits of consumption and aesthetic desires so as to make the new world more like home. The *Bildungsroman,* with its emphasis on the incorporation of the individual into society and its institutions, appears suspicious when enacted abroad. If Tancred were to develop in the Middle East, he would need to bring British institutions with him, which he does in the ultimate pages of *Tancred.* But more importantly, he would need to import new energies and habits of thinking. The *Bildungsroman* proved to be a perfect means to package these ideas. In Chapter 4, I argue that in the process of narrating the world, round-the-world travel accounts developed an ability to incorporate and disseminate the new ideology of speed in a way that ameliorated fears about the loss of space and story. Jules Verne's 1872 novel *Around the World in Eighty Days* was the most successful of this genre, for it not only abolished all fears of a faster world, but it developed a method to follow suit—inspiring an entire body of literature which, I have argued, pursues a technological way of thinking.

The ability of the novel to incorporate the world was furthered by innovations of the modernist novel. Stream of consciousness, for example, is a narrative technique which permits characters to break with the strictures imposed upon them by conventions of time and space in order to roam the world, if only in their minds. Of course, stream of consciousness developed out of earlier nineteenth-century narrative techniques; authors had always found ways to crisscross time and space, as Charles Dickens adeptly demonstrates in his novel *Tale of Two Cities,* where he moves between nineteenth-century England and eighteenth-century France with ease. Even though techniques such as the stream of consciousness made it even easier to cross temporal and spatial borders by enabling individual characters to do so at will, I would argue that the novel still remained more comfortable in the terrain of the relatively slow time and localized space of the national railway. Temporal and spatial leaps and bounds in narrative more often took place in film. I therefore conclude by reflecting on how two film versions of Verne's *Around the World in Eighty Days,* the first made in 1956 and the second in 2003, furthered the development of the narrative technologies discussed thus far.

I began by referencing David Lean's incorporation of the Suez Canal into his 1962 movie *Lawrence of Arabia,* suggesting that the Canal here dramatically symbolized a world in transition following Gamal 'Abd al-Nasir's nationalization of it in 1956. I conclude by turning to another Hollywood movie that touches upon the subject, this one appearing in the same year as the "canal crisis," Michael Todd's 1956 *Around the World in*

80 Days. A movie that seems to need no introduction was given two discrete ones when it was re-released in 1982. The 1982 film begins with a lengthy introduction by the American Robert Osborne. Todd himself built a "prologue" into his film when he had Edward R. Murrow introduce it in 1956. Thus Todd cleverly gave himself the ability to comment on the film by putting his own words into the mouth of one of the most authoritative reporters at the time, made so by his World War II reporting. Sitting behind a desk, surrounded by neatly filled bookshelves and a globe, Murrow ponders Verne's technological foresight and then considers the connections between "fiction" and "fact." Verne, after all, he says, predicted in fiction the invention of the submarine, the airplane, and the rocket. Indeed, Murrow is preoccupied with the rocket, and he kicks off the film by showing the earliest film of Verne's work, the 1902 short "A Trip to the Moon," made from Verne's novel *From the Earth to the Moon* by the French filmmaker George Méliès.

Todd uses Méliès's famous film to introduce his own for two reasons: first, to call attention to the quickly modernizing world, and second to implicate Verne's novel (and fiction in general) in that process. First, Todd made *Around the World in 80 Days* during the beginnings of the race for space: only a year after his film was released, the Soviets launched Sputnik and the United States swiftly countered by opening NASA. Todd ends his prologue with images of a real rocket launch, the type of footage that would only become familiar to American viewing audiences in the following decade. In Todd's movie, the image must have been truly awesome, especially as it was preceded by Méliès's crude fictional representation of a rocket launch a half a century earlier. If the juxtaposition of the footage purposefully shows just how far man has come, it also demonstrates the progressive relation of fiction to technological fact. In addition, Murrow's pronouncements provide a moral spin to Verne's imaginings, as he admonishes "speed is good only when wisdom leads the way," adding, "There is in this power of destruction also the promise of hope. Man has discovered a method of destroying most of humanity or of lifting it up to high plateaus of prosperity and progress never dreamed of by the boldest dreamer."

That Todd was a bold dreamer himself is the message of Robert Osborne's 1982 introduction in which he ponders the innovations that were the products of Todd's dreaming. Most importantly, Todd pioneered the Todd-AO process, a wide-gauge panoramic presentation method, a technology that better enabled him to incorporate landscapes into his travelogue. He also invented the cameo role, which permitted him to procure a star-studded cast without overspending. Osborne's interest in Todd's innovations stems from his desire to shift the focus away from the film and to its making, away from Verne's vision to Todd's. This shift is noted in his introduction: "The story of the making of the film is as wild, implausible, and entertaining as the film itself." According to Osborne, nobody believed that Todd, who had never made a movie before, could pull off such an ambitious one: "By all odds everybody expected this movie to be a disaster." Critics said that he would never raise the money, he wouldn't get the stars, and he wouldn't be able to pull off the world-circumnavigating plot. Yet he "begged, borrowed, and cajoled" to raise the money to get his movie made. Moreover, he managed to land the "wealthiest and the most independent" actor in the world, the Mexican comedian Cantinflas, to play the role of Passepartout, a coup, Osborne explains, because Cantinflas had hitherto turned down all requests to play roles in English. Despite all setbacks, the story goes, Todd triumphed. He won the Oscar for best picture, and Osborne adds the final punctuation to his story by concluding with these words: "He wooed and won Elizabeth Taylor as his wife."

The story is by now familiar. Todd's tale not only echoes the life of Phileas Fogg but of all of the fictional and real-life entrepreneurs that made Fogg possible such as Doyce/Clennam and Lesseps. And it shows just how far that figure, has come—from its humble origins in the much-maligned characters of George Hudson and Mr. Merdle to the culturally coveted position of producer/director. Osborne reveals the entrepreneur to be the engine that motors modern technology. And he brushes away all remaining moralism surrounding that figure, clarifying that it does not matter how one organizes the productive factors just as long as they get ordered. Whether one "cons" or "charms," as does Todd, the entrepreneur is the hero of the modern age.

If Osborne propagates the myth of the entrepreneur who overcomes all difficulties to accomplish great feats, the film itself reveals a different, if not more accurate, story. Fogg is wholly dependent upon his valet, Passepartout, to circle the globe, for it is Passepartout's propensity to embroil himself in adventures that speeds up the circumnavigation process, as I have argued in Chapter 4. It takes two to circle the globe in record time. Imperialism is indeed a joint venture. Throughout this book I have shown the ways in which various partnerships enabled imperialism; among them I discussed how the coupling of French theory and British practice informed the making of the entrepreneur. I have argued that the romance and the novel joined forces to imaginatively conquer the Middle East. I pointed out the manner in which British market moralism and greed became paired in the coupling of Tancred and Fakredeen in order to ensure the cleansing of the investor figure. I demonstrated how the familial pairing of Lucy Duff Gordon and her servant Omar obscured unfair labor practices and promoted the consumption of cheap products abroad. And I intimated the ways in which Fogg and Passepartout combined English capital and French ingenuity to conquer the globe.

Disney's 2003 remake of *Around the World in 80 Days* adds a new twist to global partnership, one that reflects a more modern world in which an ascending global power joins forces with a descending one. In it Jackie Chan plays a Chinese Passepartout, while Steve Coogan plays Fogg—no longer the English gentleman, but an American-style antiestablishment inventor/entrepreneur. While at first glance this movie appears to be as different from Todd's film as it is from Verne's novel, that difference is superficial. This movie also accelerates what David Harvey theorizes as "time-space compression," bringing the technological innovations that marked the genre of global circumnavigation from the beginning to their logical conclusion.

Not surprisingly, then, the film is nearly impossible to watch, for it packs adventures into every scene, crowding out any attempt at plot development. The plot is simple enough to be summarized in a few lines: Chan must return a jade Buddha to his village in China before a pack of Chinese thugs headed by an evil Chinese warlord stops him. Therefore, he races around the globe en route to China, using an unsuspecting Fogg, who is innocently circling the globe, as his cover. As can be surmised by the plot summary, this movie shifts the focus from Fogg to Chan, who was clearly chosen for his fame as an actor in action films. Chan propels this movie from one adventure to the next, allowing nothing, not even plot, to get in the way. Landscapes that had been so stunningly filmed in Todd's movie have no place here, and the world becomes reduced to a smattering of interchangeable adventures in which place loses all distinction. While Todd dallied in the countries that Fogg visited, especially India, to film breathtaking scenes from the window of the train as it rolled through the countryside, taking advantage of his new Todd AO method to capture the broadest of vistas, Disney too makes the most of the technology that it pioneered. In Disney's movie, landscapes are replaced by animations of landscapes. The animations, in turn, enable Fogg and Chan to speed up the tempo, to zip across India without entering a train—to move from Calcutta to Hong Kong without crossing the water.

Disney has literally captured the landscape by turning each locality into a corporate production of space—an animation produced and owned by Disney. Yet we are not so far from where we started. The round-the-world travel narratives, made possible by the new global routes, reproduced technology wherever they went and called that technology Western, as we have seen. But the difference is that while their writers circled the globe in record time and found room for story, Disney's did not. The most recent retelling of Verne's 1872 classic was a box-office flop. This, perhaps, could be explained in the ways that various reviewers have suggested: poor marketing, a relatively unknown actor playing Fogg's role, the overuse of slapstick, or Chan's recent lack of appeal. As right as these assessments may be, I suggest that the movie's poor reception stems from another source—that the movie itself is exemplary of a genre that has perfected its techniques of spatial and temporal conquest to the point of playing itself out. It represents a genre that has been overwhelmed by its own technology.

Such confidence in a purely technological vision of the globe leads to a failure of corporate imagining, as they cannot fathom what Verne's Londoners predicted would surely delay Fogg's swift journey around the world—those Indians who would "stop the trains," "plunder the carriages," and "tear up the rails" (19). Corporate culture cannot picture those unpredictable events—rejections, reclamations, and rebellions—caused by the peoples that they are so riotously globalizing. Thus technology is not as totalizing as it has been believed to be, and the triumph of technology as a way of thinking invites its own catastrophe.

Notes

NOTES TO THE INTRODUCTION

1. According to Leo Marx the "organizational complexity" of the transcontinental railway is what makes it exemplary of the concept of technology: "As a business enterprise, a transcontinental railroad was much too large and complicated, and required the synchronized efforts of too many experts, to be operated within the framework of the traditional family-owned firm. It was much better suited to the new, bureaucratized, corporate mode of organization" (466).
2. Of "time-space compression" Harvey writes, "I mean to signal by that term processes that so revolutionize the objective qualities of space and time that we are forced to alter, sometimes in quite radical ways, how we represent the world to ourselves. I use the word 'compression' because a strong case can be made that the history of capitalism has been characterized by speed-up in the pace of life, while so overcoming spatial barriers that the world sometimes seems to collapse inwards upon us" (240).
3. See Henri Lefebvre for a discussion of how space gets produced differently in each historical period because the elite of each era produce a space that satisfies their political, economic, and social needs.
4. See Timothy Mitchell for a discussion of Cairo's Haussmanification. Mitchell argues that the reproduction of the Western city of Paris in Egypt during the nineteenth century was actually a means to conquer Egypt.
5. See Mike Davis for a discussion of how British modernization actually exacerbated famine in Egypt, China, and India during the century. See Michael Landes for a discussion of how the West's unfair loaning practices led to Egypt's bankruptcy.
6. I would like to maintain that modernism brings both great gains and great losses, as Marshall Berman so eloquently argues. However, within the context of colonialism, the gains and losses are so unevenly split between colonizer and colonized, rich and poor, men and women that it would be hard to justify such an argument.

7. See Anthony Gorst and Lewis Johnman for an analysis of the importance of nineteenth-century events in understanding the nationalization of the Canal in the twentieth century.
8. In *Orientalism* Said also argues that the "idea" of the Canal was the "logical conclusion of Orientalist thought" (91). I am suggesting, however, that the full comprehension of that idea is also the logical conclusion of an altered business ethos. For this reason I focus on the act of purchase, rather than on seizure.
9. The British finished building a railway line from Cairo to Suez in 1859, the year that work on the Suez Canal began.
10. Disraeli purchased 40 percent of the Canal shares, making England the largest shareholder.
11. New Imperialism is a term used to understand the expansionist policies of Europe during the last three decades of the nineteenth century. The beginnings of New Imperialism are often contested, as is the idea that anything was new at all about imperialism in the century. However, among those who distinguish between the imperialism of the early century and what came after, it has been proposed that Britain's new age of imperialism alternatively begins in 1867–1868 with the Abyssinian expedition, in 1872 with Benjamin Disraeli's proimperialism rallying cry embedded in his Crystal Palace speech, in 1882 with Britain's bombardment of Alexandria and invasion of Egypt, and in 1888 with Britain's participation in the scramble for Africa.
12. A canal was built in the twentieth or nineteenth century B.C.E. to Lake Timsah which was then the northern end of the Red Sea. Xerxes I had the canal extended. It was restored several times until the eighth century C.E. when it was closed and fell into disrepair.
13. It is telling that the British do not include in their history the Saint-Simonian plan to build a canal. It was, after all, the Saint-Simonians who popularized the idea of an isthmian canal throughout the 1830s and 1840s and Lesseps was clearly influenced by them. He, however, cut them out of the project when he received the 1854 concession.
14. Compare this modern definition of "traffic" to older ones, such as this one dated to the sixteenth century: "The transportation of merchandise for the purpose of trade; hence, trade between distant or distinct communities; commerce" (*OED*). Here is another definition from the same period: "The buying and selling or exchange of goods for profit; bargaining; trade" (*OED*).
15. There is, of course, much overlap between financial journalists and novelists in the period, as Mary Poovey argues in "Writing about Finance in Victorian England: Disclosure and Secrecy in the Culture of Investment." Here, however, I am emphasizing what the differences in the forms of economic journalism and novelistic prose enable.

16. Jürgen Habermas, for instance, sees the genesis of the bourgeois public sphere in the traffic of commodities and news created by early capitalist long-distance trading. And Michael McKeon gives global travel an important place in the history of the novel when he argues that the Royal Society's interest in dictating travel narrative format in the seventeenth century had an impact on the novel form.

NOTES TO CHAPTER ONE

1. The importance of the forging of "national character" at midcentury has been discussed by Mary Poovey and Lauren Goodlad. Poovey argues that it is the novelist and his portrayal of writing characters (such as David Copperfield) who put forth the "professional" as a model for middle-class identity and national character. Goodlad challenges what she sees as a lack of nuance in Poovey's perception of the middle class in the period and argues that national character can be best understood as a contest within the middle classes between the professional and the entrepreneurial ideals.
2. It wasn't until the centennial of his death that the second biography of Hudson appeared. A.J. Peacock's 1971 biography, introduced by E.P. Thompson, is by far the most critical of the Railway King. Recently there has been a renewed interest in Hudson's life, and in the last two decades three Hudson biographies have been published. See Brian Bailey, Robert Beaumont, and A.J. Arnold and S.M. McCartney.
3. One senses that the issue may not have been so definitively decided during the period. *Punch,* for instance, writes in the same year: "We are almost prepared for the time when Mr. Hudson's reputation will be made so very 'pleasant,' that a remorseful and conscience-stricken generation will appear by deputy at Albert Gate, to present Mr. Hudson the keys of the Bank of England" ("Hudson Takes a Step Forward" 70). And D. Morier Evans writes forgivingly about Hudson at the end of the decade.
4. Yet even more humorous is an episode reported by *The Times:* "The King . . . retorted with a demand, in which the magniloquence of the opening was strangely contrasted with the diminutiveness of the close. "In the name of the prophet—figs!" (3 August 1846).
5. Carlyle's negative treatment of Hudson should be considered in relation to his positive treatment of the industrialists outlined in "Captains of Industry" in 1843. In this essay, Carlyle calls for the "captains of industry" to form a new aristocracy with the aim of "managing the working classes" (267). He envisions their leadership as a way to protect the country from the "chaos" which would ensue if labor organized itself. Although Carlyle does not mention Hudson in this piece, he does posit his ideal industrialist as a solution to a seedier sort—those who, like Hudson, raise money

through speculation. Carlyle clearly separates making goods from making money, praising the practitioner of the former while castigating anybody who partakes in the latter.

6. Hudson's obituary reads: "There was a time when not to know him was to argue one's self unknown; now he is only a tradition" (*The Times* 16 December 1871).
7. One can read Evans's 1859 *Facts, Failures and Frauds: Revelations Financial Mercantile Criminal* as an attempt to evaluate the character of the ten most notorious speculators, bankers, and businessmen of the 1830s, 1840s, and 1850s.
8. Harold Perkin argues in *Origins of Modern English Society* that the "entrepreneurial ideal" emerged in the beginning of the nineteenth century and that by the 1850s it held sway. Soon, however, tension developed between the new middle class in the developing professions and the capitalist owner-managers. In *The Rise of Professional Society* Perkin tells the story of how the professional class gained precedence by 1880.
9. Of the power of Hudson's name D. Morier Evans writes: "In the early days of the mania, his name seemed to possess talismanic value; the mere fact that it was associated with any scheme being alone sufficient to cause a demand for shares, and a consequent rapid advance in prices" (2).
10. For the most complete essay on Hudson during the nineteenth century, see D. Morier Evans's *Facts, Failures, and Frauds* (1859).
11. Taken from sketches that appeared in *Fraser's Magazine, Tait's Edinburgh,* and *The Times.*
12. In most other ways his accumulation of his wealth conforms with nineteenth-century narrative norms: a marriage to the draper's daughter explains his rise to partner in the firm, and an inheritance further boosts his social position.
13. In 1844 a sharp increase in railway company rivalries coupled with a large number of railway bills in Parliament prompted William Gladstone, president of the Board of Trade, to set up a House of Commons committee of inquiry into the railways. Many railway proprietors saw this as the beginning of state control, and Hudson headed a campaign of opposition. In a private meeting with Gladstone a compromise was made which removed the immediate prospect of railway nationalization (Reed).
14. The *Yorkshireman* is the most notable exception to the press's laudatory treatment of Hudson before 1846, as they themselves point out upon his fall: "Hudson's whole life has been one vast aggregate of avaricious and flagitious jobbing for the accumulation of wealth . . . We are, and have been, right for years. Single-handed, and contrary to the tone and disposition of the whole press of the kingdom, we have endeavoured to drag Mr. Hudson to the bar of public inquiry and opinion, and there to leave him to the mercies of the duped shareholders" (qtd. in Beaumont 119).

15. The word, Merdle, is a scatological pun. But even as such its meaning is opaque. Christopher Herbert argues that Merdle "is money incarnate" (202). Merdle's transformation from gold to shit during the course of the novel follows the famous Freudian formula of the equivalence of money and excrement. Herbert uses Merdle to reveal the taboo nature of money during the century, challenging James Frazer's notion of "taboo" originating in "primitive" societies. Frazer, studying Polynesian societies, argues that the concepts of the sacred and the filthy are originally the same, while Herbert, studying Victorian England, points out that money for the Victorians was a taboo in that it was considered both divine and polluted.
16. Merdle arises from the novel if we accept Bakhtin's definition of the novel as a diversity of social speech types and individual languages, as opposed to other genres which rely heavily upon authorial input. If we couple Bakhtin's definition with his idea that the novel is the only form in direct contact with developing reality, we can see why Merdle is produced stylistically as a heteroglossic composite and why he is the most "novelistic" of Dickens's productions.
17. This may be a function of what Mary Poovey calls the "cultures of investment." Poovey argues that beginning in the late 1840s novelistic plots began to incorporate features of the financial journalism that arose in the 1840s, such as the normalization of what she calls the "dynamic of disclosure and secrecy." Financial journalism is characterized by a style that both reveals information necessary to a functioning economy, and keeps hidden business secrets. Novelists adopted this style. Poovey argues that the inexact knowledge about business that circulates in this text is an example of financial journalism's influence on the novel.
18. At no period in history does the *OED* record "invest" as having a negative connotation. Commenting upon the positive valuation of the word, invest, in the early nineteenth century, Mary Poovey argues that words like invest helped to normalize radical business cycles of the first half of the century because they created the illusion that there were "good" as well as "bad" investments (called speculations.)
19. Timothy Alborn shows how "speculation" in early railways in the 1830s and 1840s was qualitatively different from trading in other sorts of company shares due to railways' unique political circumstances which involved winning parliamentary approval. The result was that "during the long period between projection and incorporation, railway investors were traders" (189). This (along with increases in volume and amount of people trading) explains the anxieties surrounding the manias of the 1830s and 1840s, and it also explains the widening difference between the words "speculate" and "invest" in the period: "In railways there was a clearer distinction between the 'speculative' period when the line was still being debated in Parliament and when cost estimates were being bandied about,

and the 'construction' period when permanent investors settled down to pay calls and collect dividends" (189–190).

20. Elaine Freedgood's theorization of risk in the nineteenth century is useful here. She argues that England is textually constructed as "safe" between 1832 and 1897 so that risk could be either avoided in England or engaged on a voluntary basis. In contrast to Anthony Giddens, Niklas Luhmann, and Marshall Berman, who believe that modernity is characterized by an acceptance of risk, she argues that it is characterized by risk's geographical containment in space constructed as "safe" in a wide range of literatures.
21. The nature of the Clennam business is never clarified in the text. Wenying Xu argues that the silence on this matter suggests that the Clennams were trading in opium. Clennam's disgust with the family business reflects his guilt as well as the nation's guilt about being involved in the drug business.
22. I am not suggesting that Meagles is the first positively presented businessman in a Dickens novel. The Cheeryble brothers of *Nicholas Nicholby* are presented in a positive light.
23. The word "career" depends upon modern ideals of personal advancement and only obtains its current meaning in the nineteenth century. The *OED* defines "career" in its most modern sense as: "A course of professional life or employment, which affords opportunity for progress or advancement in the world," and dates it to the early nineteenth century. That it is first used in the context of the diplomatic career, "a more difficult negotiation than you have ever had in your diplomatic career" (Wellington *Disp. II.* 424 1803), suggests the nationalistic undertones that the word must have carried when applied to other types of employment.
24. Lauren Goodlad's argument that by 1850 middle-class identity could be understood as a contest between entrepreneurs and officials may help us make sense of this situation in which the business community accepted and the government officials rejected Lesseps.
25. Samuel Smiles records that Stephenson said, "I have surveyed the line . . . I have traveled the whole distance on foot, and I declare there is no fall between the two seas. Honourable members talk about a canal. A canal is impossible—the thing would only be a ditch" (*Lives* 463).
26. Maxine Berg points out that G. Koolman argues that it was not until the 1830s that British political economists recognized the role of the entrepreneur. G.P. Scrope, Samuel Read, and George Ramsay took the idea of the entrepreneur from the French philosopher J.B. Say, who claimed the entrepreneur as his own concept at the turn of the century (Berg 123).
27. Before the advent of the nineteenth century the most common word used to describe the entrepreneur was "undertaker" or "adventurer." Adam Smith, for example, chose the word "undertaker" to translate the French word entrepreneur; however, by the nineteenth century the economic

sense of undertaker became obsolete and only the funerary sense remained (Hozelitz 243).

28. Consider, for example, this 1667 usage by S. Primatt: "There are as many Projectors (who have more of fancy and imagination in their Designs, than of any real operation) that do undertake in the dreining these and other sorts of mines" (Hoselitz 242).
29. Since the English had no word for entrepreneur when Prinsip first translated Say's *Traité* into English, he chose the word "adventurer." The English did not distinguish between the supply-of-capital function and the enterprise function (Koolman 273). Say's theorization of the entrepreneur is important because it creates a new identity for and appreciation of what was once called an "adventurer" and was now being called variously capitalist, projector, speculator, and promoter.
30. See Harold Perkin's *Origins of Modern English Society* and *The Rise of Professional Society.*
31. Smiles's story of the eighteenth-century canal engineer James Brindley, and the projector of his canals, Francis Duke of Bridgewater, further illustrates this point. The Duke raises the capital and pulls the political strings, while Brindley hones his practical skills and perseveres at his work. When the Duke ran out of money in midproject, Smiles writes that he inquired of Brindley: "'What's to be done now? How are we to get at the money for finishing the Canal?' Brindley, after a few long puffs, answered through the smoke, 'Well, Duke, I can't tell; I only know that if the money can be got, I can finish the Canal, and that it will pay well'" (*Lives* 109).
32. J. L. Austin describes the performative utterance as one that enacts what it seems to be describing. Something is performative when the saying of it makes it so. Austin's classic example of the performative utterance is the wedding vow, "I do."

NOTES TO CHAPTER TWO

1. The Suez Canal was purchased in 1875, but Queen Victoria was named Empress of India a year later. The temporal conflation that this scene enacts, alongside its spatial referencing of England, Egypt, and India, suggest the relation of the canal purchase to the project of imperialism. In addition, the overlaying of a marriage plot onto the scene intimates the way that generic conventions can be used to package political ones.
2. It should be noted that Disraeli did, however, lose the election in 1880.
3. Just how new " New Imperialism" was has been the object of much historical debate. John Gallagher and Ronald Robinson's 1953 article, "The Imperialism of Free Trade," broke with the widely held belief that imperialism began in the 1880s when the abandonment of free trade necessitated

the extension of markets abroad through formal annexations. They argue instead that imperialism, which they redefine as having political as well as commercial causes, was continuous throughout the century and that "formal" annexations were only resorted to when "informal" methods failed, as in the case of Egypt.

4. Here it is evident that Eldridge understands imperialism to be premeditated physical expansionism. More recently, the definition of imperialism has been reevaluated to include the role of financial expansionism. P.J. Cain and A.G. Hopkins, for example, argue that it is through the growth of the service sector, especially after 1850, and the exportation of service through what they call "Gentlemanly Capitalism" that imperialism takes hold. Cain and Hopkins downgrade the importance of formal acquisitions, favoring the explanation that commerce and finance were the most dynamic elements in the nation's economic thrust overseas.
5. Eldridge here is guilty of exoticizing Disraeli, as are many writers, including Disraeli himself. I am suggesting that this general exoticization of Disraeli works to both "other" empire *and* embody it in a literary form.
6. See Charles Richmond and Paul Smith (eds.), *The Self-Fashioning of Disraeli, 1818–1851.*
7. In *Tancred* Disraeli creates Fakredeen, a character who was praised by contemporary reviewers for being "amusing" and "original." I shall argue that just as Disraeli makes this amusing and Eastern character into the mouthpiece of imperialism, the British public portrayed "Dizzy" as an entertaining Jew for similar purposes. British anti-Semitism played into the need to other empire, so as to make it more acceptable.
8. For an alternative interpretation of Disraeli's orientalism see Patrick Brantlinger's "Disraeli and Orientalism." Brantlinger believes that Disraeli's orientalism is less unified, more hybrid, and more positive than Said recognizes. Further, Brantlinger argues that the most important feature of Disraeli's orientalism is that he orientalizes himself as a part of a "bold, aggressive defense against the anti-Semitism that he had to combat throughout his career" (91).
9. See Joseph W. Childers *Novel Possibilities: Fiction and the Formation of Early Victorian Culture* for a discussion of the ways that Disraeli's works made political discourse available to the novelistic form.
10. The Silver Fork novel, popular in England from 1825 to 1837, portrayed contemporary British aristocratic society by focusing on leisure activities, etiquette, and luxuries. William Hazlitt gave the epithet "Silver Fork" to these works in a scathing review in which he critiqued the subgenre's concern with the trivial details of upper-class life. Robert Plumer Ward's *Tremaine* (1825) is considered to be the first Silver Fork novel. The best-known representatives of the genre are Benjamin Disraeli's *Vivian Grey* (1826) and Edward Bulwer-Lytton's *Pelham* (1828).

11. In 1854 Abbas Pasha invited Robert Stephenson to build Egypt's first railway from Alexandria to Cairo, and in the same year the electric telegraph was laid along this route. Two years later a railway from Cairo to Suez was begun and was finished in 1859, the same year that work on the Suez Canal began. Egypt emerged in the 1850s as a trading country of major importance. In the years 1848 to 1860 Egypt went from twenty-sixth to twelfth place as a customer for British products, and in the period 1854–1860 from tenth to sixth place as a source of British imports (Landes 85). By 1865, England was noted for its extensive loaning practices in Egypt: "The British lent money generously—185 million francs subscribed in the space of a few years; the French had yet to admit an Egyptian loan to quotation" (Landes 271).
12. See Abbas Kelidar for an account of the new political role of the press in Egypt. See Juan Cole and Mona L. Russell for accounts of the rapid growth of Arabic-language newspapers during Ismail's reign.
13. Writers and intellectuals from all over the Middle East flocked to Egypt to take advantage of Ismail's openness. Syrian Christians, escaping from the civil war of the 1850s, especially saw Egypt as a safe haven (Allen 24).
14. McKeon calls these three stages of the questions of truth "romance idealism," "naïve empiricism," and "extreme skepticism."
15. Nicholas Daly makes a similar point when he argues that romance provides a way to "absorb, reflect upon, and codify various facets of modernization" (24). However, Daly argues that only the late nineteenth-century romances work to spread modernity. McKeon, on the other hand, believes that ever since the seventeenth century romance has been a modernizing form.
16. Mitchell claims that in Europe "the words of language had come to be considered not meanings in themselves but the physical clues to some sort of metaphysical abstraction—a mind or mentality" (141). As words lost their integral meanings, language became a separate realm, a mere representational system. In other words, language became just one more representational system that would be used to colonize Egypt.
17. Patrick Brantlinger argues that there is an "upsurge in romance writing" (231) at the end of the nineteenth century and believes this late romance is to be found in popular forms such as imperial Gothic, Wellsian science fiction, invasion fantasies, and spy stories, all of which "betray anxieties characteristic of late Victorian and Edwardian imperialism both as an ideology and as a phase of political development" (*Rule of Darkness* 236). Judith Wilt has likewise argued for the existence of links between late Victorian Imperialism and the resurrection of the Gothic romance formula (618–628).
18. This was actually a common complaint waged against writers of Silver Fork novels, for they were often written by members of the middle class who were accused of having higher social aspirations.

19. This is not to suggest that development began with the British in the 1850s. Most historians date modernization in Egypt to Muhammad Ali, viceroy of Egypt from 1805 to 1848. Muhammad Ali built upon the foundations of the Mamluks from whom he took techniques of centralization and the establishment of law and order. He introduced new policies on industry, agriculture, education, and the Egyptianization of bureaucracy. It is often said that his successors Abbas (1848–1854) and Said (1854–1863) reduced his programs although they did continue to develop railways and telegraph lines. When Ismail became Khedive (1863–1879) he reimplemented some of Muhammad Ali's initiatives, and invited foreigners to invest extensively in new projects. For more on modernization in Egypt throughout the nineteenth century see Afaf Marsot, Michael Brett, Timothy Mitchell, Mona L. Russell, and Lisa Pollard.
20. Jameson argues that Greimas's methodology is important because it can show a disjunction between the narrative surface and the underlying *actantial* mechanisms. Further, Greimas's method is most useful "in those instances in which the surface unity of 'character' can be analytically dissolved, by showing . . . that a single character in reality conceals the operation of two distinct *actants*" (*The Political Unconscious* 126). Jameson performs Greimas's process in reverse, showing that a single *actant* in reality conceals the operation of two distinct characters. He uses Greimas's findings to argue that both Propp's and Greimas's narrative systems are most productive when they deviate from their basic schema. Because of its particular relation to the surface character of the hero, the donor function becomes the key for Jameson to locate this deviation.
21. Disraeli's purchase of the Canal was applauded in the press across the political spectrum. Hepworth Dixon's portrayal of the event in *Gentleman's Magazine* is typical: "I have seen nothing to compare with the fever of London society during the past and present week. . . . When we are agreed, our unanimity is wonderful! In these early days of December, 1875, England appears to have only one thought. She has done a great thing, and made her neighbors stare" (38).
22. Disraeli's positive spin on Fakredeen's debts belie the real-life dependency that debt would come to represent in the Middle East. While debt is portrayed as Fakredeen's greatest ally, prompting him on to great deeds, it would plague the reigns of the Egyptian rulers Said Pasha (1854–63) and Ismail Pasha (1863–1879), finally causing the bankruptcy of Ismail's government in 1876. Said is known for stepping up the modernization process begun under Mohammed Ali, and slowed under Ali's successor, Abbas Pasha (1849–1854). Said's initiation and support of many modernization projects, including improved streets in Alexandria, better water transport, irrigation projects, cotton cultivation, the dredging

of the Mahmoudieh canal, and the granting of the concession for the Suez Canal, caused him to seek two substantial foreign loans in the early 1860s, which propelled him into debt. Ismail inherited that debt, which grew exponentially under his reign: from £3,300,000 to £91,000,000 in the period from 1863–1877. Ismail's pursuit of huge public works, empire in Africa, and the completion of the Suez Canal were some of the factors that contributed to the growth of debt under his government. In the West, Ismail gained a reputation of being a profligate spender—a reputation that should be evaluated within the context of debt production, rather than morality, as it so often has been.

23. Moretti uses marriage as a metaphor for the social contract: "It has been observed that from the late eighteenth century on, marriage becomes the model for a new type of social contract: one no longer sealed by forces located outside of the individual (such as status), but founded on a sense of 'individual obligation.' . . . It is not only the foundation of the family that is at stake, but the 'pact' between the individual and the world, that reciprocal 'consent' which finds in the double 'I do' of the wedding ritual an unsurpassed symbolic condensation" (*The Way of the World* 22).
24. It is interesting that Fakredeen gains access to Besso's capital at this point. Besso believes that Fakredeen saved his daughter from the Ansarey; therefore Besso promises him unlimited loans as a reward. One would think that Tancred's new filial relation to Besso would give him new access to Besso's capital, as it would in a novel plotted in England. However, Tancred has always had access to Besso's capital. The twinning of the protagonists, then, which began as a function of romance, is what allows for the transfer of Tancred's reward to Fakredeen. The remnants of the romance convention of twinning serve to produce a sense of brotherhood between the two, and all that that connotes—fairness, equality—when the romance resolves into a *Bildungsroman.* The real inequality of access to capital is elided by the adoption of the new literary form.
25. Moretti places the "everyday" realm "to the side of" the bustling world, as opposed to in the past, in the precapitalistic community, where it is often placed by theorists: "aesthetic organicity, and happiness that comes with it belong not only to a past that precedes capitalist production and the 'mechanical' state, but endure in modern times as well. Except that now they are shifted 'to the side of' the great collective institutions, which they engage in a silent and unending border war" (*The Way of the World* 33).
26. Taking his cues from Lukacs and Simmel, Moretti writes: "It is fairly difficult for modern 'personality' to reach its goal in a professional occupation alone, that is to say, work. Work has become too fragmented in its nature and also too 'objective,' too impervious to 'living meaning.' Those

who devote themselves to modern profession must give up their own personality" (41).

27. In 1891 plum pudding is referred to as "our most national of dishes" in *Black and White,* which printed a story about Lord Byron very similar to Disraeli's account of the colonel. While Byron was in exile in Italy, he experienced "a sudden yearning" for plum pudding and had his Italian cook prepare it ("National Dishes of the Civilized World" 12).

NOTES TO CHAPTER THREE

1. See Briony Llewellyn, who argues that John Frederick Lewis and Frank Dillon were the only two professional British artists working between 1840 and 1870 to have focused on private and secular buildings in Cairo rather than on its public and religious places.
2. Here I disagree with Pollard. I don't believe that it was the discovery of the Khedive's debauched family life that motivated the British and French to invade Egypt. This was rather one of many justifications for the invasion. The British and French deposed the Khedive because they wanted to take control of Egypt's finances.
3. The actual introduction of modern housing into Egypt is described by Timothy Mitchell, who discusses the first model villages drawn up by French engineers in 1846. With the modern house, the Europeans introduce a concept of space that relies upon fixing an interior and exterior, or breaking space up into containers to create legibility, a process which he calls "enframing." The traditional Egyptian house was not conceived of as a container; rather it was a "charged process." Mitchell argues that through "enframing" and the introduction of the modern house, Egypt was colonized.
4. The type of change that I am discussing is often registered in the titles of the travel narratives. In the first half of the century, titles frequently announced an interest in ancient monuments, as does Isabella Frances Romer's *A Pilgrimage to the Temples and Tombs of Egypt, Nubia, and Palestine in 1845–46.* After 1850, interiority is more often stressed, as it is in Isabel Burton's 1875 *The Inner Life of Syria, Palestine, and Holy Land: From my Private Journal.*
5. All three of Lott's accounts of her observations of Ottoman harems received bad reviews: *The Governess in Egypt: Harem Life in Egypt and Constantinople,* 1865 (republished under similar names in America in 1865 and 1867); *The Mohaddetyn in the Palace: Nights in the Harem; or, The Mohaddetyn in the Palace of Ghezire,* 1867; and *The Grand Pacha's Cruise on the Nile in the Viceroy of Egypt's Yacht,* 1869. Contemporary reviewers objected to her overly detailed accounts. According to Michael Wojcik, "Lott's books brought her little profit or recognition" (235).

6. Briony Lewellyn suggests that the reason that Frederick Lewis was able to represent the Egyptian interior so authentically was because he lived there for nine years: "Clearly the settings of Lewis' domestic scenes are convincing because they are real; he could portray them accurately and with assurance because he had lived within them" (151).
7. According to Billie Melman there were only four books written by European women on the Middle East from 1500 to 1821. By 1911, however, after having reached a peak in the 1890s, that number had reached 241.
8. See Derek Gregory for a discussion of Nightingale's treatment of nature. He argues that she presented Egyptian landscapes as unnatural, beyond natural, and even supernatural.
9. Only a few years before the women arrived in Egypt, the first general collection of photographs of the Middle East was published, Francis Frith's 1858 *Egypt and Palestine, Photographed and Described.* For a discussion of the importance of photography in the colonizing of Egypt see Timothy Mitchell, who argues that Europeans' obsessive photographing of Egypt was part of their desire to make it readable because colonial power needed a country to be legible.
10. I am borrowing the idea that the "everyday is a wartime" from Mary A. Favret (606).
11. Another exception may be found in mass tourism guides such as John Murray's. However, these details are of a different sort than those found in Duff Gordon's work. Because guides need to appear current, they only include information which does not change; therefore, they cannot contain details subject to the fluctuations of everyday life.
12. Recently there have been many good studies of the relation of liberalism to empire. See, for example, Uday Singh Mehta's *Liberalism and Empire: A Study in Nineteenth-Century British Liberal Thought* and Jennifer Pitts's *A Turn to Empire: The Rise of Imperial Liberalism in Britain and France.*
13. It would be interesting to know why Lott's racist work was often criticized for being overly cruel to her subjects while Nightingale's equally racist work was not.
14. I am referring to Marshall Berman's argument in *All Things Solid Melt into Air* that modernist thought begins with Marx.
15. See Malek Alloula for an analysis of Western male depictions of the Algerian harem. Alloula argues that the lasciviousness of the harem dwellers is at the core of Western representations, asserting that portraying the harem as such enabled Westerners to justify their own desires: the colonial conquest of the harem and of Algerian society. Lisa Pollard makes a similar argument about the depiction of the Egyptian harem. For an analysis of Western female depictions of the harem see Jill Matus, who notes that Victorian women also approached the harem as a spectacle of sensuality. However, she argues that the harem provoked British women's

own anxieties about domestic life in England (65). Thus women represented the dullness and sloth of the harem to comment upon their own ambivalence about the separate, domestic sphere (75). For similar reasons Victorian women focused on polygamy and confinement within the harem.

16. In the West, the harem is understood to be "the part of a Muslim dwelling-house appropriated to the women" or "the occupants of a harem collectively" (*OED*). Lott, however, conveniently extends the spatial definition of "harem" to include the whole palace, even those rooms designated to men. She even spies upon Ismail in the bathroom. Since in the West the harem was also understood to be a private and/or a sacred space, Lott's total penetration is significant.
17. See Melissa Lee Miller for a comparison of the ways that Lott and Duff Gordon represent the harem.
18. See Timothy Mitchell for an analysis of the reconstruction of Cairo. In 1867–68, he writes, Ali Mubarak, an Egyptian administrator, teacher, and engineer who visited the Exposition Universelle in Paris was appointed Minister of Schools and Minister of Public Works on his return home. What followed, under Mubarak's leadership, was the "greatest period of construction and demolition in the city since the growth of Mamluk Cairo in the 1300s" (65).
19. This is in contrast to what has been said about Lucie Duff Gordon by Faiza Shereen in the *Dictionary of Literary Biography* and in the account of her in the *Dictionary of National Biography.* Both articles depict Duff Gordon's critique of modernization as unproblematic.
20. Henry Ross was a director of the Sudan Company, later known as the Egyptian Commercial and Trading Company, established in 1863 to trade with Upper Egypt, the Sudan, and the Red Sea. Janet Ross wrote in a letter to *The Times* on April 7, 1863 that the company had "brilliant prospects," and stood to gain an average profit of 200 per cent per annum. Duff Gordon wrote that Ross "stands to win pots of money" (84), but later she said that Ross did not understand the situation in Egypt well enough to direct such a company.
21. It was not uncommon for Europeans living abroad to imagine familial and affective ties with their native household servants. Ann Laura Stoler demonstrates through a series of interviews with Dutch colonials about their home life in Indonesia during the colonial period that many nostalgically referred to the Indonesian domestic servants who worked for them as "family." None of the domestic workers whom she interviewed, however, shared their boss's affection. Many of them could not even recall their employers' names; they did, however, remember in detail the dull chores and hard work that they preformed in the Dutch households. Stoler's interviews reveal just what the word "family" can mask in the colonial setting.

22. See Melissa Lee Miller, who cites Duff Gordon's dismissal of her eight-year-old slave because of her refusal to eat pork as evidence of Duff Gordon's cultural imperialism.

NOTES TO CHAPTER FOUR

1. Globe-trotters can be thought of in the context of the rise of organized tourism dated to the 1840s in England, the period in which guidebooks were published and tours were organized by a developing industry. Although undeniably a part of this new phenomenon, the round-the-world narratives differ from other tourist tomes in their teleology. Their journey is defined by their destination, which is always the shortest way back home.
2. "Globe-trotter" was commonly used self-referentially by round-the-world travelers beginning in the 1870s. The American traveler E.K. Laird uses it in his 1875 account: "These are the sentiments of a 'globe trotter,' whose business it is to see sights" (Laird 223). And the British traveler William Simpson also uses it in his 1877 account when discussing Europeans in China in 1872: "There are only those belonging to the Legations and the Missionary institutions, except an occasional 'globe-trotter' like myself" (219).
3. A fourth technological enterprise that facilitated global travel was the Mont Cenis Tunnel, opened in September of 1871. It was the first tunnel to cut through the Alps, facilitating travel between France and Italy by reducing the time it took to cross over the Alps to a period of less than ten minutes.
4. The Great Indian Peninsular Railway Company was founded in 1845. This company built the first railway in India from Bombay to Thana in 1853. The cross-continental line from Bombay to Calcutta was completed on March 7, 1870.
5. Simpson writes that in 1859 it took him ninety days to travel from England to Calcutta around the Cape of Good Hope, and that that was considered a quick voyage. The cutting of the Suez Canal reduced the time it took to travel from England to India to less than a month.
6. These are the advantages of the new cross-continental railway according to Phileas Fogg, the protagonist of Jules Verne's *Around the World in Eighty Days.*
7. See John Gallagher and Ronald Robinson's article "The Imperialism of Free Trade." Breaking with the widely held belief that imperialism began in the 1880s when the abandonment of free trade necessitated the extension of markets abroad through formal annexations, they argue instead that imperialism was continuous throughout the century, and that "formal" annexations only were resorted to when "informal" methods failed.
8. Arendt argues that after government power began to be exported in the last quarter of the century, the position of financiers, particularly Jewish

financiers, weakened. Then a native bourgeoisie took over. As an example, she cites Cecil Rhodes, who although an absolute newcomer, "in a few years could supplant the all-powerful Jewish financier in first place" (136). If she is correct, this adds a racial dimension to the argument that I made in the first chapter, for only after the native bourgeoisie become financiers does this position lose its taint.

9. Karl Marx and Friedrich Engels date the bourgeoisie's entry into the political realm much earlier than Arendt does. In the *Communist Manifesto* they indicate that by 1850 the bourgeoisie was thoroughly entrenched in state power.
10. Harvey, following Marshall Berman, argues that literary modernism arises during the nineteenth century to represent the crisis in space and time invoked by capitalism. I am suggesting that the round-the-world narratives are modernist texts in that they emerge to resolve that crisis.
11. Geo. M. Towle and N. d'Anvers published the English translation in 1873, but biographers claim that British and American newspapers published excerpts from Verne's serial publication of the novel that began on December 22, 1872 even earlier.
12. M. M. Bakhtin uses "chronotope" to mean "time-space." Chronotope explains the connectedness of temporal and spatial relationships that are expressed in literature, and it defines genre and generic distinctions.
13. This is not to say that journeys around the world altogether stopped. Henry Kratz in his introduction to Adelbert von Chamisso's journey around the world (1815 to 1818) suggests that circumnavigations increased during the mid-eighteenth century, citing various round-the-world expeditions including that of Samuel Wallis and Louis Antoine de Bougainville, who led the first French expedition to travel around the world in 1766–1769; Captain James Cook, who led three British expeditions in the second half of the century; and Adam Johann Von Krusenstern, who led the first Russian expedition around the world in 1803 to 1806 (Chamisso xii).
14. I am not suggesting that all of the circumnavigators lack seriousness. Some of them are indeed serious about their mission, as is the American C.C. Coffin, who travels around the world in 1869, and William Simpson, who travels in 1872. However, more often than not, authors downplay the seriousness of their travels as they play up the joyfulness and ease of a journey around the world. Even Coffin and Simpson, who are serious about their work, lack a rigor of study that is found in earlier circumnavigations. That is to say that Coffin and Simpson's work resembles journalistic prose much more than it resembles scientific writing.
15. Compare Laird's flippancy to the much more serious Aldebert von Chamisso, who traveled around the world in 1815–1818: "My chief occupation now, using time and the good nature of scholars industriously, was to inquire what gaps in our scientific knowledge a voyage such as the one in

prospect might hope to fill" (14). Or consider James Holman who traveled around the world in 1834: "I have been conscious from my earliest youth of the existence of the desire to explore distant regions, to trace the varieties exhibited by mankind under different influences of different climates, customs, and laws, and to investigate with unwearied solicitude the moral and physical distinctions that separate and diversify the various nations on the earth" (2).

16. Thanks to Enrique Lanz Oca for sharing with me his unpublished paper on the British travel industry and the military in the late nineteenth century.
17. See John Pudney, who writes of Cook, "After the battle of Tel-el-Kebir, he undertook to transport all the wounded and sick from Cairo to Alexandria by water without making any other charge than the actual cost of running steamers" (198).
18. James Buzard and Piers Brendon both hypothesize that Jules Verne may have gotten the idea for his novel from Cook's 1872 expedition. And Cook's biographers Allotte de la Fuye and Bernard Frank also suggest that Cook's advertisement of his journey inspired Verne's book. But Verne had contemplated round the world navigation long before he sent Phileas Fogg racing around the world. Verne wrote *Captain Grant's Children: A Voyage Round the World* in 1865. And in his 1864 novel *Twenty Thousand Leagues Under the Sea* he sends Captain Nemo and his crew circumnavigating the globe in a submarine. Verne's idea was much more likely to have come from a variety of sources.
19. See also Adelbert von Chamisso's narrative: *A Voyage Around the World with the Romanzov Exploring Expedition in the Years 1815–1818 in the Brig Rurik.* Captain Fisher A. Newell's too demonstrates this trend: *Two Brothers Narrative of a Voyage Around the World in the Bark 'Sea Breeze'* (1850).
20. Lenin uses the export of railways around the globe to argue his thesis about New Imperialism. Capitalism, he asserts, inevitably leads to monopolies and imperialism. The girdling of the globe with railways in the 1890s was a sign of monopoly capitalism and the New Imperialism: "Thus, about 80 per cent of the total existing railways are concentrated in the hands of the five Great Powers (U.S., British Empire, Russia, Germany, France). But concentration of the ownership of these railways, of finance capital, is much greater still: French and English millionaires, for example, own an enormous amount of stocks and bonds in American, Russian, and other railways" (98).
21. American accounts of round the world travel were numerous. The Union Pacific Railway company came out with *Around the World by Steam, via Pacific Railway* in 1871 enabling many to easily take the journey. William P. Fogg went around the globe in 1869–71 and described his tour in a series of letters to the *Cleveland Leader* and published *Round the World: Letters*

from Japan, China, India, and Egypt in 1872. The American railway builder George Francis Train went around the world four times, once in eighty days in 1870. An American boy, Emmit Carr traveled the world in 1874 with his grandfather and mother and published *All the Way Round* (1876). The sixteen-year-old Ellen Walworth circled the globe with her uncle and published *An Old World, as Seen through Young Eyes* in 1877. The most famous circumnavigations of them all were Ulysses S. Grant's *General Grant's Tour Around the World: With a Sketch of his Life* (1879) and Nellie Bly's record-breaking narrative, *Around the World in 72 Days* (1890).

22. Lesseps reserved 5 percent of the canal shares for investors from the United States, but American investment in the project was actually much less (Farnie 51).
23. Notice how closely this skeletal route coincides with what R. Calwer called the "main economic areas" at the turn of the century: Central Europe, Great Britain, Russia, East Asia, America. Calwer's map furnishes insights into an economic understanding of the structuring of this particular route.
24. Hinchliff decides to go to South America precisely because it is not on the circuit. He writes that he wanted "to avoid following the example of the great majority of modern travelers, who, for some unknown reasons, appear almost unanimously to exclude South America from their programme" (viii).
25. This is not to say that he never mentions the weather. He does, for example, when he passes through the inferno of the Red Sea. However, weather intrusions are relatively rare, especially when compared to other types of travel narratives, where weather and weather patterns make a daily appearance.
26. See Marshall Berman for the importance of "smoothness" to development. He discusses Haussman's use of macadam to pave his new boulevards. Berman makes the point that while macadam was good for horse and carriage traffic, it was a travesty for the pedestrian, who got mired in the filth that it threw up (158).
27. Compare this to the typical hassles of the English traveler described in Murray's 1836 guidebook: "Of all the penalties, at the expense of which the pleasure of traveling abroad is purchased, the most disagreeable and most repugnant to English feelings is that of submitting to the strict regulations of the continental police, and especially to the annoyance of bearing a passport" (*A Handbook for Travellers on the Continent* xv).
28. One sure way that a story can go wrong, Franco Moretti suggests in *Atlas of the European Novel,* is to fail to incorporate borders and border-crossings (what he calls complexity). This is where the English novel gravely erred. England's production of a genre that lacks border-crossing is what Moretti says has made England into an island.

29. See, for example, Vladimir Propp's *Morphology of a Folktale.*
30. Marx uses this statement to describe the bourgeoisie, but I am suggesting, rather, that technology develops as an ideology to relieve the bourgeoisie of taking responsibility for their destructive actions.
31. Most round-the-world travelers cite three cultural reasons for the Chinese resistance to Western technology: the burial mounds, the practice of audience rituals such as kowtowing, and the belief in Fung Shuey.
32. Fogg is not a typical globetrotter, whose "business it is to see sights" (Laird 223). But he is typical of the railway sojourner, who according to Wolfgang Schivelbusch detached himself from the outside world, preferring a good book to a distant view. Phileas Fogg, then, is the cliché of the railway passenger in the nineteenth century, who often was referred to as a "human parcel" who dispatched him/herself to his/her destination by means of the railway and steamboat. Indeed, Verne intermittently refers to Fogg as a commodity and merchandise.
33. Lenin wrote that beginning in the 1870s capitalism veered from its roots in "free trade" and became increasingly monopolistic. Lenin used the railways as an example of the expansion of monopolies around the world. For him, both the component parts of the railway—coal and steel—and the railways themselves that by the 1890s were found in nearly every space of the globe were evidence of the monopolistic developments of capital.
34. George Bradshaw began to publish the *Series of Railway Timetables* in 1839. By 1847, he expanded them to include the continent, and his timetables became indispensable for railway and steamboat travel (Buzard 78).
35. These are the adventures that are met along the way: Passepartout's pagoda melee, an elephant ride through an Indian jungle, a suttee rescue from fanatics, apprehension and trial for the pagoda incident, storm at sea, Passepartout drugged and passed out in an opium den, missing the *Carnatic,* a typhoon, Passepartout's bout as a Japanese acrobat, an election day brawl, train leap across a broken bridge, a duel on a speeding train, a Sioux attack, a Sioux rescue, missing the train, a sledge ride, missing the *China,* a boat hijack involving locking up the captain and taking over his crew, dismantling and burning a boat for fuel, taking a mail boat, an arrest, and imprisonment.
36. The odd character triad–Fogg, Passepartout, and Fix–that Verne propels into motion around the globe mirrors another strange triad that Hannah Arendt understands to be vital to the development of New Imperialism. Arendt argues that during the 1880s superfluous capital and superfluous labor first joined hands and left the country with the aid of the state.
37. It also opens up the spy novel, that other globe-trotting genre, which represents a network of spies and suspicion propelled into the world at the selfsame moment that England was firming up its hold upon the globe.

38. Not surprisingly, adventures are even more profuse in the film versions of Verne's novel. Indeed, in these the plot becomes reduced to a stream of adventures, and plenty of new adventures are introduced to the plot.
39. Verne's body of work is geared towards pushing this temporal limit of circumnavigation. In *Twenty Thousand Leagues Under the Sea* (1869), he sends captain Nemo's submarine though a secret passageway under the Suez Canal, and they speed from the Red Sea to the Mediterranean in twenty minutes only.
40. Here we can return to Elaine Freedgood's theorization of risk in the nineteenth century. England, she argues, was textually constructed as "safe" between 1832 and 1897 so that risk could be either avoided or engaged on a voluntary basis. Freedgood argues that modernity is characterized by risk's geographical containment in space constructed as "safe" in a wide range of literatures.
41. American imperialism began to differ from the British variety in this period when America turned to economic means of conquest rather than military ones. Verne suggests that Fogg may well be an American hero when he has Captain Speedy compliment Fogg by saying: "Well, Captain Fogg, you have Yankee blood in you."
42. See Yvette H. Ward's *Around the World in 32 Days* (1958).
43. Five years earlier Wiley Post records the eight-day flight of Winnie Mae in *Around the World in Eight Days; The Flight of Winnie Mae* (1931).

Bibliography

Adams, D.D. *A Voyage Around the World.* Boston: Henry Hoyt, 1871.

Alborn, Timothy L. *Conceiving Companies: Joint-stock Politics in Victorian England.* London: Routledge, 1998.

Alder, Judith. "Origins of Sightseeing." *Annals of Tourism Research* 16 (1989): 7–29.

Allen, Roger. *The Arabic Novel: An Historical and Critical Introduction.* New York: Syracuse University Press, 1982.

Alloula, Malek. *The Colonial Harem.* Minneapolis: University of Minnesota Press, 1986.

Anderson, Amanda. *The Powers of Distance: Cosmopolitanism and the Cultivation of Detachment.* Princeton: Princeton University Press, 2001.

Anderson, Benedict. *Imagined Communities: Reflections on the Origin and Spread of Nationalism.* London: Verso, 1983.

Arago, Jacques. *Voyage Autour du Monde.* Paris: Berquet et Pétion, 1842.

Arendt, Hannah. *The Origins of Totalitarianism.* Cleveland: Meridian Books, 1958.

Armstrong, Nancy. *Desire and Domestic Fiction: A Political History of the Novel.* New York: Oxford University Press, 1987.

Arnold, A. J., and S. M. McCartney. *George Hudson: The Rise and Fall of the Railway King.* London and New York: Hambeldon and London, 2004.

Austin, J.L. *How to Do Things with Words.* Cambridge: Harvard University Press, 1981.

Bailey, Brian J. *George Hudson: The Rise and Fall of the Railway King.* Gloucestershire: Alan Sutton Publishers, 1995.

Bakhtin, Mikhail. *The Dialogic Imagination.* Austin: The University of Texas Press, 1981.

Ballou, Maturin Murray. *Due West, or, Round the World in Ten Months.* Boston: Houghton Mifflin, 1885.

Beaumont, Robert. *The Railway King: A Biography of George Hudson.* London: Review, 2002.

Benjamin, Walter. "The Storyteller." *Illuminations.* New York: Schocken Books, 1968.

Berg, Maxine. *The Machinery Question and the Making of Political Economy 1815–1848.* London: Cambridge University Press, 1980.

Berman, Marshall. *All That is Solid Melts into Air: The Experience of Modernity.* New York: Penguin Books, 1988.

Blakesley, J. W. Rev. "M. de Lesseps and the Suez Canal." *Macmillan's Magazine* March 1860: 407–416.

Blessington, Marguerite. *Hughenden Papers* 22 March 1848: 36.

Bly, Nellie. *Nellie Bly's Book: Around the World in Seventy-Two Days.* New York: The Pictorial Weeklies Company, 1890.

Brainbridge, Lucy Seaman. *Round the World Letters.* Boston: D. Lothrop & Co., 1882.

Brantlinger, Patrick. "Disraeli and Orientalism." *The Self-Fashioning of Disraeli, 1818–1851.* Ed. Charles Richmond and Paul Smith. Cambridge: Cambridge University Press, 1999. 91–105.

———. *Rule of Darkness: British Literature and Imperialism, 1830–1914.* Ithaca: Cornell University Press, 1988.

Brassie, Annie. *Around the World in the Yacht Sunbeam.* New York: Henry Holt and Company, 1878.

Brendon, Piers. *Thomas Cook: 150 Years of Popular Tourism.* London: Secker and Warburg, 1991.

Brett, Michael. "Continuity and Change: Egypt and North Africa in the Nineteenth-Century." *Journal of African History* 27 (1986): 149–162.

Buck-Morss, Susan. "Semiotic Boundaries and the Politics of Meaning: Modernity on Tour—A Village in Transition." *New Ways of Knowing: The Sciences, Society, and Reconstructive Knowledge.* Ed. Marcus G. Raskin and Herbert J. Bernstein. Totowa: Rowman and Littlefield, 1987. 200–236.

Burchell, Williams. *Travels in the Interior of Southern Africa.* London: Longman, Hurst, Rees, Orme, and Brown, 1822.

Burlingame, H.J. *Around the World with a Magician and a Juggler.* Chicago: Clyde Pub., 1891.

Burton, Isabel. *The Inner Life of Syria, Palestine, and Holy Land: From my Private Journal.* London: Henry S. King, 1875.

Burton., Sir Richard F. *Personal Narrative of a Pilgrimage to Al-Madinah and Meccah.* New York: Dover Publications, 1964.

Buzard, James. *The Beaten Track: European Tourism, Literature, and the Ways of Culture, 1800–1918.* Oxford: Clarendon Press, 1993.

Cain, P.J. and A.G. Hopkins. *British Imperialism, 1688–2000.* New York: Longman, 2002.

Campbell, John. *Travels in South Africa.* London: Francis Westley, 1822.

Carlyle, Thomas. "Captains of Industry." *Past and Present.* Boston: Houghton Mifflin Company, 1965. 267–273.

———. "Hudson's Statue." *Latter-Day Pamphlets.* Freeport: Books for Libraries Press, 1972. 220–248.

Carr, Addis Emmit. *All the Way Round; or What a Boy Saw and Heard on His Way Round the World.* London: Sampson Low, Marson, Searle, & Rivington, 1876.

Chamisso, Adelbert Von. *A Voyage Around the World with the Romanzov Exploring Expedition in the Years 1815–1818 in the Brig Rurik, Captain Otto Von Kotzebue.* Honolulu: University of Hawaii Press, 1986.

Childers, Joseph W. *Novel Possibilities: Fiction and the Formation of Early Victorian Culture.* Philadelphia: University of Pennsylvania Press, 1995.

Coffin, C.C. *Our New Way Round the World.* Boston: Fields, 1869.

Cole, Juan. *Colonialism & Revolution in the Middle East.* Princeton: Princeton University Press, 1993.

"A Contrast." *The Times* 23 March 1846: 4e.

Cook, Thomas. *Letters from the Sea and from Foreign Lands, Descriptive of a Tour Round the World.* London: Routledge/Thoemmes, 1998.

Daly, Nicholas. *Modernism, Romance and the Fin de Siècle: Popular Fiction and British Culture, 1880–1914.* Cambridge: Cambridge University Press, 1999.

Danziger, Christopher. "The First Suez Crisis." *History Today* September 1982: 3–7.

Davis, Mike. *Late Victorian Holocausts: El Nino Famines and the Making of the Third World.* London: Verso, 2002.

De Certeau, Michel. *The Practice of Everyday Life.* Berkeley: University of California Press, 1984.

Dickens, Charles. *Little Dorrit.* London: Oxford University Press, 1953.

Disraeli, Benjamin. *Tancred; or The New Crusade.* New York: Alfred A. Knopf, 1934.

Disraeli. Dir. Alfred E. Green. With Florence Arliss and George Arliss. Warner Brothers, 1929.

Dixon, Hepworth W. "The False Move on Egypt." *Gentleman's Magazine* January-June 1876: 38–44.

Duff Gordon, Lady Lucie. *Letters From Egypt, 1862–1869.* New York: Frederick A. Praeger, 1969.

Ekins, Herbert Roslyn. *Around the World in Eighteen Days and How to Do It.* New York: Green & Co., 1936.

Eldridge, C.C. *Disraeli and the Rise of the New Imperialism.* Cardiff: University of Wales Press, 1996.

Farnie, D.A. *East and West of Suez, The Suez Canal in History.* Clarendon Press: Oxford, 1969.

Favret, Mary A. "Everyday War." *ELH* 72:3 (2005): 605–633.

Fitzgerald, Percy Hetherington. *The Great Canal at Suez: its Political, Engineering, and Financial History. With an Account of the Struggles of its Projector, Ferdinand de Lesseps.* London: Tinsley Bros., 1876.

Fogg, William Perry. *Round the World: Letters from Japan, China, India and Egypt.* 1872.

Francis, G.H. "Outlines in Parliament. The Railway Potentates—Mr. Hudson, Mr. Chaplin, Mr. Rusell, Mr. Strutt." *Fraser's Town and Country Magazine* August 1847: 213–227.

Freedgood, Elaine. *Victorian Writing about Risk: Imagining a Safe England in a Dangerous World.* New York: Cambridge University Press, 2000.

Frith, Francis. *Egypt and Palestine, Photographed and Described.* London: J.S. Virtue, 1858.

Frye, Northrop. *Anatomy of Criticism.* Princeton: Princeton University Press, 1971.

Gallagher, John and Ronald Robinson. "The Imperialism of Free Trade." *Economic History Review* 1.1 (1953): 1–15.

Goodlad, Lauren M.E. "A Middle Class Cut into Two": Historiography and the Victorian National Character." *EHL* 61.1 (2000): 143–178.

Gorst, Anthony and Lewis Johman. *The Suez Crisis.* London: Routeledge, 1997.

Grant, Ulysses S. *General Grant's Tour Around the World: With a Sketch of his Life.* Chicago: Rand McNally, 1879.

Gregory, Derek. "Between the Book and the Lamp: Imaginative Geographies of Egypt, 1879–50." *Transactions of the Institute of British Geographers* 20:1 (1995): 29–57.

Greimas, A.J. *Semantique Structurale.* Paris: Larousse, 1966.

Habermas, Jürgen. *The Structural Transformation of the Public Sphere: An Inquiry into a Category of a Bourgeois Society.* Cambridge: MIT Press, 1989.

Haddad, Emily. "Digging to India: Modernity, Imperialism, and the Suez Canal." *Victorian Studies.* 47.3 (2005): 363–396.

Hamley, William. "Egypt and the Story of the Suez Canal." *Blackwoods Edinburgh Magazine* 106 December 1896: 730–745.

Harcourt, Freda. "Thomas Waghorn (1800–1850)." *Oxford Dictionary of National Biography,* Oxford University Press, 2004 [accessed 29 Oct. 2004: http://www.oxforddnb.com/view/article/28397]

Harper, Lila Marz. "Gordon, Lucie Duff, Lady Duff Gordon (1821–1869)" *Oxford Dictionary of National Biography,* Oxford University Press, 2004. [accessed 27 Sept. 2004: http://www.oxforddnb.com/view/article/8175]

Harvey, David. *The Condition of Postmodernity: an Enquiry into the Origins of Cultural Change.* Oxford: Blackwood Publishers, 1990.

Heidegger, Martin. "The Question Concerning Technology." *The Question Concerning Technology, and Other Essays.* New York: Garland Publishing, Inc., 1977.

Herbert, Christopher. "Filthy Lucre: Victorian Ideas of Money." *Victorian Studies* 44.2 (2002): 185–212.

Herbert, Mary Elizabeth. *Cradle Lands.* New York: The Catholic Publication Society, 1869.

Hinchliff, T.W. *Over the Sea and Far Away being a Narrative of Wanderings Round the World.* London: Longmans, 1876.

Hobson, J.A. *Imperialism.* Ann Arbor: The University of Michigan Press, 1972.

Hoffman, William. *The Monitor; or, Jottings of a New York Merchant During a Trip Round the Globe.* New York: Carleton, 1862.

Holman, James. *A Voyage Round the World, Including Travels in Africa, Asia, Australasia, America.* London: Smith, Elder, and Co., 1834.

Horn, Edward. *Around the World; a Narrative of a Tour of the Earth.* Cincinatti: Press of Jennings and Pye, 1904.

Hoselitz, Bert F. "The Early History of Entrepreneurial Theory." *Essays in Economic Thought: Aristotle to Marshall.* Ed. Joseph J. Spengler. New York: Rand McNally & Co., 1960. 234–254.

"Hudson Takes a Step Forward." *Punch* 1850: 70.

Huebner, Baron de. Trans. by Mary Elizabeth Herbert, *A Ramble Round the World.* London: Macmillan & Co., 1874.

Jameson, Fredric. *Marxism and Form: Twentieth-Century Dialectical Theories of Literature.* Princeton: Princeton University Press, 1974.

———. *The Political Unconscious: Narrative as a Socially Symbolic Act.* Ithaca: Cornell University Press, 1981.

———. *The Prison-House of Language: A Critical Account of Structuralism and Russian Formalism.* Princeton: Princeton University Press, 1972.

Kelidar, Abbas. "The Political Press in Egypt, 1882–1914." *Contemporary Egypt: through Egyptian Eyes: Essays in Honour of Professor P.J. Vatikiotis.* Ed. Charles Tripp. London: Routledge, 1993.

Kennedy, Paul. "Continuity and Discontinuity in British Imperialism 1815–1914." *British Imperialism in the Nineteenth Century.* Ed. C.C. Eldridge. New York: St. Martin's Press, 1984.

Kinglake, Alexander William. *Eothen, Or, Traces of Travel Brought Home from the East.* London: J.M. Dent, 1844.

Koolman, G. "Say's Conception of the Role of the Entrepreneur." *Economica* 151 (1971): 169–286.

"Lady Duff Gordon's Letters from Egypt." *Edinburgh Review* July 1865. 108–119.

Laird, Egerton K. *The Rambles of a Globe Trotter.* London: Chapman & Hall, 1875.

Lambert, Richard S. *The Railway King, 1800–1871: A Study of George Hudson and the Business Morals of his Time.* London: George Allen & Unwin LTD, 1834.

Landes, David S. *Bankers and Pashas: International Finance and Economic Imperialism in Egypt.* Cambridge: Harvard University Press, 1958.

Lane, Edward Williams. *Manners and Customs of the Modern Egyptians.* London: Dent, 1954.

Lawrence, T.E. *Seven Pillars of Wisdom; a Triumph.* Garden City: Doubleday, 1938.

Lawrence of Arabia. Dir. David Lean. With Peter O'Toole, Alec Guiness, Anthony Quinn, Omar Sharif. Horizon Pictures, 1962.

Lenin, Vladimir Ilich. *Imperialism, The Highest Stage of Capitalism.* New York: International Publishers, 1939.

Lewellyn, Briony. "Two Interpretations of Islamic Domestic Interiors in Cairo: J.F. Lewis and Frank Dillon." *Travellers in Egypt.* Ed. Paul Starkey and Janet Starkey. London: Tauris Parke Paperbacks, 2001.

Lott, Emmeline. *The English Governess in Egypt: Harem Life in Egypt and Constantinople.* London: Bentley, 1867.

Marsot, Afaf. *Egypt in the Reign of Muhammad Ali.* Cambridge: Cambridge University Press, 1984.

Martineau, Harriet. *Eastern Life, Present and Past.* London: E. Moxon, 1848.

Marx, Leo. "'Technology': The Advent of a Hazardous Concept." *Negotiations of America's National Identity.* Ed. Roland Hagenbüchle and Josef Raab. Tübingen: Stauffenburg Verlag, 2000. 464–470.

Matus, Jill. "The 'Eastern-Woman Question': Martineau and Nightingale Visit the Harem." *Nineteenth-Century Contexts* 21 (1999): 63–87.

McKeon, Michael. *The Origins of the English Novel, 1600–1740.* Baltimore: Johns Hopkins University Press, 1988.

Mehta, Uday Singh. *Liberalism and Empire: A Study in Nineteenth-Century British Liberal Thought.* Chicago: University of Chicago Press, 1999.

Melman, Billie. *Women's Orients: English Women and the Middle East, 1718–1918: Sexuality, Religion, and Work.* Ann Arbor: University of Michigan Press, 1992.

Miller, Melissa Lee. "The Imperial Feminine: Victorian Women Travellers in Egypt." *White Women in Racialized Spaces: Imaginative Transformation and Ethical Action in Literature.* Ed. Samina Najmi and Rajini Srikanth. Albany: State University of New York Press, 2002.

Milnes, Monckton R. "Mr. D'Israeli's Tancred—The Emancipation of the Jews." *The Edinburgh Review* 86 (1847): 138–155.

Mitchell, Timothy. *Colonising Egypt.* Berkeley: University of California Press, 1988.

Moir, Edith. *The Discovery of Britain; The English Tourist. 1540–1840.* London: Routledge and Keagan Paul, 1964.

Montagu, Lady Mary Wortley. *Embassy to Constantinople: The Travels of Lady Mary Wortley Montagu.* New York: Amsterdam, 1988.

Moretti, Franco. *Atlas of the European Novel, 1800–1900.* London: Verso, 1998.

———. *The Way of the World: The Bildungsroman in European Culture.* London: Verso, 1987.

Morier, Evans, D. *Facts, Failures, and Frauds: Financial Mercantile Criminal Revelations.* New York: Augustus M. Kelley 1968.

Murray, John. *A Handbook for Travellers on the Continent.* London: John Murray and Son, 1836.

———. *A Handbook to India & Ceylon.* London: John Murray, 1892.

———. *A Handbook for Travellers in Egypt: Including Descriptions of the Course of the Nile Through Egypt and Nubia, Alexandria, Cairo, The Pyramids and Thebes, The Suez Canal.* London: John Murray 1875.

"National Dishes of the Civilized World." *Black and White.* 6 February 1891: 12.

Newell, Captain George. *Two Brothers Narrative of a Voyage Around the World in the Bark "Sea Breeze."* Norwalk: Whale House Press, 1961.

Nightingale, Florence. *Letters from Egypt, 1849–1850.* New York: Weidenfeld and Nicolson, 1987.

Parsons, Timothy. *The British Imperial Century.* Totowa: Rowman and Littlefield, 1999.

Peacock, A.J. and David Joy. *George Hudson of York.* Yorkshire: Dalesman Book, 1971.

Perkin, Harold. *The Origins of Modern English Society, 1780–1880.* London: Routledge & Kegan Paul, 1969.

———. *The Rise of the Professional Society.* New York: Routledge, 1989.

Pitts, Jennifer. *A Turn to Empire: The Rise of Imperial Liberalism in Britain and France.* Princeton: Princeton University Press, 2005.

Pollard, Lisa. *Nurturing the Nation: The Family Politics of Modernizing, Colonizing, and Liberating Egypt, 1805–1923.* Berkeley: University of California Press, 2005.

Poovey, Mary. *Uneven Developments: The Ideological Work of Gender in Mid-Victorian England.* Chicago: University of Chicago Press, 1988.

———. "Writing about Finance in Victorian England: Disclosure and Secrecy in the Culture of Investment." *Victorian Studies* 45.1 (2002): 17–41.

Post, Wiley. *Around the World in Eight Days; the Flight of the Winnie May.* New York: Rand McNally & Company, 1931.

Pratt, Mary Louise. *Imperial Eyes: Travel Writing and Transculturation.* Durham: Duke University Press, 1999.

Propp, Vladimir. *Morphology of the Folktale.* Austin: University of Texas Press, 1968.

Pudney, John. *Suez: De Lesseps' Canal.* New York: Praeger Publishers, 1970.

———. *The Thomas Cook Story.* London: Michael Joseph, 1953.

"The Railway King has Exceeded the Very Liberal." *The Times* 3 August 1846: 4.

Reed, Michael. "George Hudson [the Railway King] (1800–1871)." *Oxford Dictionary of National Biography.* Oxford University Press, 2004. [accessed 29 Oct 2004: http://www.oxforddnb.com/view/article/14029]

Reeve, H. "The Suez Canal." *Edinburgh Review.* January 1856: 120–136.

Richardson, D.N. *A Girdle Round the Earth: Home Letters from Foreign Lands.* Chicago: A.C. McClurg and Company, 1887.

Richardson, James. *The Mysteries of Hudson's Railway Frauds Exposed.* London: C. Mitchell, 1850.

Richmond, Charles and Paul Smith, Ed. *The Self-Fashioning of Disraeli, 1818–1851.* Cambridge: Cambridge University Press, 1999.

Romer, Isabella Frances. *A Pilgrimage to the Temples and Tombs of Egypt, Nubia, and Palestine in 1845–46.* London: Richard Bentley, 1846.

Ross, Janet. *The Fourth Generation: Reminiscences.* London: Constable, 1912.

Russell, Mona. *Creating the New Egyptian Woman: Consumerism, Education, and National Identity, 1863–1922.* New York: Palgrave Macmillan, 2004.

Said, Edward. *Culture and Imperialism.* New York: Vintage Books, 1994.

———. *Orientalism.* New York: Pantheon, 1978.

Schivelbusch, Wolfgang. *The Railway Journey: The Industrialization of Time and Space in the Nineteenth Century.* Berkeley: University of California Press, 1977.

Schwarz, Daniel R. "Disraeli's Romanticism: Self-Fashioning in the Novels." *The Self-Fashioning of Disraeli, 1818–1851.* Ed. Charles Richmond and Paul Smith Cambridge: Cambridge University Press, 1999. 43–65.

Shereen, Faiza. "Lucie Duff Gordon." *Dictionary of Literary Biography.* 166 Detroit: Bruccoli, 1996. 157–164.

Simpson, William. *Meeting the Sun: A Journey All Round the World, through Egypt, China, Japan, and California.* London: Longmans, 1874.
Smiles, Samuel. *Lives of the Engineers.* 3 vols. London: John Murray, 1862.
———. *Self Help.* London: Sphere Books Ltd., 1968.
———. *Round the World: Including a Residence in Victoria and a Journey by Rail across North America/by a Boy.* New York: Harper & Brothers, 1872.
Stephen, Leslie. "Mr. Disraeli's Novels." *Fortnightly Review* 22 October 1847: 351–353. Reprinted in *Nineteenth-Century Literature Criticism.*
Stoler, Ann Laura. *Carnal Knowledge and Imperial Power: Race and the Intimate in Colonial Rule.* Berkeley: University of California Press, 2002.
Taylor, W.C. "The Hebrew, The Saracen, and the Christian." *Bentley's Miscellany* 21 April 1847: 385–389.
"Testimonial to George Hudson." *The Times* 6 October 1845: 3e.
The Times 19 November 1845: 3c.
The Times 2 April 1847: 5b.
The Times 15 August 1863: 6b.
Thompson, E.P. *Customs in Common: Studies in Traditional Popular Culture.* New York: New Press, 1993.
Trollope, Anthony. *The Way We Live Now.* Oxford: Oxford University Press, 1999.
Troup, George. "The Hudsonian Eclipse." *Tait's Edinburgh* 20 May 1849: 319–324.
Union Pacific Railroad Company. *Around the World by Steam, via Pacific Railway,* 1871.
Verne, Jules. *Around the World in Eighty Days.* Oxford: Oxford University Press, 1995.
———. *Twenty Thousand Leagues Under the Sea.* London: J.M. Dent, 1908.
Virilio, Paul. Translated by Marc Polizzotti. *Speed and Politics.* Los Angeles: Semiotext(e), 2006.
Wall, Samuel W. *Round the World with Train. A Typhoon. Being the Confessions of a Private Secretary Concerning a Tour of the World in Sixty-Seven Days.* Boston: Round the World Co., 1891.
Waller, J.F. "Novels and Novelists of the Day." *Dublin University Magazine* 30 September (1847): 253–267.
Walworth, Ellen H. *An Old World, as Seen through Young Eyes; or, Travels Around the World.* New York: D. Appleton and Co., 1877.
Ward, Yvette. H. *Around the World in 32 Days.* Hudson: Star-Observer Print, 1958.
Wedgwood, Sir Ralph L. *International Rail Transport.* London: Oxford University Press, 1946.
Weir, William and W.H. Wills. "Shortcuts across the Globe i." *Household Words* 13 April 1850: 65–68.
———. "Shortcuts across the Globe ii." *Household Words* 11 May 1850: 167–168.

White, Rev. James. "A Testimonial in Praise of Testimonials." *Household Words* 7 February 1857: 121–124.

Wilt, Judith. "The Imperial Mouth: Imperialism, the Gothic and Science Fiction," *Journal of Popular Culture* 14 (1981): 618–628.

Wojcik, Michael. "Emmeline Lott." *Dictionary of Literary Biography* 166. Detroit: Bruccoli, 1996. 235–239.

Xu, Wenying. "The Opium Trade and Little Dorrit: A Case of Reading Silences." *Victorian Literature and Culture* 25:1 (1997): 53–66.

Index

For Product Safety Concerns and Information please contact our EU representative GPSR@taylorandfrancis.com
Taylor & Francis Verlag GmbH, Kaufingerstraße 24, 80331 München, Germany

www.ingramcontent.com/pod-product-compliance
Lightning Source LLC
Chambersburg PA
CBHW071408100726
47908CB00004B/1096

* 9 7 8 0 4 1 5 5 4 0 7 9 7 *